Meaningful Relationships

**SAGE SERIES ON
CLOSE RELATIONSHIPS**

Series Editors
Clyde Hendrick, Ph.D., and
Susan S. Hendrick, Ph.D.

In this series...

ROMANTIC LOVE
by Susan S. Hendrick and Clyde Hendrick

COURTSHIP
by Rodney M. Cate and Sally A. Lloyd

ADULT FRIENDSHIP
by Rosemary Blieszner and Rebecca G. Adams

TWO CAREERS/ONE FAMILY
by Lucia Albino Gilbert

SELF-DISCLOSURE
by Valerian J. Derlega, Sandra Metts,
Sandra Petronio, and Stephen T. Margulis

SEXUALITY
by Susan Sprecher and Kathleen McKinney

FACEWORK
by William R. Cupach and Sandra Metts

MEANINGFUL RELATIONSHIPS
by Steve Duck

REMARRIED FAMILY RELATIONSHIPS
by Lawrence H. Ganong and Marilyn Coleman

Meaningful Relationships

Talking, Sense, and Relating

Steve Duck

Sage
Series
on Close
Relationships

SAGE Publications
International Educational and Professional Publisher
Thousand Oaks   London   New Delhi

For information address:

SAGE Publications, Inc.
2455 Teller Road
Thousand Oaks, California 91320

SAGE Publications Ltd.
6 Bonhill Street
London EC2A 4PU
United Kingdom

SAGE Publications India Pvt. Ltd.
M-32 Market
Greater Kailash I
New Delhi 110048 India

Printed in the United States of America

Library of Congress Cataloging-in-Publication Data

Duck, Steve.
   Meaningful relationships : talking, sense, and relating / author, Steve Duck.
     p. cm.—(Sage series on close relationships)
   Includes bibliographical references and index.
   ISBN 0-8039-5702-5.—ISBN 0-8039-5703-3 (pbk.)
   1. Interpersonal relations. 2. Interpersonal communication.
I. Title. II. Series.
HM132.D81943 1994   94-1742
302—DC20   CIP

94 95 96 97 10 9 8 7 6 5 4 3 2 1

Sage Production Editor: Yvonne Könneker

If truth in hearts that perish
Could move the powers on high,
I think the love I bear you
Should make you not to die.

Sure, sure if steadfast meaning,
If single thought could save,
The world might end to-morrow,
You should not see the grave.

This long and sure-set liking,
This boundless will to please,
—Oh you should live forever,
If there were help in these.

But now, since all is idle,
To this lost heart be kind,
Ere to a town you journey*
Where friends are ill to find.

*Reprinted from *A Shropshire Lad* (XXXIII), by A. E. Housman, 1990, New York, Dover Publications. Original work published in 1896. Reprinted from Dover Publications, Inc.

Contents

ॐ

Series Editors' Introduction

When we first began our work on love attitudes more than a decade ago, we did not know what to call our research area. In some ways it represented an extension of earlier work in interpersonal attraction. Most of our scholarly models were psychologists (though sociologists had long been deeply involved in the areas of courtship and marriage), yet we sometimes felt as if our work had no professional "home." That has all changed. Our research not only has a home, it has an extended family, and the family is composed of relationship researchers. Over the past decade, the discipline of Close Relationships (also called Personal Relationships and Intimate Relationships) has emerged, developed, and flourished.

Two aspects of close relationships research should be noted. The first is its rapid growth, resulting in numerous books, journals, handbooks, book series, and professional organizations. But as fast as the field grows, the demand for even more research and knowledge seems to be ever increasing. Questions about close, personal relationships still far exceed answers. The second noteworthy aspect of the new discipline of close relationships is its interdisciplinary nature. The field owes its vitality to scholars from communications,

family studies and human development, psychology (clinical, coun-
seling, development, social), and sociology, as well as other disciplines such as nursing and social work. It is this interdisciplinary
wellspring that gives close relationships research its diversity and
richness, qualities that we hope to achieve in the current series.

The **Sage Series on Close Relationships** is designed to acquaint
diverse readers with the most up-to-date information about various
topics in close relationships theory and research. Each volume in the
Series covers a particular topic or theme in one area of close relationships. Each book reviews the particular topic area, describes
contemporary research in the area (including the author's own
work, where appropriate), and offers some suggestions for interesting research questions and/or real world applications related to the
topic. The volumes are designed to be appropriate for students and
professionals in communication, family studies, psychology, sociology, and social work, among others. A basic assumption of the Series
is that the broad panorama of close relationships can be best por-
trayed by authors from multiple disciplines, so that the Series
cannot be "captured" by any single disciplinary bias.

The current volume, *Meaningful Relationships: Talking, Sense, and
Relating* by Steve Duck, is an important theoretical statement on
personal relationships. The volume is an intensive search for foun-
dational concepts and root metaphors that form the bases for adequate theories of personal relationships. The volume begins with an
exploration of talk, meaning, and metaphor as these concepts apply
to relationships. Discussion moves to consideration of basic issues
of segmentation, change, and constancy in the flow of relationship
experience, followed by an analysis of time and language in the
construal of relationships. The complexities of similarity are woven
into the context of the nature of meaning in relating, leading again
to the centrality of talk in relationship construction. Lessons for the
researcher abound. Steve Duck has provided the community of
relationship scholars with a definitive point of view and great
breadth of topical coverage that should serve as a rallying point for
theory formation and empirical research on close relationships.

CLYDE HENDRICK
SUSAN S. HENDRICK
SERIES EDITORS

Preface

By a stroke of curious coincidence, I wrote much of the final version of this book while listening to one or another of Ralph Vaughan Williams's two musical settings of Bunyan's *The Pilgrim's Progress*, which is a book beginning with a strikingly appropriate apology by the author:

> When at first I took my pen in hand
> Thus for to write, I did not understand
> That I should make a little book
> In such a mode; Nay, I had undertook
> To make another; which when almost done,
> Before I was aware, I this begun.

For at least the past 18 months when people have asked me what I was doing, I first answered that I was trying to do a book on "metaphor in relationships," but later my answer was that I was trying to put down in writing a new conceptualization of relation-ship processes. This book is now about the nature of relationships although it started out being about metaphor. As I wrote the book I began to see metaphor as involving a process that also runs through relationship making: the process of making meaningful connections between ideas (· · · people) that started out as separate and different. The notion of metaphor itself became a metaphor for relationships for me and helped me to pull together several different strands of thinking that I had done over the past few years. The book thus crystallizes the thinking about relationships that I have done during what may turn out to have been the first half of my career.

The book now offers an argument about relationship processes that is based on personal meaning, and it attempts to move us away from the dominant paradigm where relationships are today ex-plained most often in terms of emotions, feelings, disclosures, or knowledge—or else by reference to social structure or early devel-opmental experiences. Instead, I place most emphasis on the in-triguing fact that people express themselves and communicate with one another about the above emotions, feelings, and so forth. As I was writing this book I became convinced that relationships are solidly based in the ways in which we represent the world to ourselves and to other people, using dialogues, conversations, and talk.

Also I wanted to emphasize that relationships are not the done deals that we often read about in research—stable and arid things labeled as perpetually close and full of certainty (or else as perpetu-ally "unstable," casual, and difficult relationships). For me relation-ships are continually unfolding and in need of perpetual responsive action and construction. Relationships can be processes that continu-ally (under the right circumstances) reproduce themselves in their own image, and that is what has led us to view them as stable entities. But they do not have to be like that: The state of a relationship today is often a poor guide to tomorrow's emotional hurricanes and delights. I argue that it is in the transactions of discourse, daily speech, talk, and conversation that people construct their relationships.

This book might therefore seem to be about language and its role in relationships, and of course I shall say something about that. Nevertheless the scope of the book is broader than that and depends on the distinction between language and speech, or the terms that I prefer, namely, between language and everyday talk or conversation. It is also about the meaning that people distribute and broadcast in such talk. It is about the ways in which people develop the sense that they are in a personal relationship with someone else, and it is about *sharing meaning*, by which I mean the deep processes of understanding someone else's ways of thinking about their experiences in the world. I am concerned not with what it *is* to be in a relationship so much as what it means, and not just what it is to be a person in a relationship but what it means.

To ask what it means for two people to have a relationship to each other is to travel along, but ultimately to step off, some traditional pathways. I have become increasingly diffident that present methods and approaches will explain entirely what two people are up to when they snuggle up, remain loyal under duress, or arrange to go to a party on a date. Likewise, I do not feel confident that the presently dominant views can explain why I always write books about relationships to the music of Ralph Vaughan Williams, but both sets of questions can be illuminated by the meaning of the enterprises to the persons involved.

This book has a somewhat unusual feature in that its arguments do not unfold in the traditional strict linear fashion, where Point A leads to Point B and so on to The Conclusion. Instead it will revisit points from different angles and show their simultaneous relationships to different contexts, reposition them, and in some cases revise them. This is an important stylistic recognition of, and metaphor for, some of the points that I wish to make in the book's argument. In relationships as in conversation, we do not know how things will turn out or where they will go. We may have some idea of the topics that will come up, the sequences in which they may be encountered, or the path that will be taken. Yet these very notions of topics, sequences, and paths are themselves something of a conventional contrivance that can create the false impression that things have only one logical, spatial, or emotional relationship to one another. Just as countryside can be seen from different angles as we pass through it, or as people may be seen in different lights at different times, or relationships may be reevaluated in reflective moments, so too this book treats its subject matter as continually unfolding and as understandable from different perspectives serially or simultaneously. In part, this vantage point helps me to make the implicit case that the different disciplines that make up the field of personal relationship research can all simultaneously add something to our understanding without us having to make choices about which one is more "accurate" or more valid. Questions of validity and "accuracy" make sense only once one has defined both the purpose *for which* and the context *in* which one asks the question. Neither is it true that such a position commits us to the notion that all viewpoints are equally valid—merely that for a given purpose at a given time and in a given context each may have a validity that others do not simultaneously possess for that purpose, time, or context. By analogy, there is no universally superior way to cook food, but, with particular foods, some ways yield more satisfying results in some circumstances than others do.

So if you are looking for the traditional linear wham-bang book, put this one back on the shelf and browse elsewhere. For those who persist, we will travel together through the rich land of metaphor, talk, meaning, intimacy, similarity, and a few other everyday common-or-garden experiences. Traditional landmarks of the PR field will be seen from different angles and annexed to different owners while others that are lying in neglect will be uprooted and transposed to a more favored location. All this will, I believe, help to explain both why I have stuck at this field for the past 22 years and also why I still see another 22 years of work there to be done.

🐚 Acknowledgments

I think I eventually succeeded in saying what I wanted to say, although at the outset I am not sure that I knew what that was. As the editors can heroically attest, this book emerged from a tormented process of Hendrick-facilitated gestation where both structure and content changed many times. Many readers added thoughts that I had not had, acted as obstetricians for ideas I could not express properly until they told me what I meant, or suggested reorganization of poorly formulated notions. Among those people were many colleagues, students, and friends who challenged my thinking and sharpened it up. I am particularly grateful to the following for reading the whole, or large parts, of the manuscript in one or several of its configurations: Linda Acitelli, Irwin Altman, Leslie Baxter, Anne Beall, Dan Canary, Carl Couch, Perri Druen, Kathleen Farrell, Clyde and Susan Hendrick, Bill Ickes, Zoltan Kovecses, Renee Lyons, Catalin Mamali, Mik Monsour, Karen Prager, Laura Stafford, Peter Stromberg, and Julia Wood. To all of them I owe an especial debt of gratitude and a fervent hope that I have learned from what they tried to teach me.

STEVE DUCK

1

Talking Sense
Shared Meaning and Talk as
a Basis for Relationships

Why is it that scientists know a good deal about what it is to be an organism in an environment but very little about what it is to be a creature who names things and utters and understands sentences about things?

W. Percy (1975, p. 8)

Ben, my son, was 15 months old when I first noticed something about our interactions that made me ask questions about the nature of relationships. I had been pointing hopefully to the lights in our kitchen and saying "light" in the hope of helping him to associate the object with the word *light*, which I understand as a symbol for the object. As I pointed upwards, he resolutely stared at the end of my finger, grinning gleefully and proudly at his understanding—but from my perspective he really didn't get the point (as it were). Apart from being the only child who will grow up thinking that he has two thumbs and eight lights on his hands, he did not take my pointing as a sign saying, "Go beyond here and look further." The *meaning* of my action, which would be taken for granted by adult members of my culture, had not then been absorbed by little Ben.

When I unraveled the above scenario as a scholar rather than as an overoptimistic parent, it seemed even more beguiling. I was using language and Ben wasn't (yet); I was trying to get him to make connections and he didn't make the same ones; I tried to share meaning with him and he didn't get it (though he constructed another meaning of his own). Behind such observations lie a number of very important assumptions and circumstances. I have information that Ben does not yet have. More than that, I have *knowledge* that he does not yet have (i.e., I have information that is *organized* into a system): For instance, I possess a complex cultural symbol system for portraying the world that he does not. Beyond that, I have an organized system of *personal* meaning that goes well beyond what he has so far acquired; for instance, I have had a lot of experiences that he has never had, have thought about things that he has not come across, have been a child, grown up, gone bald, et cetera. My meaning system is inevitably personal to me and is part of what makes me an individual. Ben will never entirely participate in it, even though it is composed of culturally based symbols that he will one day acquire. Likewise, he will organize these cultural meanings in personal ways for himself—within the context of his own experiences of his life.

This latter point has a parallel in relationships between adults: Each relational partner has a personal system of meanings (a "personality," values, opinions, attitudes) and organized knowledge (about the past, events, goals) that the other never fully acquires. Relationships are based on the extent to which two partners deal with that fact. In a sentence, this whole book is devoted to exploring the relational processes that are based on comprehension of others' meaning systems and the implications that lie beneath the processes of comprehension.

I chose to write this book because of these issues and their ramifications. My acquaintance with interdisciplinary research on personal relationships (as well as my own experiences in them) convinced me that certain prevailing scholarly views of relationships are misguided and woefully partial. I believe that there are presently unseen deficiencies in the predominant orientation that seeks to explain relationships in terms of general market forces of cost, reward, and interdependence. As an alternative, I will show the ways in which relationships are created and constantly held in being—like a human pyramid in the circus—by the active constructive interaction of relational partners and others in their network or culture. I will discuss and critique these ideas in the chapters that follow and will develop the proposal that the creation and maintenance of a relationship are continual processes of mutual comprehension and transformation through the agencies of meaning and talk.

Equally I am persuaded by clues and hints in existing work that some very important issues have not yet captured adequate attention from researchers. First, human beings face real, practical dilemmas in the conduct of their daily lives—not disembodied, lab-generated, temporary dilemmas from which they can walk away at the end of the study, but real issues they have to manage with real blood, real sweat, real tears, and real sleepless nights. Second, any approach to understanding relationships either explicitly or implicitly has a view of the nature and the influences of these human experiences already built in, and I will spend many pages exploring what they mean for relational partners as well as for researchers. My own approach is based on the obvious fact that human life is continually unfolding—something obvious from experience but rarely built into theory. People are continually changing, whether as a result of aging or of moving to new projects or of adapting their behavior as a result of experience.

Critiquing the former approaches and building a case for the latter are two other related goals that steer the purposes of the present book. As a further twist, I will discuss all of the above matters, including the ubiquity of change, on two levels: (1) their *significance in the life of real relationships* between real people, which is to say that I will deal with their implications for real people's actual conduct of everyday relationships; and (2) their *significance for the process of enquiry* in future scholarship and clinical work about relationships. In addition, I am convinced that we should not pay mere lip service to the idea that the study of personal relationships is multidisciplinary. Instead, we should attempt a serious integration of thinking from psychology, communication, sociology, clinical work, literature, and elsewhere.

Let me restate the above points in a different way. Relationships are composed of two individuals who come to one another with some linguistic, cultural, human, and individual baggage, but nevertheless can proceed, through their interaction, to create substantial shared understandings of the world, which they frame in their talk with one another and enact in their everyday relational behavior. Scholars of relationships would be wrong to ignore that linguistic baggage. Like other baggage, it is not only a hindrance (since it restricts the freedoms that relaters have to discuss, construct, and transform their relationship experiences) but also may contain paraphernalia that provide opportunities, as well. We would also be wrong to overlook the kinds of enterprises, projects, and activities that characterize the human experience of individuals as a whole. It is against that human background that two relationship partners come to relate their two separate spheres of action and thought into one coordinated and interdependent unit. Everyday talk and routines reify, sustain, develop, and in some cases diminish, the coordinated interdependence that constitutes a relationship.

Therefore, I center this first chapter on the ways in which our choice of language terms frames and organizes both our thinking and our experience, whether on the level of ordinary experience of emotions or on the scholarly level of discourse about research. Chapter 2 follows up by discussing the broadest possible context: the enterprise of living a human life. How are our relationships and relational concerns and terms focused by the fact that human beings inevitably live in an unfolding world of contingencies and surprises, as well as regularities, that must be coped with? In Chapter 3, I will add the notion that the passage of time itself produces weighty effects on our experience of the world and others in it (e.g., making it a certainty that other people's behavior will evolve, change, and be as inconsistent or variable as our own). So how do we come to understand the variations in others' relational behavior as well as the apparent stabilities? Chapter 4 deals with a central element of many explanations of relationships, namely the almost irresistible power of the assumption of similarity (especially psychological similarity) between people. Chapter 5 rounds out the argument by tracing the roles of talk and meaning in relational life, while Chapter 6 offers some ideas for future research.

The style of this book itself sends its own messages that the above points have several different connections to one another. I will therefore inevitably revisit the points from several different angles as we go along. Like a car journey where the vehicle moves continually forward, the argument will move on to visit new points, but the driver and passengers will also look off to the side while still moving ever forward. So, too, can they look backward in the mirror and review scenes previously passed through, in order to gain fuller perspective on the ground they have covered. Our destination is the unraveling of the role of personal meaning and everyday talk in the conduct of everyday relationships against the continual concerns of human beings getting on with their unfolding lives. My key contention will be that *understanding* (of what is meant) and *sharing of meaning* (a social process involving understanding-plus-similar-evaluation) are essential elements of relating and that everyday talk is part of the system of communication that creates them both.

I shall depict human beings in general as striving to understand and as driven by an "effort after meaning" (Bartlett, 1932). I shall propose, with several important caveats, that relationships are processes where partners strive to understand one another's evolving personal meaning system and attempt to understand the other person in his or her own terms—that is, trying to access the other person's system of personal meaning.

I also base the idea of "personal meaning" on another important notion that relates metaphor, similarity, and meaning to other relationships. The human enterprise is essentially forward-driven and "extensive" in that it is restlessly inferential and perpetually full of motion. Everything points somewhere else as well as having intrinsic content, whether it is a word, a metaphor, a situation, a personal characteristic, a remark, a comment, an attitude, a belief, a personality, or a gesture to a 15-month-old son. Everything can be extended to something else, some other realm of meaning not inherent in itself. Every statement is situated in contexts that offer meaning, whether these be culturally agreed, relational, individual, or personal meanings. More than this, every context points somewhere else and relentlessly leads us on to new ground, new implications, new extensions of meaning. Thus context does not merely embed another concept, word, gesture, person, attitude, idea, or relationship; it also pushes forward some related topic of conversation or thought, or it develops some connection or implication that an active human mind can work on. No human symbol is inert, no word without implied action, no behavior without descendants. Attempts to understand other people are based on the agitated and irresistible extensiveness that such an idea implies.

❦ Understanding Other People

The repeated experience (that Ben did not comprehend my meaning) sparked in me the general question: How does one person's understanding of another person's meaning develop or constrain the relationship between the two of them? In everyday life we take understanding for granted in our relationships, and mutual understanding really founds the basis for our dealings with one another. Yet information comes in lots of contexts that help us to interpret it and is not something with the same absolute value to everyone, as Ben and I discovered. Its organization into knowledge depends on the fact that it means to people whatever they can make of it.

As Ben grows up, he will come to comprehend general background knowledge that other people know. The acquired knowledge not only will extend his developing identity in new directions but also will grant him an admission ticket to a broader thought-language community. He will be able to presume knowledge in other people who display similar tickets. Ben can then hope to be able to make more sense of what they say and do, as he begins to try to construct social relationships with them. In close personal relationships in the future he will do even more than this: He will build up an organized encyclopedic knowledge of the specific thinking, behaving, and speaking patterns of his close friends, parents, romantic partners, colleagues, playground peers, and classmates, and so on—even of his enemies and rivals. Ben will likewise develop specific frames of reference to help him comprehend the subtleties of what other people say to him, on one occasion as distinct from another. Planalp and Garvin-Doxas (1994) describe this state of affairs as the process of partners becoming experts on one another. This useful notion of expertise, however, contains two further distinguishable parts: knowledge and understanding. Knowledge organizes bits of information into a system, so I can know lots of items of information about you that make sense *to me* (i.e., viewing you "from the outside"). In understanding you, however, I go a step further: I organize my knowledge of you in a way that includes knowledge of how you make sense of things (i.e., viewing you "from the inside"). The switch from knowing someone to understanding the person is an important one in relationships.

knowing → outside
understanding → inside

Contexts That Give Information Meaning

Obviously the scene with Ben set me thinking about the different ways in which people comprehend one another, the ways in which relationships between people absolutely depend on such understanding, and what it is that comprehension itself depends on. We may be used to thinking of relationships as between two separate individual characters or identities that come together to "enter into" a relationship, but really there is a lot more to it. For one thing, the metaphor of "entering" a relationship is misleading insofar as it implies that relationships are "there" and persons go inside together: Instead this book looks at how individuals create, sustain, or transform relationships. For another thing, individuals' identities (in terms of their psychological characteristics and ways of thought) form a part of any relationships that they create, and—obviously— different individuals treat information differently from one another on the basis of their own particular psychological frameworks for interpreting meaning. Further, relationships do not simply add two persons together but also transform: As human processors gather information, they also reorganize it, whether information about others, about self, or about other aspects of experience. Thus while a relationship is a creation made by two people, the two people are themselves also somewhat transformed in the process of relating. In getting to know more about someone, our comprehension of ourselves may be modified by our interactions with the person as well as by the discussions that we have concerning our respective knowledge. Personal relationships transform and reorganize meanings, and are therefore not informationally inert.

Neither are people inert. One complicating fact of real life experience is that human beings change, develop, and learn. Thus any process of comprehending someone else will be an essentially unfinished task as we, and they, change. The book will draw on the theoretical claims of George Kelly in this matter, as well as in some others. Kelly (1969b) argued that human beings constantly develop new attempts to find improved workable explanations that, for the time being, "enable us to get along gratefully with whatever it is we are trying to do" (p. 44). Kelly, as a personality psychologist—and a clinical psychologist at that—focused on the individual and the ways in which each person creates a general "personal construct system"

(Kelly, 1955)—that is, an organized system of personal constructions of experience, a system of personal meaning. While we tend to think of "personality" as relatively fixed, Kelly by contrast saw it as evolving. He represented human beings as constantly enquiring, constantly looking for meaning, constantly attempting to understand their circumstances in better and better ways.

For Kelly, human activity—behavior, not just thought—is an empirical process of curiosity and inventive solution: "It is through behavior that questions are posed" (Kelly, 1969b, p. 44). For Kelly, therefore, behavior is a person's way of proposing and testing comprehension. The process does not stop once one has some sort of explanation, because there may always be a better one. Individuals can be constantly modifying their explanations and their views and predictions about people, relationships, themselves, their partners, and standards for behavior as events continue to unfold and present them with new possibilities for interpretation. Such an unending task is especially complicated in relation to other human beings, therefore, because they too are changing and evolving.

Another reason why comprehending others is a perpetual task is that adults comprehend one another in many different ways, whether in terms of identity and character, psychological characteristics, physical behaviors, roles, or something else. As we get to know someone else, so we come to comprehend them in different ways; we do not just acquire more and more information about them that leaves our understanding unaffected. We can deal with people as colleagues, as partners, and/or as individuals, based on our perceptions of their motives, our attributions about them, their self-disclosures, and so on. Perceptions are based on "information," but more than this they are forms of meaning that we attach to objects in our social worlds as we engage other persons. When we become experts in other people, such expertise involves contextual knowledge: familiarity with various contexts that help us to interpret other people. In the case of relationships, one obvious context is culture. For instance, adults can usually comprehend one another's gestures, but we do so only because we share an ability to place behaviors in a cultural context. Certain gestures (e.g., touching the top of the thumb with the top of the index finger while extending all other fingers) mean one thing in one culture ("perfect") and other things in another culture (crude sexual insult). Behaviors are symbolic within a cultural context, and it follows that cultural knowledge is a strong and explicit scene against which we understand our relationships.

That general scene is only one example of many other more particular scenes that influence our ability to participate in the relationship bazaars of life. Other such contextual scenes are our own personality styles and identities (or meaning systems), the history of the relationship, the present situation, individual relationship goals, the stage of the relationship, and many other scenes that add meaning to relational perception. In all cases the scene represents a subtle organization of bits of information and the organization of them constructs their sense. As Ben learns more about me and about these social scenes, so will his organization of this new knowledge help him to see things differently, to coordinate his behavior with mine on different levels, and to add something to his developing view of the world as a whole.

To some extent, though, our knowledge about, and relationship to, others are not only clarified but also defined and limited by the way in which we understand those particular persons in context. I will argue that the extent of Ben's ability to (re)organize his personal meanings for things and to comprehend others' frames of reference will liberate *and/or constrain*, develop *and/or contain*, or create *and/or destroy* his relationships with those whom he meets, from the moment he greets them and shakes them by the lights (!), right through to the development of deepest intimacy. What matters is the extent to which he understands other people's personal meaning systems and the ways in which the owner organizes his or her own thought. Thus a major thesis of this book will be that the extent of a person's ability to comprehend another person's meaning is the basis, channeler, and limiter of relationships with the person. A guiding question for the book is therefore how we come to understand other people's personal meaning systems—what are the necessary (pre)-conditions and mechanisms for such personalized understanding?

❧ Some Words About Talk

The fact that we know lots of information about our relational partners may be interesting, but it is not half as interesting as the fact that most of our acquisition of such information occurs through the rich and culturally embedded form of symbol: spoken (or written) language (and also, incidentally, from one of its opposites, namely silence—pregnant pauses, significant omissions, or the unspoken). In our everyday lives we form, develop, and dissolve relationships largely through talk; we conduct relational business primarily through talk; we express personality, give social support, indicate power, demonstrate interdependence, persuade, cajole, quarrel, invite, reject, divorce, propose, proposition, and propitiate primarily in talk. Talk presents our attitudes and beliefs and allows us to disclose information about ourselves, express emotion, and reveal how we think. Talk is also performative and produces actions by others (e.g., it gets them to do things: "Shut the door!"). Indeed, talk has many functions, and we should attend to them carefully if we are to understand relationships. Bochner (1984), for example, lists expression as only one of five functions of relational communication: (1) to foster a favorable impression in the mind of the listener; (2) to organize a relationship (i.e., to create a power and control structure); (3) to construct and validate a conjoint worldview; (4) to express feelings and thoughts; (5) to protect vulnerabilities.

Talk as a Source of Information About Other People

The disembodied social psychological concepts that we read about as impression management, self-disclosure, interdependence, and social exchange are also created or served mostly in talk. Talk toils for us and helps minds and people to come together. Talk works through symbols that are shared, but it works only if we can presume that the persons to whom we talk will be able to figure out what we mean because they share our symbols and our universe of discourse (Mead, 1934/1967). In short, talk is a prime source of information about people's meaning systems and concerns, and we need to think a little bit about how talk works. Alas, humans are so complex that talk can not only illuminate but also bedim, can not only reveal but also dissemble, and can not only guide but also mislead. In fact, on occasions ambiguity or equivocation are important for successful relating (Bavelas, 1990; Duck, 1994d). Luckily, talk occurs in the social context of other acts, and most observers will agree that such actions can speak louder than words. However, this statement does not mean that talk does not matter, any more than it claims that talk is all there is: Rather, talk has to be interpreted in light of what else is known or observed about the person's meaning system (Berger & Bradac, 1982).

Talk enacts most social psychological concepts, yet can have many foci simultaneously or consecutively in the course of a single conversation. While partners obviously do talk *about* themselves and their relationship directly (Acitelli, 1988, 1992, 1993), talk *in the context of* the relationship also does much else that provides evidence of a person's psychological geography and styles of thinking (Duck, Rutt, Hurst, & Strejc, 1991). As persons relate, they display themselves and their views of the world in their talk, both in context and style, both in what the talk says and what it does not, both directly and indirectly. Of course, people use talk to ask each other direct and specific questions, find out information, and self-disclose both thoughtfully and unintentionally. Through talking, people conduct other routine relationship business (Duck, 1994c); check out one another's lusts, desires, and attitudes; announce their values; reveal the structure of their concerns; uncover their attachment styles; and otherwise discourse freely on a multitude of topics that both openly and subtly reveal their own, and give clues to other people's, meaning. Even arguments, complaints, and regrets are verbal displays of meaning. Persons vocalize their feelings, utter their desires, and speak their minds in ways that inexorably evidence their thought structures to an observing mind. They also manage the dark side of their relationship against the light side by talking (Duck, 1994d) and arrange their relational paraphernalia of disputes and hassles (Bolger & Kelleher, 1993). That is not all that they do in talk, which is by no means used simply to transmit serious information and can be coarse, playful, teasing, cute, jocular, witty, and fun. People also laugh, play, josh, snigger, parody, revel, frolic, caper, fool, and sport in their talk, and we should not overlook these roles of talk in relationships, since they may evidence meaning as much as do serious, gray-suited, bespectacled monologues.

Talk as a Persuasive Tool

Over and above its variety, its social force, its style, and the content of its subject matter, talk has another interesting quality: It is used to *persuade* (Duck & Pond, 1989). Normally we do not focus on this quality, and we tend to see talk as using language that we normally consider a neutral tool for describing reality. We see it as representing things, defining ideas, pointing to objects, naming things and people. Words are symbols for things and for actions; for example, sentences symbolize thought and a lot else beside. However there is another view of language, that it is instead *presentational* and offers possible characterizations that may be disputed or reconsidered or flatly denied by other speakers. In such a view the speaker, not language itself, is accountable for what is said. For example, once something (like an attitude, value, or opinion) gets into the public domain of a conversation, it becomes a site of contest and constitutes a rhetorical focus for other speakers and thinkers: You have to defend your speech!

Nuances of meaning not only are the responsibility of the utterer, rather than of the language, but also are illustrative of the way the speaker construes and understands the world rather than descriptive of the world itself. A speaker's talk is symbolic of a view of the world, and it presents that view as an offering, which others can accept, challenge, reject, or assimilate. Speech, even everyday speech, is presentational, it argues for a view of things, it uses the metaphors and terms that a person finds helpful, it preaches the speaker's viewpoint, it is "sermonic" (Hauser, 1986). By underappreciating this point, previous research on relationships has, by and large, given talk a raw deal. Talk's body of functions has been concealed like Cinderella beneath dull and monochromatic raiment, its relational importance veiled, and its social force bundled up in a straitjacket.

We can also see the very *act of talking* itself as a symbol. Even the simple occurrence of daily chatter about nothing in particular sustains relationships (Duck, Rutt, et al., 1991). Of course, such chatter occurs in an important context of cultural, relational, and individual knowledge that lards words with some of their fatty personal and intimate meaning. The hearer who shares the speaker's symbol system understands the talk more or less as the speaker does, just as my son Ben will one day understand pointing in the same terms that I do.

Talk, like other symbol usage, is also constraining. It is formed from words that have some socially created significance that imposes limits on the uses that can be made of them (usually!). A "spade" is a "spade," whatever else it is, and we do not have Humpty-Dumpty freedom to make words mean whatever we like, at least if we wish to communicate with other people at large. In

discourse with the wider social network and in most of our discourse with partners, we generally stick close to the prevailing
social definitions and uses of words—or else the words cease to
convey meaning usefully.

In personal relationships there is, however, some evidence that
people do develop personal idiomatic meaning for words as a way
of solidifying and adding a special character to their relationships
(see below). Partners in relationships do, must, and cannot avoid
developing their own "culture" (Wood, 1982), even if relationships
are founded on shared meanings and ability to communicate together through bases of common, taken-for-granted assumptions
(Garfinkel, 1967; Goffman, 1959). In talk we express our own thoughts
in a generally shared form of the language so that others can comprehend them; in relationships we often express our thoughts in
the framework of privately shared knowledge, but the principle is
the same: Communication requires a basic framework of shared
meanings and *the belief that these meanings are shared*. The mandate
here is that partners believe that they do share meaning and that
their interactions do not belie this assumption, since the discovery
of such a difference in meaning can itself be a reason to break off
a relationship. Thus another guiding question of the book deals
with the role of talk as a promoter of understanding: How does
talk frame our relationship activity and our awareness of others'
meanings?

Talk as a Vantage Point

Talk is more than just a behavior; it is a symbolic presentational
force that persuades as well as exposes, displays, and informs. Talk
both takes a cultural vantage point (in the words and meanings built
into it) and can be superintended in a way that allows persons to
use it in their own way to express their own personal meanings. Talk
uses a common language; language uses both common and personalized symbols; symbols use meaning; meaning uses sharing; sharing uses people; people use talk. Thus we not only need to include
talk in our thinking about relationships, but we also need a theory
about the jobs that talk performs and the ways it does them. Talking
is not merely the conveyance of carefully wrapped packets of information, a mere transferrer of objective or neutral information, or a

simple medium for building of encyclopedic inventories of other people's thinking. Talk also serves many other purposes simultaneously, some strategic (e.g., the denial of other counter positions; self-presentation; impression management, and so on), some individual (e.g., enacting, expressing, or making real an individual's particular goals in interaction; acknowledging others' beliefs and values), and some relational (e.g., allowing discussion about similarities; purveying disagreement; indicating affection; making relational propositions).

In later chapters, I will conjoin talk theoretically not only with several rhetorical functions of speech but also with fundamental social processes involving dilemmas in everyday behavior. Speech, even daily talk, functions to influence others and presents a position as well as providing a means for one to recognize and acknowledge another person's system of meaning. In everyday talk the framework of a person's thought is presented to others symbolically so that the two partners may, if they are able, detect, recognize, create, and respond to similarities of interpretation of the world. In this way they achieve the intersubjectivity that is the essence of relating and of being a social person (Ickes & Gonzalez, n.d.). Such intersubjectivity is not so much an interdependence of behavior and cognition as the perception of commonalities and the witting comprehension of each other's personal system of meaning. However, achievement of intersubjectivity is not an inert knowledge state, but at the moment of its occurrence it modifies construction of the persons themselves. Sharing of meaning is not merely an overlap of content but also an interpretative, constructive, organizational matter involving the assimilation of new shared meaning into individuals' preexisting systems, which is, of course, a process of transformation.

Although I have not used the terms until now, the previous outline is consistent with there being an unfinished series of ebbs and flows of mutual understanding during the course of a relationship's life. Such ebbs and flows have relevance not only to comprehension of each partner by the other but also to comprehension of the relationship that they are creating and re-creating between the two of them (Genero, Miller, Surrey, & Baldwin, 1992). Just as I will claim that other aspects of relationships and human life as a whole are unfinished business characterized by comparison and assimilation *people aren't in relationships; relationships are in people.*

of alternative constructions, so I claim the sharing of meaning is a continually variegated and perpetually incomplete business, even in established relationships. People are not in relationships; relationships are in people, and in that sense, relationships therefore evolve as people's beliefs or memories about them change—but people themselves are also evolving. Thus the changes that occur in relationships are substantially intertwined with changes in the meaning of the relationship or the partners (including their circumstances) or the future of the two partners together as well as with the evolution of the persons themselves. That is to say, such transformations reflect an alteration in the vantage point taken to view and characterize the joint enterprise. That we should take this point seriously is the whole argument of this book.

❦ Meaning in Relational Context

The immediate and rather superficial reflection on the scene with my son Ben has raised a number of interesting features of communication and relationships to do with symbols, understanding, and talk. But it also raises the issue of how people share meaning. To explore the sharing of meaning systems we must identify the interplay of personal meaning, on the one hand (from whatever sources and tools it is constructed and organized by each person), and the transactions of meaning that occur between two persons through communication, on the other hand. While it is easy to think of individuals exchanging meanings that they have constructed for themselves, the process is not that simple and is one that first requires us to explore how individuals come to understand and use symbols that are also understood and used by other people generally.

It will perhaps be clear already that I am not here considering the nature of meaning, as the philosophical problem concerned with the relationship of sounds to objects. Meaning is not relevant in this book in the sense of whether and how a "signifier" relates to the "signified." My concern is with the fact that people act as if words mean things and also act as if other people have internal logics that can be understood on the basis of the meanings that they express. Thus I am concerned with the way in which two persons understand one another, whatever the philosophical basis of meaning may be.

Sharing Meaning

How do people use and share meanings in relationships? I do not mean: "How are people similar?" nor "How or why is similarity the basis of relationships?" I do not focus only on the fact of similarity between two meaning systems in itself. Rather I place the emphasis instead on the social transactive process, the act of comparison, transfer, extension, or connection between the two meaning systems—the act of sharing. It is this distinction between the relationship of two things (similarity) and the transactive social consequences of it (sharing) that, I will argue, are significant to understanding social and personal relationships. Sharing between people depends on the social use of similarity, the interpersonal process of association, and the doing of inference, rather than on similarity as an abstract logical relationship itself. The expression of meaning may be an individual act, but the processes of reading one another's minds are fundamentally social. Thus while two of us may be similar in that we express the same sorts of words about a given topic, all the same, it is the flashing perception of that similarity and the actions of common acknowledgment of it that have a social and relational significance. The mere existence of cognitive similarity is of meager consequence until we "go beyond it."

Readers familiar with the psychological research on attitude and personality similarity in relationships (see Chapter 4) will recognize that the above apparently simple and harmless view is somewhat radical. It will take two chapters (Chapters 4 and 5) to elaborate the position in full, but it is a direct outgrowth of my earlier points. The existence of similarity is a meal set before a person, but it is the recognition of similarity that is the enjoyable and socially useful part—eating the meal together. The *use* of similarity is the process that extends its meaning and carries it across, to a place where it exerts most relational influence in real relationships. The process is based in talk that, through its use of the common meanings and perspectives embedded in itself, allows cross-reference between the systems of meaning embedded in individualized thought (Chapter 5).

Meaning as "Going Beyond the Given"

I have already noted that life, people, and language restlessly point somewhere else and extend beyond the immediate. Even words themselves are always contextualized by this restless urge to go beyond the given. Any meaning of a word inevitably implies more than it says directly, and it does this because the speaker or the listener knows more than is said in any given word that a speaker chooses. (As a simple example, the selection of a particular word already implies a more extensive knowledge of a language that contains the word.)

As I repeatedly witnessed the scene with Ben in growing parental exasperation, it dawned on me that there was another implication of this notion and that I was like Ben in one respect. Like Ben, I took a limited view of things (in my case, relationships, similarity, metaphor, language, and memory) and had failed to realize that it could also be usefully extended to another level. In their own ways, all of the items in the above list (relationships, similarity, etc.) are not just single things like my fingers or simple acts like pointing, but they likewise serve another indicative, extensive purpose. Each concept (relationship, similarity, etc.) indicates some connection between two meanings through an association. Each implicitly contains an urge to extend and "go beyond the given" in order to increase understanding. A relationship brings together two previously independent beings and, by connecting them, creates something new from their sharing—something that presumably feeds back into each individual and affects the ways in which each thinks about the other in the future. Similarity and sharing each brings together two separate entities by indicating a connection of comparison that can be made from some exterior vantage point. Metaphor illustrates one area of thinking by indicating the relevance of another area, as when we think of two people falling in love (thus relating love to loss of control and all that this would imply). Memory ushers the past into the present and indicates significant implication or relevance of one to the other (it being particularly a compelling human rhetorical tendency to refer to history or precedent as a context for action; e.g., Megill & McCloskey, 1987).

There are many other important instances of this fact that what seem to be simple, single things restlessly and continually point somewhere else. I will contend that a relationship (and the very use of language itself) is such an instance. Relationships are always "ongoing" (Bennett, in press) and are sometimes ended just because one partner feels the relationship is not going anywhere. Also, to use a

word as a symbol is not only to go beyond sound waves to the object
that it suggests but is also to bring along all the other social associations
that a given word can carry. Thus, to say "I love you" is not only to
express an emotion but is also to tag along the baggage of relationship
definition ("Should we become romantically involved?"), of social
appropriateness ("But you are my teacher!"), and of a host of other
social, cultural, organizational, dyadic, and personal paraphernalia.
These three little words entail a huge social context in which their
meaning is understood and their implications enacted.

   This process of *associative inference* or *implication* is a striking one
that this book will apply to relationships. It relies on the fact (1) that
the human mind readily moves from one realm of meaning to
another and constructs connections; (2) that human thinking also
restlessly and continually moves from a present "place" to another
one—you cannot *not* imply; (3) that humans often hold two realms
of discourse in mind at once and make higher order comparisons
between them. Moreover, at the social level, we understand one
another through talk based on the three previous facts. None of
these items is in itself a new observation, but I extend them to the
psychological processes of meaning sharing that are the bedrock of
human relationships.

   I shall claim in this book that "relationships," "similarity," and
"meaning" are *processes* created by the interaction of minds through
communication. Processes, not products! Rather than being abstract
concepts, relationships, similarity, and meaning are things that humans do and do continually. Humans do them through the means
that separates them from animals and flies: Humans talk to one
another and present their thinking/meaning in words. Talk is not a
merely insignificant oral activity through which the really important
social relational processes occur. It is the primary process through
which humans construct and communicate images of the world. Furthermore, it is by means of talk and symbols that humans present one
another with both direct and indirect evidence of how they think about
life, themselves, each other, the world, and everything in it. From such
evidence a listener may draw inferences about the mind of the speaker.

   Just as my attempts to extend Ben's thinking were implicitly
based on an assumption that our two viewpoints could connect
somehow, so human action extends itself through inference and
relationship by constructive use of multiple viewpoints. One mind

can view things in more than one way (whether by imagination, memory, or experience), and two minds can stand at diverse vantage points to see things in different ways that beg for discussion. Indeed, the very notions of inference and extension presume the possibility of different vantage points, whether these be one person at two times, one person imagining things from another standpoint, or two persons simultaneously viewing things from their individual perspectives. The ability to recognize different perspectives lies at the root of social and personal relationships. Indeed, the very term *relationship* implies a viewing mind that constructs a connection between things over and above the perception of the single items that are perceived. This second-order perception of the relating of two "objects" is essentially a different level of vantage point for cognition, one that some thinkers (e.g., Mead, 1934/1967) have regarded as distinctive of human consciousness.

Linking Different Sets of Ideas

One striking instance of the processes of transactive extension and inference is offered by the human use of metaphor. Metaphors (from the Greek μεταφερειν [*metapherein*], meaning "to carry across") are superficially just ways of inferring, extending, or carrying across one realm of discourse or content to another in a vivid and evocative way that enlivens speech and writing. When writers used to refer to the "ship of state" instead of using the word *government* (incidentally, this is derived from the Latin, *Gubernator*, a ship's helmsman [helmsmen all *were* men in those days]), the writers were being metaphorical. The state is not a ship, neither is the President a helmsman, but we all have some idea of the point that is being made. These writers carried over their understanding of sailing and applied it to the topic of government, thereby adding something to the way in which they visualize government as a directed, purposeful enterprise taking a group of people through uncharted waters to new places and experiences (and possibly making them all sick!).

Likewise, when we think about relationships being "close," we are actually being metaphorical. *Closeness* is a term that refers literally to spatial distance and the bringing of two things together (it derives from the Latin *claudere*, meaning to shut—to bring together a box and its lid, for example). Our common present-day usage of the term to apply to *emotional* distance is itself a vivid extension of the spatial term from its original setting to a new one. Interestingly, in order to give meaning to the personal relationship, we adapt or extend our thinking from another realm of knowledge (knowledge about spatial relationships).

Thus there is more to the processes underlying metaphor than the mere vividness of a helpful imagery that offers new understanding or vision: Metaphor requires an ability to reflect on a topic and take a vantage point outside of one topic in order to connect it to another one. There is also more to a relationship than the mere behavioral patterns and discrete interactions between two people. Rather, each of the persons or observers must be able to reflect on the behaviors, and interactions, take a vantage point outside of them, and construct a mental connection between them.

Another similarity between metaphors and relationships lies in the fact that they both comprise the activities of minds trying to grasp or constitute the world. In a metaphor we attempt to find a simple way to understand something complex more clearly by momentarily and simply comparing it with something else that we already comprehend well. When Shakespeare writes of death as "that undiscovered country from whose bourne no traveller returns," the metaphor helps us to see death as a place to which we go after life. This metaphor does not require us to wrestle with complex metaphysical concepts about transformation of essence or transfiguration of souls or metamorphosis of Being-with-a-capital-B or complex and abstruse views of death that we find hard to grasp. Rather, it presents death as simply a destination, somewhere else, a place we could find, a location where we will arrive in due course (presumably along with all the tax collectors and mosquitoes that have ever lived). This familiar and simple image of "a destination" is one we already know a lot about and therefore can comprehend rather easily.

Just as our choice of such metaphors may enrich understanding, so too does it also limit what we perceive. If I think of death as a destination, then that constrains me at that time not to think of it as, say, sleep that brings rest, peace, and an end to the "thousand natural shocks that flesh is heir to" (even though Shakespeare does explore these terms in the same speech in *Hamlet*). The destination metaphor certainly prevents me from simultaneously thinking of death as a transfiguration to another form of life, as some Eastern religions hold to be true. Thus, by adopting a new frame of reference, I both shape and limit my understanding of phenomena to certain aspects rather than others for the time being. Likewise, in a relationship with Person A, I also probably limit my talk to those areas where I know we share common ground, and I forgo discussion of those that are outside the range of our shared knowledge. With Person B, I follow a similar general tactic although the topics themselves may differ.

Linking People and Minds

In developing and acting out a new construction of experience in a relationship, we do many things that metaphor does for us also. Relating and the use of metaphors are thus illustrative of the same psychologically important process. On the one hand, in a metaphor we have two realms of meaning (e.g., shipping/government or space/emotion), and we extend from one to the other in order to recast our understanding of one in terms of the other. On the other hand, in relationships we start with two personally organized systems of meaning, one each for each person entering the relationship—we can think of these systems of meaning as "personalities" for the time being—and by creating connections between those systems, the two partners may eventually come to see themselves as psychologically and behaviorally interdependent. By various processes of negotiation, the two persons construct a shared, but new, entity. That new creation somehow extends the awareness of the two original persons as well as influencing their behavior, thoughts, and emotions, and in this sense the new creation transforms their thinking. Relationships are expansive in that sense, just as metaphors are. The complex of relational interdependences arises, in part, through the transaction of shared meanings based on the two original sets of mental foundations provided by the two individual minds.

Metaphors also, like relationships, are embedded in a time and culture. Nowadays we generate almost no metaphors about our state's leader being a good shepherd, for instance, though this was a common metaphor 2,000 years ago. Metaphors, like relationships, are crucibles for the creative extension of thinking, meaning, and understanding that depend on the context in which such extension

2meaning systems working together ⇒ a shared identity

occurs. Likewise, relationships also have a context derived from culture and a place in time. Thus, the attempts to equalize relationships between men and women in the present day would probably astonish our ancestors, who saw a different "natural order."

Within the contexts of time and culture, relational partners thus do several things rather similar to metaphors: They start out with two minimally connected universes of thought (their two separate minds), and they create bridges between them that expand, limit, and transform comprehension and identities. There is a parallelism between the use and appreciation of metaphor, on the one hand, and the activity of two human minds as they create, sustain, and develop social and personal relationships on the other hand. In metaphor one realm of discourse is translated to another; in relationships two separate minds draw on a context of knowledge to make transfer, comparison, inference, and overlap with each other.

It will take me the rest of the book to explore these instances of the tendency to "Go beyond here and look further," but the point is essentially the same for metaphor, relationships, similarity, exchanges, meaning, and a number of concepts used in relationship research. Inference and extension lie beneath each one of them, yet each of them requires not only the existence of two entities between which the relevant transfer occurs (two realms of reference in the case of metaphor, two minds for relationships, a symbol and its object for meaning), *but also an awareness or construction* of the connection between them. Such an awareness implies the ability to (mentally) stand outside the objects, people, events, and experiences being compared and, from that vantage point, to comprehend them differently.

For extension to take place in a figure of speech, different elements must be simultaneously present in the same person's mind. If I accept for the moment the usefulness of calling the government a ship, then I simultaneously have to think I know something basic about ships and about government. I have to see a useful connection between the two realms of discourse, and I have to be able to work with the connection. So in relationships, to create extended mutual comprehension or a world of shared meanings, I have to be able to detect what is in my partner's mind, to compare it to what is in my mind, to be able to see the connection, and so be able to work with the connection. Naturally, in general, one would expect that in relationships we would find it easier to grasp someone else's mean-

*example of metaphor + "go beyond + look further"

ing and mind to the extent that their thinking is similar to something we already understand well: our *own* thinking. Such grasping of others' meaning in this way depends on some other processes that are well illustrated by a fuller consideration of metaphor.

❦ Metaphors as Guides for Relationships and Research

It is superficially interesting to look at the metaphors, images, and symbols that people use in relationships and talk, as above, or to look at relationships as the interesting co-presence of two persons in the same interconnected universe of behavior. However, I have just been pointing out that the parallelism between metaphors and relationships as interpersonal processes based on meaning extends beyond such interconnections and serves a constructive outcome. The important and transformative ("extensive") psychological process of inference creates the basis from which one mind transforms or influences another and the grounds on which two persons can jointly construct something new, which then becomes the new base of operations.

Metaphors as Figures of Thought About Relationships

It is not original nor particularly interesting to recognize that the terms in which people often speak about relationships connect one realm of discourse with another realm. It is so common to talk in such a way about relationships that we usually do not even notice it. We speak of bonding, we talk of couples, we describe marriage as union or conjugal (from the Latin for "putting cattle together in the same yoke"!). We hear of relationships breaking up because of relational friction or getting burned out. Alternatively people might tie the knot, or click instantly, or have the right chemistry. All of these everyday phrases are metaphorical and are derived from culturally and historically important areas of the experience of our ancestors, such as blacksmithing, boating, or agriculture. Many are now so familiar that we simply do not recognize their origin in metaphor, and many of the metaphors, having lost some of their original immediacy, have become merely quaint. Nonetheless, metaphors are Venus's-flytraps. They captivate with their vividness and then entice the user into particular ways of thinking. This assertion is true in the relationship sphere as much as it is anywhere else, and it is true of relationship scholars as much as of other human beings. Something apparently superficial (vivid language) is actually deeply structured into human thinking, and this deep structure shapes behavior.

Lakoff and Johnson (1980) and Lakoff (1986) proposed that metaphors are not simply figures of speech, if that means that they are florid linguistic devices that enliven an otherwise dull and monotonous discourse—even though that is the view that had been held to be true about metaphors for some 2,000 years. By contrast, Lakoff (1986) proposed that metaphors are figures of thought: That is, they are presentations, which happen to be expressed most often in speech, of the ways in which humans *talk about, develop,* and *extend* their thoughts. Although they represent categories useful in pure analysis of language, metaphors also reveal something about the mind that expresses itself through them, just as clothing does more than cover the body—it also reveals something about the wearer.

A number of scholars in relationships have studied how human beings use metaphors to portray relationships, but I focus on only a selected set of authors. The selected authors include Kovecses's (1991) work on metaphors of love; Owen's (1984, 1985) work on metaphors and relationship development; Baxter's (1987, 1992b) work on relational symbols and metaphors; and Harvey, Weber, and Orbuch's (1990) work on accounts of breakup in relationships. There are several other works on this general area such as McCall's (1982) discussion of metaphor in the framing of feelings about disengagement from relationships; Bernard, Adelman, and Schroeder's (1991) consideration of marketing metaphors for meeting mates; and my own discussion (Duck, 1984, 1987a) of the metaphors chosen by researchers to represent development of relationships or to conceptualize the whole set of topics that compose this area. There is also a journal devoted to *Metaphor and Symbolic Activity,* and enough books on metaphor to fill several large tea-chests. The topic can run away with one, but the selected research illustrates a few simple points that I need to make.

Metaphors of Love

Our language is rich with metaphors of love, such as insanity metaphors ("I am crazy about you," "He's mad about her," "She's nuts over him"), nutrient metaphors ("I'm love-starved," "I hunger for you," "I can't live without you," even the nicknames, "Honey," "Honeypie," "Sugar," and "Sweetie"), fire metaphors ("All aflame with passion," "Burning with love," "Hot stuff"), and many others explored by Kovecses (1986, 1991). In these cases the metaphor represents love as something else, such as insanity, fire, or nutrients. In part, these are persuasive images because they are physiologi- cally based, and the experience thus relates to something that is physically familiar. Feeling on fire sometimes so aptly describes the visceral feeling of passion that the metaphor is irresistible. On the other hand, a creative author can help readers to comprehend a mysterious experience by relating that experience to something more familiar but that had not previously seemed to be relevant (e.g., that love is an addiction or a disease or a punishment). In either case, the metaphor is informative because of its connection of one realm of experience with another.

Of course in everyday speech we are not creative Shakepeares and do not continually employ fresh and vivid metaphors. Rather we eagerly adopt those that are already available in the culture to elucidate our experiences. The several ways of metaphorizing love that are well established in a culture thus do not create new ways of comprehending love so much as they provide socially authorized reference points or norms for thinking about it. Both new and old metaphors, however, help construct the love emotion for individu- als by providing images and benchmarks against which to interpret the experience (e.g., as hot and engulfing).

Another aspect of metaphors is that they lead to inferences that can expand comprehension of the concept of love. For example, if love is insanity then the person who experiences love (or hears others describe it) would be quite likely to infer that it may entail loss of conscious control or tendencies to act in ways that seem irrational. Particular metaphors may thus shape both behavior and expectancies and/or may help define norms just as much as they may reflect them, because the range of metaphors is not infinite and some sorts of metaphors are culturally preferred over others.

Kovecses (1991) explores the underlying prototype of any emo- tion (in this case, love) that is contained in the metaphors and built into common sense (the "folk-mind") about the topic. Kovecses treats metaphors as folk-theoretical descriptions of love, cases that embody conceptual views of the emotion that are shared by the members of the culture. Specifically he argues that love is a complex emotional experience composed of many parts that are occasionally mysterious for people, both as collections of parts and as parts taken separately. People readily and naturally refer to the cultural guidance that metaphors offer: They use metaphors as ways to define and explain their experience of the emotions. For Kovecses, then, to study metaphors of love is to unravel a complex set of beliefs held by a given culture to define and understand mysterious emotional experiences.

Kovecses's method is essentially language-based. By grouping together various instances of metaphor uses, Kovecses identifies common threads running through the linguistic fabric. For instance, a common thread of nutrition is discovered in the set of metaphors: I need love; She's love-starved; I can't live without love; He hungered for love. From such an analysis Kovecses develops the argument that the concept of love as nutrient is an important component of folk wisdom about the essential character of the experience of love: Love satisfies and sustains a lover; to be without love is to be less than you could be or to fail to thrive.

Kovecses (1986, 1991) suggested that metaphors amount to strong conceptual models of the nature of love and psychological influences on one's experience of love. Rather than treating the terms and usages as mere fripperies, Kovecses makes the important point that metaphors are, in effect, lay theories. We adopt a metaphor because it captures and explains something about the essence of phenomena in a manner that expands our understanding of them in particular ways that we find valuable. As with other types of theories, lay theories focus us on particular aspects of phenomena (heat, sustenance) and exclude others. As with other theories, lay theories shape our conceptualization of things and point us in particular directions while also explaining. They serve as mental reference points of the sort referred to in other work on relationships as "prototypes" (Fehr, 1993). However, Kovecses's approach is based entirely on linguistic analysis and, as he himself recognizes (Kovecses, 1986, pp. 84-85), this sort of analysis does not by itself demonstrate that "people actually live their love experiences in terms of the models that have been recovered from conventionalized language use." We think in terms of metaphor, but do we act in terms of metaphor?

Yes, we do. In showing how metaphorical modeling is related to the other ways of experiencing love, Marston, Hecht, and Robers (1987) developed relevant evidence in their studies of "ways of loving." They used a method that tied linguistic usages to other aspects of love as an emotional experience. Marston et al. collected evidence about love as an experience, using metaphors such as colors, and also explored the ways of expressing romantic love. They depicted love as a set of polyvalent and interdependent perceptions involving cognition, feelings, and behavior. They claimed that the experience of love is so complex as to defy reduction to a single realm of human affect, or behavior, or cognition. This complex experience of love involves a wide variety of linguistic, emotional, behavioral, and cognitive elements, and the interdependence of these elements is sustained by communication. The exploration of this possibility through examination of "love ways" focused on linguistic definitions of love (e.g., love is doing things together), physiological experiences of love (e.g., love makes me feel warm), and communicative dimensions of love (e.g., I express love by telling my partner "I love you").

The results showed a wide range of experiences of love that persons communicated to others by means of six preferred "ways of loving" such as collaborative love (feelings of energy and intensified emotional response) or committed love (togetherness as a way of communicating love). The ways in which people truly experience emotion or a relationship are closely tied to the language in which they describe and communicate about the experience. The terms contain the experience but also direct it in some ways: The terms of metaphors (and other kinds of thought) are part of the sense-making that humans do in coming to comprehend a complex experience. In fact, later work by Hecht, Marston, and Larkey (1994) further indicates that individuals experiencing love as "committed" have higher quality relationships. Thus the language is not an irrelevance: It is tied closely to the experience of love.

language used to describe a relationship affects & is affected by the experience

Metaphors of Relationship Change

Critics may argue that such conclusions may not be true of the experience and conduct of relationships as a whole, but are true only of emotional components, such as love. Nevertheless, several bodies of research suggest a close correspondence between linguistic descriptions of relationships as a whole and the ways in which people think about and act in developing relationships over time.

Owen (1984) observed seven themes that are present in the discourse of persons describing their relationships: commitment, involvement, work, uniqueness, manipulation, respect, and fragility. He argued that such themes represent the organization or prototypic structure of a person's view of experience. Others (e.g., Honeycutt, 1993) have similarly suggested that MOPs (memory organization packets) store relational knowledge in organized ways that affect behavior in relationships and judgments about relationships (e.g., judgments about whether they are developing "at the right pace"). Owen (1985) developed these themes by showing that such thinking can be extended to relationship construction and behavior. He argued that episodic themes that account for specific limited events (e.g., falling in love) are also bound together into themes (such as commitment) that account for transitions between limited events or states (e.g., between dating and marriage). Owen contended that "knowing a couple's metaphors helps us to construct a richer image of the communication in relationships" (1985, p. 10). Owen also showed that metaphors have psychological force in affecting the ways in which a person or a pair of persons (and, indeed, research investigators themselves) construct the relationship. Lately he has also shown how metaphors construct the experience of relationship dissolution (Owen, 1993). Language is thus constitutive because it affects and influences the ways in which we report and engage in experience.

Of course, "language" is not just something abstract but is the basis of real human talk, and as Wood (1982, p. 75) put it, "It is through talk that persons define themselves and their relationships and through talk that definitions once entered into are revised over the life of a relationship." For instance, relational partners often create "personal idioms" or their own shorthand ways of coding experience (e.g., by making up nicknames for other people or for private activities such as sex), as Hopper, Knapp, and Scott (1981) pointed out. Hopper et al. showed that couples used such terms as a way of "celebrating" their coupling as a special dyad. Bell, Buerkel-Rothfuss, and Gore (1987) showed that these personal idioms are reconstructed and developed as relationships develop and that they function to create, as well as to express, the closeness of the developing relationship. These idioms construct relationships through the development of a system of communication that is shared between the partners alone and so is private to them and excludes other people. The use of language thus creates a boundary that defines the relationship in a way that has important behavioral and psychological consequences.

Other research classifies the ways in which persons symbolize their relationships and use language to construct them. Baxter (1992b), for instance, has used metaphor as a means for understanding the ways in which people make sense of their developing romantic relationships. She examined metaphors underlying descriptions of romantic development by relational partners themselves, taking the position that such metaphors are part of the sense-making activity by which persons organize their relationships. Baxter looked for root metaphors, the fundamental organizing themes of metaphorical expression that essentially capture and convey persons' experience—or experiential gestalts, or patterns of perception. Baxter argues that metaphors help people to express what is otherwise difficult to express at a literal level. A metaphor's vividness is something that helps a partner "get" (and so share) the meaning that one wishes to convey. What did Baxter (1992b) find? She found that three root metaphors dominated the discourse of persons describing their romantic relationships. *Relationship development as work* was represented by such phrases as "it was hard getting into the groove . . . we worked through our problems . . . it didn't come without work." *Relationship development as a voyage of discovery* emphasized the disclosure of more facts about partners and the negative consequences of "going onto automatic pilot . . . not getting any excitement out of the relationship . . . as things went on holding pattern." By contrast, things went well because people "keep finding out new things . . . and keep rediscovering." *Relationship development as an uncontrollable force* produced such concepts as "the relationship engulfed us totally . . . and I let other things slip because I just couldn't help it . . . because this was meant to be."

Baxter (1992b) also found other powerful, though less common, root metaphors such as *relationship development as danger* (need to be cautious at first . . . playing with fire . . . I have to have my guard up),

[margin annotations: relationship metaphors ↓ 1. work 2. discovery 3. uncontrollable force 4. danger]

relationship development as economic exchange (we make compromises . . . we split everything equally . . . we bargain and negotiate), *relationship development as a living organism* (birth of the relationship . . . growth to maturity . . . survival of feelings . . . it is a relationship that has never died out), and *relationship development as a game* (we played cat and mouse, alternating between pursuer and pursued . . . the relationship became a mind game . . . I won him over).

Baxter's study thus illustrates that metaphors powerfully influence people's experience of relationships. She also emphasizes the uses and functions of metaphorical images in the actual development of relationships and relational behavior. She also made a valuable theoretical contribution by conjecturing that different images predominate at different stages of relationships or that different types of relationships compel different sorts of images as distinct from others. By understanding the different folk-logics, Baxter suggests, we can get a better understanding of some of the cognitive and logical forces that attend behavioral development of relationships.

Metaphors of Relationships and Relationship Problems

McCall (1982) noted that the metaphors used by persons reporting on their relationship losses contained useful information indicating how a person construes the predicament. His insight was that such metaphors indicated a possible line of treatment for the person or repair for the relationship. Thus someone who feels that the relationship is "coming apart" will be satisfied with different sorts of advice than someone who feels that it has "become a cage." Indeed, some therapists and other counselors (Mair, 1976) have stressed the important roles of metaphors in human beings' representation of their other miseries also. The argument of such practitioners is that the metaphor not only represents, but also shapes, the responses of the patient to the problem. It does so by presenting a version of what is happening in a way that frames and carries some implications.

As an extension to the work on development of relationships, Harvey et al. (1990) offered a related study of the breakup of relationships, especially the ways in which people use accounts of breakups. It has been recognized (e.g., Owen, 1993) that metaphors play an important role in the accounts that people produce for relationship breakdown. It has also been suggested (Duck, 1982b) that such metaphorical discourse helps persons to do "grave dressing," or the social burial of relationships, after their demise and so to cope with the aftermath as well as prepare for new relationships in future. Harvey et al. (1990) have focused more extensively on accounts—meanings organized into stories—to explain the loss of close personal relationships. They have shown how such stories not only explain events but also help the person to structure a response to grief by offering rationalizations and justifications for the occurrence that caused the loss. Thus again the linguistic forms used by people in suffering are also practical guides to the business of coping.

Harvey et al. emphasized *homo narrans* (see also Fisher, 1985), or humankind as storytellers, and this fits well with the points being developed here. The ways in which people represent their circumstances linguistically are not just superficial indicators of something unimportant in psychological life. These representations offer direct evidence about the ways in which persons experience, and prepare themselves to deal with, their circumstances. In brief, accounts and stories focus people on particular issues or concerns and so encourage them to see events in terms of those issues and concerns. But as well as being personal versions of events seen in a particular frame, such accounts draw on existing cultural models and frameworks. The storyteller, the metaphor user, and the employer of language all draw on a cultural linguistic store in order to construe their own personal experiences. These personal and cultural stores are important shapers of experience in relationships (McAdams, 1993). Rather than just being amusing batteries of terms that enliven our speech, metaphors are actually culturally and personally organized psychological structures that not only express our thoughts but also "structure how we perceive, how we think, and what we do" (Lakoff & Johnson, 1980, p. 4).

Metaphors in Relationship Research

While the above discussion has focused on the activities of human relaters, I do not want to exclude human relationship researchers from the same analysis. Not only do relaters use metaphors, but so do scholars: We all use a language to conduct (research on) relationships, and such language frames the (research on) relationships, both extending and restricting the ways in which people think about (research on) relationships. Just as metaphorical frameworks for thinking about emotion frame relaters' thoughts, so researchers' frames of thought are channeled by the metaphors that they choose to describe relational phenomena. For example, researchers who conceptualize developing relationship as "a trajectory" (e.g., Surra, 1984) naturally go on to look for "turning points" or "changes of direction" (Surra, Arizzi, & Asmussen, 1988). It is even true that the singularity inherent in the metaphor of a trajectory constrains present research to focus on *the* trajectory of a relationship and not on whether we should begin to explore the separate trajector*ies* of several components to the experience of relationships (Duck, 1980, p. 118). If you begin by conceptualizing a thing (a relationship) as having a route (a trajectory), then it does not make any sense to look for it having several separate parts. Far less would you be encouraged to suppose that each part takes a different route simultaneously or progresses along its track at different rates separately, rather like the Conestoga wagons that all took different routes across the prairie to the same eventual new Western towns in the 1870s. Yet studies have recently shown that knowledge, intimacy, similarity, and evaluation take different tracks simultaneously (Duck, Rutt, et al., 1991). A trajectory metaphor runs the risk of narrowing the vision of the possibilities and directing attention only to the finding of the one True Path for a relationship's development. The metaphor also constrains researchers to operationalize a relationship's development by means of growth in intimacy as if that is the most important or even the only endpoint for relationships to be striving to reach (Allan, 1993). The trajectory metaphor is therefore perhaps one of those that Fitzpatrick (1993) had in mind when she urged us that "today's illumination may well become tomorrow's dogma" (p. 284).

For another example, researchers sometimes write of the decline of relationships as a "film shown in reverse" (Altman & Taylor, 1973), which suggests that relationship decline is the precise reverse of relationship development. In some ways it may be true (e.g., affect decreases, attachment reverses, time together declines, intimacy diminishes). In other respects the metaphor misleads us into ignoring other aspects of relating during relationship decline. For instance, amount of information about someone does not decline during relationship disengagement, but rather the information's significance may be reinterpreted (Duck & Lea, 1983). The film analogy does not alert us to look for such transformations, however. Likewise, those researchers who focus on relational development as passage through a conceptual roadway from low intimacy to high intimacy are inclined to ignore the possibility that relationships are *transformed* (rather than simply magnified in some quality like intimacy level) by their development (Conville, 1988). As I have noted before (Duck, 1984), the life of relationships could just as well be metaphorized to the life cycle of frogs (eggs, tadpoles, frogs) or insects (egg, larva, pupa, adult), where each previous state is completely different in form from the later ones, yet the individual frog or insect is still the same individual. Since such transformations are rather hard to operationalize in relationship research, however, the tadpole and insect metaphors are probably never going to be applied to relationships, even if they are a truer reflection of what actually happens in relationships.

The perspective of the researcher is framed in the metaphors used to describe phenomena, and the parallelism between researchers' activities and those of other human beings should not be minimized (Duck, 1987a). In both cases, as with other attempts to communicate with someone, we presume a frame of reference and a background of assumptions. The frame both informs and limits the ways in which we shape up to the phenomena. This is essentially the same issue as that in physics: Observation cannot be neutral. Every view of phenomena essentially presumes a view*point*, and the relativity of different viewpoints can help us to see something fundamentally important about relationships just as it does in physics. Likewise, in the personal relationships field, relational assessment devices are not neutral devices, but they too also presume and encapsulate a viewpoint. Like metaphor, this process frames and shapes the sorts of things that we count as "data" and the sorts of explanations that we will find satisfying.

The above position has many unseen implications for relationship research. For one thing, as argued by Bernard (1972), Olson (1977), Duck and Sants (1983) and Duck (1990), and now becoming fashionable as a view of relationships (Noller & Guthrie, 1992; Surra & Ridley, 1991), insiders and outsiders viewing the same relationship events can form quite different views of what occurred. This difference has apparently surprised some researchers who thought that there was one true way to view relationship events and have been puzzled by the reasons why their subjects did not obey this evident law (Christensen, Sullaway, & King, 1983). Such researchers, adopting a scientific metaphor for their own work, seek a single true way of looking at the things that happen in relationships. Some take the view (alternative to the one here) that differences between observers' views are evidence that one observer (usually the one who is not a scientist) must be wrong. For example, notice the emphasis on objective truth and the privileged perceptions of an investigator that are contained in Berscheid and Peplau's (1983) claim that:

> the degree of correspondence between the participants' *beliefs* about the relationship and an investigator's *description* of the *properties* of the *actual* relationship activity encompasses a huge set of interesting questions. However, to be useful, relationship *descriptors* must ultimately be *true* to the *properties* of interconnected activity *patterns* that can be *recorded* and agreed upon by *impartial* investigators. (p. 13, emphases added)

By contrast my position here suggests that the usefulness of investigations is likely to be related to the degree of correspondence between the investigator's descriptions and those that have meaning to the persons in the relationships, not those that have meaning only to the investigator, the investigators' colleagues, or other academic culture-members. It is unlikely, however, that investigators who do not look for personal meaning (as distinct from "objective reality") will ever find it or find it to be influential in relationships.

All the same, Duck, Pond, and Leatham (1994) demonstrated that lonely persons see the results of their interactions quite differently from those in which outsiders (or the lonely person's partner) see the events. In particular, lonely persons tended to draw negative conclusions about their interactions and to feel that the interactions adversely affected their relationship even when other observers saw no such result. The differences are differences in the construction of events or in the meaning assigned to them, not in some misconception or error: Lonely persons' perceptions of events are just as personally valid as anyone else's as a way of understanding the world, even if that understanding fosters unhappiness that some other perceptions might not. Attention to the organization and importance of such

constructions would emphasize their role in the creation and sustenance of the experience of loneliness for the lonely person.

However one interprets these and a growing band of similar
studies, the essence of their message is that relationship events are
like other events in the sense that people's views of them are
structured by their starting points and the context from which they
see things. Individual perceivers differ in their interpretation of
such events, and the differences in part *are* the experience of the
relationship that the perceiver takes away. Such studies make the point
that alternative constructions of events are a part of life so familiar to
us that we fail to notice their existence only when we are being
"scientific" and begin to believe that reality takes only one shape. In
everyday relationships, the encountering of alternative viewpoints is
a fact of life as we talk with other people. Yet it is a fact that relational
partners must creatively resolve in order to communicate better.

Likewise, scholarly researchers are human too, and show the
same tendencies to structure their thought and use terms that support and produce the structure. Just as metaphor and relationships
reach out to new areas and extend persons' understandings of the
world, so too do scholars extend their research to one another by the
adoption and use of shared terminology. Thus scholars' terms,
metaphors, and viewpoints are susceptible to the same analysis as
are the terms, metaphors, and viewpoints of other individual human
beings. Such terms, metaphors, and viewpoints are as illustrative of
human activity as are the terms, metaphors, and viewpoints of
ordinary people living ordinary lives. Both serve essentially the
same purpose: trying to make sense of the world and to find others
who attach the same sorts of intelligible meaning to it.

Another incidental but important consequence of the present
approach is that it also accepts Kelly's (1969b) argument that theories of human behavior have to be reflexive—that is, they have to
explain what the *theorist* is up to when formulating a theory about
human behavior. Any theory of human behavior should be able to
explain the behavior of the theorist in the theory's own terms or else
it is not a general theory of human behavior (Mair, 1970). Likewise,
theories of relationships must be able to explain not only the past
regularities but the future transformations of relationships. In particular, theories should encompass the fact that many relational events
that have the greatest significance to people are *not* those that are

straightforward repetitions of the past but are those that have not happened before and are transforming of identity and meaning (e.g., first kiss, birth of a child, a wedding, the ending of a relationship, death of a partner, first sexual experience together). It is often in looking forward to such impending events that human beings guide their relational behavior in the present, and in this sense things in the future can have an effect before they happen.

Moreover, any theory, just as any other human utterance, should be understood as an invitational statement about the theorist's (speaker's) views of the world rather than as a revelation of objective fact. A theory or utterance articulates a "rhetorical vision" (i.e., a persuasive image) that is offered to others and invites them to accept that viewpoint. Those theories that acquire fashionable currency are accepted presumably because they resonate with the views of the world then held in common by other human beings and these people accordingly accept the invitation. Or at least the theories shift readers toward a vantage point where that resonance becomes more possible and acceptance more likely.

❦ Summary and Conclusions

This chapter started with a point about extension and inference, then looked at talk and metaphor, and ended with the ways in which language frames our thoughts and acts as a process by which meaning is created by one or two persons, whether scholars or other human beings. Although originally made as points about metaphor and language, these insights equally pertain to relationships and relationship research and are particularly relevant to *behavior*. Just as we exhibit our thoughts through communication and these influence our own behavior and the behavior of others, so too does this transpire in relationships. In relationships we talk to partners and so exhibit our thoughts in such a way that we can relate to one another. Just as metaphors present a particular framework for viewing a given matter, so talk in relationships is a way of *presenting* our views of, or our thoughts about, the world, rather than a simple mechanism for letting thoughts out of their cage.

In sum, this chapter proposes contexts for understanding the value of symbol-sharing. It has taken metaphors as a first example of symbols that indicate a general human approach to thinking about and acting in the world. It also drew on the general point of rhetorical theorists who claim that any statement or piece of talk about anything implies, presumes, and has built into it a view, a perspective—even a theory. As we have seen, many social scientific methods and theories also have built into them some (often implicit) perspective about the underlying nature of human life, which I have elsewhere termed "theorettes" (Duck, 1992c). These theorettes guide, shape, or constrain the things that researchers do and see, just as metaphors do. If I reach for a hammer rather than a wrench then it is partly because I see the problem in a particular way, and see a hammer as more useful than a wrench *for that particular job*, not because a hammer is universally a better tool than a wrench. The same argument holds true for social scientific methods such as questionnaires or specific tests, and it also holds for methods of study and concepts about relationships (Duck & Montgomery, 1991). Likewise, any theory of relationships structures its data gathering in the world in a certain way that contains a "theorette" (Duck, 1992c).

Any theory also presumes an underlying view of the essence of human nature. A theory speaks, usually silently, about the ways in which human beings are carrying out their daily business of being human. In just this same way an individual forms a personal viewpoint of the world and creates relationships with that viewpoint more ready to hand than any other—at least to start with. Thus the business of relating occurs in and through transacting such frameworks and assumptions. We should explore them and the ways in which they work specifically through talk. It is as if each partner has one lens of a stereoscope and the relationship is brought to life by the partners placing the lenses together and seeing everything afresh in 3-D.

This chapter thus outlined the case that relationships are based on the transaction of meaning and that talk is a key activity through which relationships are created, sustained, and developed. The chapter has begun to lay out the position that the interaction of minds occurs in a semantic context where meaning is shared and where the appreciation of the actions, gestures, language, nonverbal behavior, and other symbolic communicative forms is shared between the participants.

I have also laid out the claim that the transactive extension of meaning from one area of thought to another is characteristic of relationships, in that the two minds that come to relationships extend one another in the processes of coming together. The chapter also claimed that the same principle is evident in the workings of the process of metaphor, which (like relationships) causes a transactive extension of meaning, is likely to be somewhat constrained by the context from which it originates, takes account of linguistic influences on thought, and ends up extending the meaning system from which the metaphor is made.

The process of linking things together by use of common reference points or by linking together different realms of discourse or different points of understanding is a key process not only in understanding how people talk to one another but also how we can relate. By use of commonly vantaged tools, talk allows individuals to realize similarities that construct pathways between minds that generate access from one to the other and then permit development beyond that. The psychological cross-referencing that takes place in the conversations of everyday life is an overlooked but important concretion that performs this function of bridging minds together, allowing them to invent collaborative new comprehension, and helping them to sustain that comprehension. Talk is the agency of social behavior through which many of the other relational processes come to life.

2

❦

Human Relational Life in Its Context Living With the Possible

If we simply live immersed in the [stream of consciousness], we encounter only undifferentiated experiences that melt into one another in a flowing continuum.

A. Schultz (1973, p. 17)

If we are to have a psychology of [a person's] own experience, then we must anchor our basic concepts in that personal experience. . . . It is only in terms of his [or her] predictions that [a person] ever touches the real world.

George A. Kelly (1969a, pp. 273-275)

Mens cuiusque is est quisque. [The mind of each person *is* the person]

Marcus Tullius Cicero, *De Republica* (49 B.C.)

The human quest is not about to be concluded. . . . [I]nstead it seems likely that whatever may now appear to be the most obvious fact will look quite different from the vantage point of tomorrow's fresh theoretical positions. . . . The human enterprise is at best a touch-and-go proposition.

George A. Kelly (1969a, p. 284)

OVERVIEW

Chapter 2 begins by noticing that humankind faces continual uncertainty. Like weather forecasters, we all live a life laced with contingency and always face an indeterminate variety of possible outcomes. The chapter argues that this background is not simply amusing or irritating, but fundamentally shapes human activity. Human activity, including relating, is significantly structured by the constant imminence of the future and is contingent on the human need to make sense of the continuous flow of onrushing experience in life as it goes wherever it is going. This chapter explores the individual and relational consequences of this context of uncertainty, ambiguity, and contingency, while also relating it to some other contexts. For this purpose Chapter 2 explores the ways in which persons segment the flow of experience, make choices between alternative ways of predicting the future, and create the sense of meaning from the continually unfinished business of living with the possible. In exploring these issues, the chapter not only continues to attempt to integrate interpersonal communication with rhetoric (i.e., to represent interpersonal behavior as persuasive and presentational) but also starts to lay out some formal theoretical statements.

❦ The Importance of Change and Constancy in Everyday Life

It is all too easy to think of human behavior but forget one of its important contexts: the future. The fact is that humans do not really know for sure how things will turn out, whether it be a cake that we are baking, a career, a friendship, or a young son. For that reason we spend a lot of our time hoping, preparing, buying planning diaries, worrying, fearing, arranging, taking out insurance, getting excited, looking forward to events, setting and organizing life around deadlines, and generally developing expectations, in an attempt to prepare for the unfolding future.

Several theorists have emphasized that the world is truly in constant flux. The Ancient Greek philosopher Heraclitus even noted that we can never step into the same river twice because it is always changing its specific form, and we also change it just by stepping into it. Since Heraclitus, one tradition of thought has taken change as a central "given" in human life. This chapter will develop the psychological implications and effects of change and uncertainty, draw-ing on the thinking of Marcel Proust, George Kelly, and Mick Billig.

Change, uncertainty, and process are often not obvious; people have many tricks to make life look stable and predictable. The novelist Marcel Proust noted that even if life is continually unfold-ing, developing, and rushing along, even if we are constantly aging, facing new challenges, resolving relational dilemmas, and dealing with daily hassles, all the same, human beings constantly devise ways to make the world seem as if it is a relatively stable place. Except in those shocking moments when we look too closely at the mirror, we usually act as if time is passing only in some theoretical or trivial sense. We describe our worlds in terms of such apparently stable concepts as "my marriage" or "my career" or "my children" or "my self." It may seem odd to suggest that these stable-sounding words actually denote things that are changing, variable, or devel-oping—but they are. In part such stabilization is achieved by the very nature of our Western language structure that focuses us on nouns ("things") rather than on continuous processes, and on a subject-predicate form of language that encourages us to identify linear connections between things. Other linguistic forms (e.g., East-ern languages) emphasize process more than we do (Yum, 1988).

Human beings typically perceive the continuous flow of experi-ence in chunks, segments, or events, and this applies also to rela-tionships that represent conveniently stable-sounding units. Yet, as Bennett (in press) has recently contended, most relational phenomena are surrounded by a "sense of 'ongoingness'" and hence are implicitly always open-ended and incomplete in our experience, even as we assume stability of the world. To comprehend the impact of recog-nizing relationships and behavior in them as a process, we need to discuss the ways in which persons deal with uncertainty, segment experience, make choices between alternative expectations for the future, are affected by life's continually unfinished feel, and express their conclusions, hypotheses, and expectations to other people.

Segmenting Experience Into Chunks and Units

The human segmentation of experience applies to almost every-thing, even though members of different cultures do not break up the flow of experience in the same ways (e.g., some cultures do not break up experience as readily into "things" as Western cultures do, preferring to focus on activities or the conjunction of forces). Instead of seeing time as an undifferentiated flow, for example, human beings have separated it into days and nights or weeks, months, and years. All the same, daylight is not the same length every day of the year, some months have 30 days and some do not, and one month even has a different length every 4 years! Where we nowadays see it as natural that there are four distinct seasons, the ancient Egyptians thought it was equally natural to perceive that nature had three seasons (Time of the Flood, Time of Heat, Time of Harvest).

Despite their original arbitrariness, referents help members of particular cultures to pattern experience in a way that anticipates its continued unfolding and makes some kinds of sense out of the experience for members of that culture. However, the nature of even such events and referents is unstable, flowing, and changing all the same. Exactly the same things do not happen on May 8th each year; *this* romantic relationship is not exactly the same as *that* romantic relationship in all respects (or even as *this* romantic relationship was 2 years ago); *you* do not see these events in precisely the same way as *I* see them all the time. Also, "a day" contains many different and unrelated events, and circumstances may be very different at the end of it than they were at the beginning.

Two interesting psychological questions then are (a) why do people characterize things as stable when they are variable? and (b) how do people make their choices about the phenomena that are "important" enough to them to be noticed as different from the background in which they occur? For example, my weight fluctuates within limits from day to day, but I notice the changes only when they get out of hand.

It is important to recognize that the segmentation of events is essentially arbitrary, but it is also *psychologically functional* for people and contributes to the "punctuation" of their communication as well as of their experience (Watzlawick, Beavin, & Jackson, 1967). Perhaps for this reason changes are marked and noted as changes between *states*, and names are applied to those states. For some cultures or religions, "a day" ends with sunset and a new day begins; for others it ends at midnight and changes to a new one; for others, yesterday ends as the rising sun makes this a new today— but cultures do mark the change one way or another, and the fact that such segmentation occurs is illustrative of an important human process of comprehension.

Segmenting Relationships Into States and Stages

We can all probably nod sagely at the obviousness of this observation, but the points about arbitrariness and variability are also true of the daily experience of stable relationships. In the same manner as above, various changes in relationships are marked and noted by segmentations. Dating leads to engagement, engagement leads to marriage after a full ceremony complete with grotesque relatives and photographs to celebrate it into the future. Other relationship passages, such as the transition to parenthood, are achieved and recognized and even reported to the newspapers. In their own ways such notable transitions are formal ways of segmenting a relational life and marking out difference by creating a sense of gradual progression from one recognized "state" to another and celebrating those "states" (Werner, Altman, Brown, & Ginat, 1993).

There is another very important point, however, that is not often acknowledged in research. Relationships, too, are variable experiences full of challenge, change, and difference as well as stability. Partners have occasional quarrels even in good relationships and spend each day dealing with that day's relational events, whatever those happen to be. In a sense we do not step into the same relationship twice. Yet at the practical psychological level people (including researchers) organize their lives in ways that make relationships seem stable, predictable, and even routine, as if the "same" relationship could be experienced a thousand times and as if one label (e.g., marriage, friendship) adequately captures the inherent variability.

Researchers typically attempt to exclude such variation from their analysis of relationships or to remove atypicality in order to focus on the stable and prototypical features. For example, most measures of intimacy and closeness are lauded for being "reliable" rather than criticized for being unrepresentative of the variability that people actually experience (Berscheid, Snyder, & Omoto, 1989). Yet a true picture of relationship experience would include assessments of such variability within them. Otherwise researchers may be doing the equivalent of finding the "true position" of a swinging pendulum or setting themselves the task of finding the exact single time-point that best characterizes or typifies this particular January 4th.

Researchers also characterize relationships as good, functional, satisfactory or bad, dysfunctional, and dissatisfying, as if such attributes were not only inherent in the relationship but also stable features. The problem is that all relationships contain simultaneously both a "bright side" and a "dark side" (Duck, 1994b). Part of the problem of continuing relationships is the difficulty of managing the dark side—irritations, squabbles, and pains—in the context of the bright side. Successful relaters *manage* the bad side: They do not just *have* one. Fixed labels dissemble the varieties that occur within experience.

The same point about segmentation is true not only of the stages of relationships but also of the types of relationships, some of which are treated as obvious in some cultures but not in others, or to some people in a culture but not to others. For example, Harré (1977) pointed out that some cultures emphasize the importance of "brotherhood" between male adults, who may even go through formal rituals to establish their bonds of loyalty to one another; yet our culture has no such formal system (except perhaps in fraternity houses and Masonic Lodges). In other cultures the central importance of the cousin is beyond dispute, yet we have no idea in our culture why anyone would privilege such a relationship over the more apparent one of sisterhood. In the Western world the obviousness of dating as a stage of relationships is not questioned, yet it is in fact a relatively new occurrence, both in form and character, having been introduced around the turn of the 20th century (Rothman, 1984). For some 2,000 years before that, two young adults simply did not go out together and eat pizza as part of the preparation for a possible romance.

Within relationships, likewise, the segmentation and characterization of relational events or "stages" is often a matter of cultural choice (Honeycutt, 1993). Modern Western culture sees a progression from dating to marriage as almost ordained from the moment of the Big Bang (e.g., Surra, 1987). But in fact only some 150 years ago a rather complex series of personal introductions, chaperoned excursions, and parental agreements was held by Western culture to be the only decent way to do it all (Rothman, 1984).

There is also a certain amount of *individual* choice about the ways in which relationships should be conducted. Respondents differ in views of what a first date is and how it might progress, for example.

Christopher and Cate (1985) showed that 7.4% of couples had sex on their first date, while 16% of people did not even kiss. People take different views of the interpretation of certain sorts of relational behavior, such as flirtation (e.g., Montgomery, 1986, showed that men tend to see flirtatious behavior as primarily sexual and women tend to see it as primarily friendly).

Finally, partners themselves do not always correspond on judgments about what they give and receive in relationships (Prins, Buunk, & vanYperen, 1993). Even reports of amounts of self-disclosure *in a given interaction* can be discrepant just as often as they are in agreement. For instance, Sprecher (1987) found that there was little actual reciprocity between self-disclosure given and received. Baxter and Bullis (1986) found that partners agreed on only about half of the key relational events or turning points in their relational history. Surra (1987) even reported that some romantic partners were unable to agree to within one whole year about the date of their first sexual intercourse!

Negotiating Segments of Relationship Experience

Choices for segmenting relational experience may also be negotiated within a dyad. Some aspects of relationships have to be agreed on between individuals, of course; two persons are going to get married, for example, only if they both agree to do so. In other cases it just plain helps if the parties happen to agree. If I think that you and I are in a serious dating relationship headed toward exclusivity and commitment, but you do not think so, then there will be some sort of showdown sometime! Likewise, if I think our marital argument was started by your particular behavior X, then my choice to punctuate the experience at that point may not coincide with your choice of segments or perception of events (Watzlawick et al., 1967). Such a discrepancy itself is then likely to become a focus for a heated relational dispute.

Researchers (e.g., Gottman, 1979) have clearly shown that many relational fights are about two things: (1) the segmentation and sequencing of events (e.g., about whose behavior started the problem) and (2) the interpretation of the segments or disputes about the two persons' roles in the discussion. Disputes about a topic where one would "expect" agreement can make the topic become a difference that is symbolic of a larger difficulty in the relationship and not just a difference of opinion. Couples with chronic distress in their marital relationships or with persistent marital problems have typically different ways of segmenting and interpreting segments of behavior, although this is often reported merely as communicative strategy differences (Noller & Guthrie, 1992; Noller & Venardos, 1986). One of the many reasons for conflict and distress in relationships is precisely because people disagree about the ways in which to describe the flow of experience and how to characterize it (Noller & Fitzpatrick, 1990). The deadening thud of this research finding ought to draw us away from judgmental analysis of who is right and who is wrong and should instead encourage discussion of the frequency with which differences in experience are reported to researchers in human sciences. The reasons for the differences need to be theorized and explained rather than condemned as subjective error, and, perhaps more importantly, researchers also need to theorize the positive functions of difference (Baxter, 1993b).

Segmenting as Experience

As Proust pointed out, the "chunking" of the flow of personal experience is, by and large, helpful and necessary for coping with life. The particular results of the chunking are open to an individual's own stylistic orientation as well as to a culture's own preferred style of thinking and acting. Obviously I do not mean this to imply that individuals' orientations are random or solipsist: They rest on the background provided by cultural or societal agreement. Nor does this claim mean that outsiders could not express and discuss their view of the value, validity, or utility of another person's perceptions. On the other hand, it does not mean that several individuals may not take the same vantage point, or all individually accept and adopt their society's way of looking at things. In some cases we have very little real choice (about the meanings of words, for example), and membership in a culture obviously implies assimilation of much of the culture's ways of dealing with things.

As members of a society, individuals partake of that society's solutions to cultural, social, and interpersonal problems, so that even an individual and the individual's views of relationships are strongly contextualized by that membership. The same holds true, up to a point, for the language terms, metaphors, and ways of thought that an individual sees as applicable to relationships. In modern Western society, for instance, we use terms like love to explain romantic arrangements between two people, whereas Eastern societies see it as a result of the confluence of forces and Karma (Yum, 1988).

There are individual differences in perceptions of relationships in our society, but one should not focus only on them to the extent of overlooking the simply stunning accord about such things. For example, Fehr (1993, p. 119) reported a program of work that has uncovered similar prototypes of love that span "subject groups from New Zealand and various parts of North America: male and female, homosexual and heterosexual, psychology students and non-psychology students, patrons of a shopping mall, government employees, and married subjects focusing on love in a marital context." Such powerful cultural prototypes construct large doses of systematically similar behavior, expectations, and interpretations in relationships and schematic attitudes about them (Andersen, 1993; Berger, 1993). Like metaphors, such prototypes offer channels for our thinking and acting in relationships.

However, the choices of behavior and attitudes or schemas are still individual in some important sense that I want to explore, even if an individual chooses to see it all the same way as does someone else. The *organization* of the behavioral and attitudinal choices could be very much an individual organization and one a new relationship partner cannot predict a priori. We are all, as it were, responsible at some level for the advice—even cultural advice—that we choose to accept or adopt and also responsible for the whole pattern of personal meaning that we create out of it. Such cultural advice as we receive comes to us through interactions with cultural symbols, structures, and practices (Allan, 1993), especially through language and through the everyday talk that we carry on with friends and others. Thus the individual conclusions that a person reaches are ultimately communicable to others and open to dispute in the always unfinished business of relating.

❦ Conducting Unfinished Business

Billig (1987) pointed out that, for behaving individuals, the conduct of life is *all* unfinished business, an observation that applies to the business of segmenting experience as just discussed. Billig sees persons as in a constant dialogue with themselves (thinking) and with others (arguing) concerning issues that bother or press them in the unfolding experience of time. People talk or think essentially by arguing with themselves or others, having dialogues in their own minds or else out in the public domain with other people. Thus for Billig the unfinished business of life is a result of the fact that humans see the future coming at them, metaphorically speaking, and are busy constructing and considering alternative ways of defining and dealing with possibilities.

Billig also explores some of the implications of the fact that people do not just *have* plans but they also *make* them. In the course of making plans, devising projects, working out routines, ordering our day, organizing our lives in either big ways ("get ahead") or small ways ("time to do the dishes"), we have to make choices between possibilities. We ponder alternatives and make a decision, but we may also reconsider it, make another decision, and then go on to ponder alternatives yet again! Even a decision that has been made and carried out can create further decisions. The deliberative, argumentative, contemplative process never stops as long as life goes on.

A Cultural Context for Unfinished Business

Individual thinking nonetheless takes place in a social context, using tools like language and metaphor that carry implications. Billig (1987) and his co-workers (Billig et al., 1988) have noted the relevance of cultural ideology to individual thinking. The broad cultural context of beliefs creates the backdrop for an individual's expression and consideration of personal opinions—even radical new opinions or statements must contest or dispute existing ones, and so must be placed in the historical context of those existing beliefs. Those who argue for alternative lifestyles or unconventional relationships will know this fact all too personally.

The maxims, values, and opinions that are widely held in a given culture or society are themselves products of conditions and beliefs that have a history. Cultural values do not simply emerge out of nowhere. Likewise, individuals' beliefs about their relationships are also embedded in the history of the individuals, of the two individuals as partners, and of the relationship, and the culture.

Beliefs about self, relationships, and so on, not only have a history but also serve present functions. These functions deal with an individual's needs in a context that reflects the assumptions held commonly at the time. We do not, for instance, evaluate the goodness of our marriages and friendships in terms of absolute standards but instead compare them to cultural ideologies about what a "good marriage" or a "true friendship" is like (McCall, 1988). Newspapers, TV, books, and magazines all provide information about such standards. "Is your marriage really a success?," "Fifteen ways to improve your friendships," and the like are common ways for magazines to influence and reify cultural ideology on such matters. Prusank, Duran, and DeLillo (1993) recently demonstrated the ways in which advice columns in magazines shifted their models of relationships in each decade from the 1950s to the 1990s, drawing on earlier work by Kidd (1975). The ideology of "good relationships" changed from 1950 to 1960 to 1970 to 1980. The 1950s ideology claimed that a good marriage was one where the wife always deferred to the husband, and it held that all marital problems would have a single solution on which all experts would agree. The later 1960s and 1970s ideologies emphasized that partners should solve their own problems by "open communication" and "being true to themselves." The most recent ideology emerging in the late 1980s stressed equality and awareness not only of self and self's own goals but accommodation to the partner's also. That one will inevitably evolve into some other new ideology in due course. Ideological evolution does not grind to a halt when it reaches the present day.

The paradox of ideology, then, is that individuals operate in a context that, like the metaphors in Chapter 1, neither wholly coerces them to believe certain things nor wholly frees them to think and behave in unfettered liberty (Billig, 1991). In relationships, as in other things, this paradox has a number of implications for the relating partners. For one thing, it always means that we can never know for sure that a new partner believes that relationships should be conducted as we believe that they should. For one thing, at the start of relationships the two partners do not know whether they share similar views about how to conduct a relationship (and as Baxter & Wilmot, 1985, indicate, it is a dangerous and unpredictable topic of conversation if handled directly). For another it means that we never know for sure what a partner will think about relationship

futures and how relationships should develop. For a third, it means
that two people in a dyad have certain freedoms to create a particular form of relationship in the way in which they want to (Berger &
Kellner, 1964), but the partners do not have completely unlimited
freedom to deviate from cultural forms in any way that they choose
(Allan, 1993). For example, a person may not "marry" a sibling.

Nonetheless, individuals, dyads, and cultures all are continually
reflective, within certain limits, and are able to consider alternatives
to their present views or segmentation of experience (as when, for
example, a culture debates whether it will now recognize new forms
of "marriage," such as between two partners of the same sex).

Personal and Audience Contexts for Unfinished Business

While culture provides a general background for relationships,
particular other contexts also sweep in and out of the unfolding
conduct of those relationships. Individuals are able to express their
views in different circumstances to different audiences or to the
same audience (or relational partner) at different times, as the
context for their statements alters around them. Thus the role of
discourse or talk *about* relationships and *in* relationships is one that
is important to place in the above contexts.

Billig (1991) noted that someone discussing the British Royal Family
with a person known to be a pronounced monarchist may tone his or
her views in a way that accommodates to the other person's views (if
the person happens to like the monarchist) or diverges from that
person (if the person dislikes the monarchist). Equally, if discoursing
with a Marxist, a person may express the same views in different ways
as a function of this audience. Billig's point is that a person's views are
a composite of different ways of expressing a core evaluation that is
itself open to continuous reassessment and varying formulations. As
time goes by, so our own thoughtful dialogues with ourselves may
bring certain aspects of these evaluations to prominence over other
aspects. People do, after all, occasionally change their minds simply
as a result of thinking about things for themselves (Duck, 1980,
discussed the role of "out-of-interaction" thinking upon relationships, for example). Also they formulate beliefs and awareness of their
relationship through dialogues with partners (Acitelli, 1988, 1993), and
such dialogues change their beliefs and their behaviors.

Statements by relational partners about their relationship, their emotions, their problems, their commitment, their intimacy level, and so on, are strongly contextualized by their individual histories; the relational history; dyadic, network, and cultural circumstances; and the situation in which discourse about it all takes place. Therefore we should be very wary of characterizing a person's relationships as states by focusing on only an invariant central core of the person's beliefs about them that may or may not give the whole picture of the person's feelings in a relationship. For instance, Hendrick and Hendrick (1993) pointed out the relevance of this observation to research: The presentation of one's beliefs about a relationship to an investigator constitutes a special type of association between a speaker and an audience. This association might generate special statements from the range of possible statements that could be made about the relationship. Further, a description of one's feelings for a partner offered in the heat of argument might be different from that offered during a proposal of marriage to the same partner, both of which might be different from passionate expression of the feelings (Duck, 1992a). The base/core feelings are in some sense enduring, but they could be expressed or evoked differently as a function of the audience, the circumstances, or the situation. The existence of variability discussed in the previous section confronts people with real choices in the ways in which they represent their experience in a given moment of time. Such temporary dating of expressions of experience has many ramifications (see Chapter 3) not only for partners' own understanding of their relationship but also for researchers' as we seek to understand relationship *processes* that are continuous despite the fact that we use methods and techniques that freeze them. In essence my argument is that such methodological segmentations focus exclusively on the shell-like outer form of relationships and too little on the squirming contents that are the life enclosed by the shell.

Relationships as Unfinished Business

Billig's work brings up a number of important points that have a bearing on the ways in which we see the operation of individual minds. On the one hand, we must see the fundamental importance of those minds' operation in a social and societal setting. To state the point in rhetorical terms, a person's utterances and expressions are "situated" (Ginsburg, 1988), that is, they can be modified to accord with the person's perceptions of the rhetorical situation or circumstances. As people conduct the unfinished business of life, so their expressions and utterances will be situated as a reflection of instant circumstances, their audience, or their present needs. But as discussed in relation to metaphors in Chapter 1, *what* they feel and *how* they interpret experience are both likely to be constrained by their contexts and circumstances (Wood, 1993a, 1993b).

In the case of relationships both the variabilities and the relationship's constant ongoingness would mean that relationships are not stable psychological fixities, but are continually unfinished processes, open to continuous reinterpretations or reformulations in the light of unfolding events. Thus they can be expressed, demonstrated, or manifested in different ways according to circumstances, moods, and situations (Duck, 1990).

Living in a relationship is thus also living with continual and sequential explanation or interpretation in a world of changing possibilities, not living with finalities and unchanging certainties that some people would prefer to find. Getting married, for instance, does not answer once and for all the question of whether the partners will stay together. The existence of a marriage is not the uniformly reliable measure of commitment that some take it to be when they write of marriage as the ultimate "close relationship" (e.g., Kelley, 1983). For instance, I know a lesbian and a gay man who went through a marriage ceremony in order to obtain a green card for the woman: They are close friends but their marriage is not close. Marriage, like any other relationship, can be "close" when it is going well, but does not always go well all the time. In some relationships (e.g., blue-collar marriages) intimacy is not the only or even the best measure of a satisfactory relationship (Krokoff, Gottman, & Roy, 1988). Neither the length of a friendship nor its simple existence, as reported by a subject on a single occasion (or even three occasions), is itself alone a satisfactory indication of its intimacy. The initial strong dislike of a work partner does not mean that one will never become close to him or her. Thus the fact that two people once disliked each other does not necessarily predict their disliking in *present* studies of their relationship (Wiseman, 1989), though it may provide a useful context for understanding their relationship as a whole.

Even in apparently fixed and labeled relationships, measures that encourage subjects to make firm and final-sounding assessments of the state of their relationship may mislead investigators into seeing relationship stages as completed business. Yet a search for reliability could be seeking a will-o'-the-wisp or else missing out on something psychologically important, namely, the fact that humans find variability in experience and yet often compress and construe that experience without the variability. Although partners in stable relationships may express strong commitment to each other on some occasions, it would be odd if the various day-to-day experiences of the relationship did not affect the feelings of intimacy and commitment in both the long and the short term.

Therefore in relationships, as in the rest of life, individuals are faced with the "ceaselessly unforeseen originality" of events, in Shotter's (1987, p. 237) elegant phrase. The question then becomes: What principles do humans invoke to make choices and create subjective stabilities about relationships and everything else in the context of unfolding change?

❦ Making Choices as Making Meaning

George Kelly contributes to the position that I am outlining by noting that individuals' thoughts and behavior are driven by ("channelized by" in Kelly's terms) the ways in which they anticipate the unfolding of the constantly flowing world of experience. For Kelly (1969b), an individual does this by continually attempting to characterize the past in ways that will help anticipate the future. Kelly put it thus: *A person anticipates events by construing their replications.* In other words, people attempt to detect patterns (segments, chunks) in the past and to assume that replicas of those patterns will recur in the future. The result is a computing assumption about possible results or outcomes, a probability assessment, if nothing else.

This idea does not necessarily imply that the same event actually ever repeats itself; indeed, part of the human problem is that we *know* events rarely repeat themselves exactly. Thus a person's anticipation of the future is a matter of that person finding some apparently recurrent theme in events or experiences from the past and basing expectations on the theme. Clearly people can differ in their abilities and styles at judging that a pattern has been detected. Kelly's (1969b) theory included some strong statements about the nature of individual judgments on this matter as well as on the person's construction of a way of organizing and using such judgments. Although Kelly's (1955) approach has become the basis for an approach to clinical psychology and therapy, he meant to apply it to every human being, not just to those whose pattern detection led them into trouble with other human beings or with their own ways of coping with life. Neither does the idea imply that two people in the same event or having had the same physical experiences will invariably construe or interpret them in identical ways. For Kelly, two people have had the same experience *when they construe things the same way*, whether or not the construction is based on "the same things" happening to them. Thus Kelly's approach to events and stimuli was closely related to that of Mead (1914, in Miller, 1980), who noted that "stimuli are opportunities or occasions for acts, not mandates" (p. 15). People have some degree of choice about their responses, even responses to Stimuli-with-a-capital-S.

Although the above discussion emphasizes anticipation of the future as a driving force in human activity, it should not be construed as saying nothing about the past. The passages above are about *all* processes of interpretation and the assignment of personal meaning to events or people. For this reason the past is not sacred. Examining the past includes the possibility of rethinking the past, reevaluating its significance, or even reformulating it in some way. Kelly emphasized the individual's *experience* of events as subjective knowledge (i.e., emphasizing what people make of events) rather than the "experiences" that happen to people as stimuli (i.e., emphasizing the sorts of things that seem to happen to people and assuming that the same event strikes different people in exactly the same way, as much Behaviorism assumes).

Kelly also strongly asserts that different views of events can coexist and that alternative constructions of events and experience (or relationship) are always possible on many levels. He labeled this fact of life as "constructive alternativism." For Kelly, the consequence of constructive alternativism is that people make choices between alternative constructions, and they compose a system of personal meaning by organizing those choices for themselves.

Choices and Contrasts

Of course an individual's choices are between or among things, by definition, and Kelly noted the psychological significance of this fact. Constructive alternativism thus included another point recognized in many theories. Full understanding of someone's personal meanings does not come merely from knowing how he or she groups things together, much as a dictionary definition does, but also from discovering how she or he distinguishes things. Psychologically, contrast is essential to clarification of a person's meaning. As Kelly (1969b, p. 9) indicates, "Sometimes what is implicitly denied is more focal to the person's intent than what was affirmed, as when the disgruntled first mate entered in the ship's log that 'the captain was sober tonight.' "

Negation or contrast or opposition is taken by many thinkers as a key ingredient in the delineation of meaning (e.g., Bakhtin; see Baxter, 1993b). Kenneth Burke, a rhetorical theorist, also testified to the importance of negation in human thought, and he characterized human beings as the inventors of the negative (see Chapter 3). Meaning is not simply the magical assignment of content to a concept but represents a *choice* of something *and a simultaneous rejection* of something else: Personal meaning is thus essentially an organizational concept based in contrasts. Nor is contrast the setting off of an act or choice against all that it is not: rather it is to understand something in terms of its contrast. In other words, it is "brought into relevant perspective by our *structured* awareness of *what it might have been*" (Kelly, 1969b, p. 12, emphasis added). For this reason, once again, it is important to note that an individual's ways of doing things need to be seen in the context of *time* (see above discussion and Chapter 3), because ways of doing those things might have been modified as a result of reflecting on experience.

Social Influences on Choices for Making Meaning

Individuals create something of their own meaning system, yet draw on cultural conventions to do so. By focusing on the individual alone so far we raise one difficult question. If people can make choices more or less without constraint, some critics may argue, how is it that people can communicate with one another? Also, by emphasizing the individual's ways of making choices, Kelly (at least so far as I have expounded his thinking to this point) seems to be denying a role to the ubiquitous interpersonal dialogues and conversations discussed earlier. Why is it that so much similarity already seems to exist in the world, and how do people use it when they find it? Does Kelly's position, some may ask, not suggest such unbridled originality among persons that it would make social life essentially impossible?

On the contrary, a careful analysis shows that human unoriginality is actually the whole basis of social life, and of the relationships that happen there (Burkitt, 1991; Goffman, 1971). Certainly, choice about interpretation can exist, and interpretation can exist at many levels, but much background similarity also is observable. A range of forces, such as socialization, adoption of a particular language system, and membership in a particular culture, ensure that individuals as a group also absorb particular ways of seeing the world as a result of such membership (Mead, 1934/1967). The existence of such commonality permits the initial possibility of communication (Duck & Condra, 1989). Cultural membership provides a huge system of shared and instilled ways of characterizing experience that is the essence of a society that uses language and symbols. Cultural membership prepares the way for the meeting of minds by providing the common language tools, but does not itself build the building, as it were.

Society is the context in which individuals present their choices and viewpoints before other people—a context that leads some people to be shy about doing so. Thus individual meanings will, casually and through happenstance, very frequently overlap with the meanings to be found in other individuals (Duck, 1992b; Duck & Condra, 1989), but these instances are by far the least interesting, especially insofar as concerns the development of voluntary personal relationships (see Chapter 4). Nonetheless, the unbounded freedom of choice perhaps implied earlier in this chapter is not attainable except at the cost of inability to communicate with others and the impossibility of *social* life. Choice, communication, and culture are closely interrelated concepts intimately connected with this book's central theme, the issue of meaning and how it is shared by persons in relationships.

Culture as a Guide for Choice

Whether one is concerned with the range of choices or with the form in which the choices are expressed, or with the sorts of stories, accounts, metaphors, and narratives that people use in describing their relationships, one comes back every time to meaning, to culture, and ultimately to communication. Some basis of mutuality and commonality of meaning has to be presumed for any communication to occur. Beyond that, the transactive extension of meaning through deliberate, dyadic action adds further psychological importance and social force to the commonalities already available. To understand this force fully we must briefly consider "culture" from another angle. Three notions of "culture" were foreshadowed by Mead (1934/1967) and have been distinguished by Philipsen (1987): *Culture as code* refers to an organized system of beliefs or values; *culture as conversation* emphasizes the patterning of lived experience that is created in normal conversation; *culture as community* emphasizes the sharing of identity based on a communal ordering of memories. In what follows, I am adopting something of a mixed model and emphasizing different aspects at different times, starting with ancient notions of *code*.

Rhetorical theorists have often pointed to the importance of δοξα (*doxa*, meaning "received opinions") within which a speaker and audience (social psychology would say "a subject and an observer") carry on their interaction. A person's individuality is expressed, indeed is meaningful, only in the context of, and sometimes in contrast with, a culture's received opinions and beliefs (cf. Hinde, 1981). If we gently extend this notion from a Culture-with-a-capital-C to a dyad's relational culture (Wood, 1982), then some quite exciting implications can be developed for the present argument. Couples can create their own minicultures made up of an "extensive set of definitions, values and rules, which [compose] a unique-to-the-relationship world order. In turn, this world order is the nucleus of the relationship and acts as an elaborate filtering schema through which partners interpret and guide themselves" (Wood, 1982, p. 77).

As individuals make choices and construe alternatives and express these choices in the presence of someone else (*culture as conversation*), so a transformation of each individual's meaning systems becomes possible. As the two individuals attempt to integrate their independent meaning systems, so some form of alteration occurs to each system. Such integration between systems is more than the juxtaposition or simple co-presence of two viewpoints: It requires active psychological work and reverberates with transformation and change. Individuals are transformed by their participation in personal relationships in this way. The integration may lead to creation of a relational world order that assimilates both initial views and creates a new background for the future actions of the partners together. That such assimilation has to be *achieved* and recognized is an important issue for consideration in Chapters 3 and 4.

The initial meeting of two meaning systems (personalities, minds, etc.) is possible only if they communicate to each other and only if "communication" means that they understand the basic frameworks within which each is operating: that is, if each one has some comprehension of the other's personal meaning system. People achieve comprehension by watching and listening to each other's expressive actions, questioning one another about intents, observing the other's response to self, and then putting meaning onto them (Berger & Bradac, 1982). At first observers (like researchers) put only their own meaning on the actions (i.e., they *attribute* meaning). Later, they may be able to infer something of the meaning of the actor, as the observer comes to delve more deeply into the actor's personal meanings. Not unnaturally in everyday life the first evidence about an actor's personal meaning typically comes from the ways in which those meanings are expressed in talk and action.

In daily life, ordinary people are engaged in debating, discussing, declaring, and deciding their views on a whole range of issues, both large and small. The style of their language betrays and declares their positions and constructions, as does the content. A simple model of communication treats it as the simple expression of inner thoughts and feelings. There are, however, some serious deficiencies in this approach, and we need a better way of looking at communication in relationships, as more than a mere representation of preexisting thought.

❦ Expressing Meaning to Others

Alternative constructions of reality are the basis for individuality, but do not exist only in some abstracted personal black hole. They have social force as soon as people open their mouths. As people behave, talk, and use symbols, they declare their constructions of experience in all manner of ways, whether through content and/or through style of talk. In talk, people do not only do big things, such as offer opinions or take formal positions on debatable matters. They also declare or "leak" their constructions and interpretations of events in many ways both verbal and nonverbal (Goffman, 1959). Such "leakages" form the basis of the polygraph lie detector test, for example, and are familiar to a host of researchers into nonverbal behavior, speech patterns, power, status, liking, self-disclosure, and clinical psychology (Keeley & Hart, 1994, review these implications for relationships). In such research it has been established that nonverbal communication conveys intimations of attitudes about self, attitudes about others, and attitudes about degree of comfort with the interaction itself, while small features of language style themselves convey liking, intimacy, and status (Duck, 1992a). In everyday real life, however, such cues are also readily available through the normal discourse of life and relationships.

Communication Is More Than Just Expression

Cues to a person's thinking are, however, evident even if we look only at an expressive function of language—"communication *at*" rather than "communication *with.*" Expressiveness is not really "communication" between two people but is like two people holding up advertising billboards in one another's presence, each declaring their internal states, view of the world, attitudes, and so forth. Such a view of communication is not as simpleminded as it first sounds. Indeed, several people who use the word *communication* actually mean little more than this expressive function ("You should communicate your feelings"). Such academic writers as Jourard (1971) focused on self-disclosure as the opening up of oneself to others to create a transparent self. Jourard (1971) regarded such open expressiveness as a sign of mental health. For some later writers self-disclosure came to be nothing more interactive than a simple declaration of feelings (see Hendrick, 1987, for a discussion). These one-sided, billboarding ways in which self-disclosure is frequently operationalized in research often lead reviewers to see the whole "self-disclosure" process as no more than the expression of feelings and experiences that characterize the discloser's inner self. In reality, self-disclosure is a much more complex process (Dindia, 1994; Spencer, 1994). It involves many declarations that in truth serve to keep the conversation going rather than offering much information per se (Planalp & Garvin-Doxas, 1994) but can also be used to control conversation or manage identity (e.g., when parents confront adolescents and require them to disclose things about their habits and behavior—Spencer, 1994).

The depiction of disclosure as declaration naturally, even if unintentionally, channels us to see self-disclosure as an essentially individual characteristic rather than an interactive or communicative one (Duck & Pittman, in press). The representation of self-disclosure as a personality trait or an individual characteristic is not itself a problem for some purposes (e.g., clinical work or the enhancement of the conversation skills of lonely persons; Jones, Hansson, & Cutrona, 1984). Yet such representation of self-disclosure becomes misleading, when other scholars treat such declarations of the self as being the same thing as self-disclosure as an *interaction*, or when scholars use it as a criterion for "good communication" in relationships or as a predictor of relationship intimacy (e.g., Berg & McQuinn, 1986). The intention of such research is to treat self-disclosure as a dyadic or relationship characteristic, but "expressiveness" is not dyadic, and such mistaken equation of self-disclosure misrepresents its contribution to the intimacy level in the relationship (Acitelli & Duck, 1987).

Simple billboarding and expressiveness probably do have important roles to play in relationships and in relationship development (e.g., in creating opportunities for reciprocity of disclosure between two interactants or making the expresser feel relaxed in the presence of the other person or providing information). However, this fact exemplifies the problem of assuming that "expression" is also "communication." For example, reciprocity of self-disclosure is not necessarily valuable (Fitzpatrick, 1988). If Person A says "I have a medical problem" and Person B responds "So do I," then the reciprocity may not be very useful on its own. The usefulness of a reciprocal self-disclosure or its importance instead depends on how each listener reacts to the expression and whether the reciprocator then launches off into a catalogue of sores, pustules, and malodorous symptoms. (There are some interesting sex differences on this where females are more likely to find a "So do I" supportive because it is communal; Wood, 1993a, for example).

Several writers (e.g., Montgomery, 1984) have pointed out that what is intimate for a speaker may not seem intimate to a listener and so may not have any effective influence on the listener's urges to reciprocate or to develop a relationship. Rather, scholars must change focus and see that it is the *perception* of a statement *as* intimate self-disclosure that creates in the listener a likelihood of reciprocity, and not the expression of a statement on its own, nor the content of the statement itself that does so. The background and social context for a behavior (such as self-disclosure)—including the role of the perceptive listener (Harris & Sadeghi, 1987)—is at least as important to its social impact as is the behavior itself.

Recent work increasingly recognizes that, to a significant degree, the meaning and impact of self-disclosure comes not from itself but partly from its impact on, and involvement of, the listener (Hendrick, 1987). To make such a claim is to note that self-disclosure is a relational force *when* it is communication between two people that is based on the use of messages that *one knows or expects will be understood* by someone else.

How might a sender come to believe that a listener will "get it" when he or she expresses something? One fair assumption is that a listener may understand simply because members of the same culture recognize the symbols and language being used. However, there is no guarantee. A sender may also help the listener by disambiguating the expression or clarifying the choice that has been made and thus the possibilities that are excluded. "I mean these, not those; she is indicating here, not there; your meaning is this, not that." Very little can be said that cannot be challenged, negated, or placed in the context of an alternative interpretation or an extended way of viewing it. Such implications and clarifications through contrast are the baggage, the threads and ropes, of meaning that senders need in order to be able to express things in a way compatible with their partner's style of looking at the world.

Speech as a Sampler of Meaning

Ambiguity of language is important because it again emphasizes the inadequacies of treating expression as all there is to communication.

Not only do some things have personal meaning to an expresser but words, places, and suggestions are often ambiguous for a listener within a relational context or can mean different things simultaneously depending on how a partner chooses to take them. For example, "Why don't we both go back to my place for some coffee" *could* just mean what it says on its face, or it could be a sexual proposition, or it could be an invitation that expresses interest in seeing what possibilities arise. The listener will have to decide what the implications of acceptance are to be in the face of such possible ambiguity. Much of relational and social life is similarly ambiguous, and the interactants' task is precisely that of determining what it is that the speaker intends (Shotter, 1987).

As the true currency of the interchanges of relational life, meaning (like talk) is much more complex than simple declaration of feelings or expression of what is in one's mind. Individual statements are always incomplete in the sense that they could be revised during the unfinished business of thinking. Individual statements do not always state clearly and exhaustively what it is with which they contrast themselves. Furthermore, few people can express the complete essence of all that they know about a given topic in a single sentence. Perhaps one should see meaning not as a single thing but rather as a well into which a given piece of speech throws a bucket. The bucket samples the water but does not bring it all up at once. Likewise, different buckets bring up different volumes, have different shapes, and sample different parts of the well. Thus a single statement samples what a person could say about a given object and thus represents a momentary choice made from all the things that a person could say about something. Such statements may or may not give an adequate picture for observers to comprehend the full significance of something. So here, too, we see that our metaphors influence our thought and action. If we believe that talk is meaning (or identity) we behave differently than if we believe talk is a sample of meaning or identity. It is through extended interaction and talk with a partner that the detail can be understood and the representativeness of any particular sample becomes more apparent.

❦ Summary and Conclusions

The social importance of talk is as an interpersonal activity, a link between *people* rather than a link between concepts or a simple expression of a mind's contents. The chapter focused us on the role of talk as both a presentation and an experience of someone's ways of dealing with the world in a context where such views are individually constructed and therefore not necessarily easy to predict or understand. Like metaphors, one person's talk helps another to understand the unknown—in this case the speaker's personal meanings. But understanding occurs only if someone else's personal meanings can be comprehended in terms of one's own experience first. Symbolic activity, especially talk, initially permits, as a commonplace, a basic understanding of one person's meanings by another. Metaphor, talk, and other ways of sharing meaning are basic to human relating because they not only indicate, provoke, and substantiate "symbolic interdependence" (Stephen, 1985) between two persons. They also simultaneously create the sense of "being in a relationship" that is the essence of relating (Duck & Sants, 1983).

The following chapters develop an interpersonal and intersubjective theory of relating based on the individual's own development of a personal meaning system and the presenting and sharing of that meaning system with other people in relationships. Thus although most considerations of talk and metaphor focus on linguistic aspects, this book explores them at the interpersonal level and as essential agencies and channels for sharing experience.

Because most statements made by persons are indicators of choice, are less than all of what they could say, and are rarely fully elaborated every time the person speaks, *listeners* must themselves devise ways to interpret and complete the statements that they hear in order to divine the speaker's meaning. Initially, the listener presumably attributes significance in terms of his or her own system of thought, projects intentions, and does a lot else besides just being a receptacle for sound waves. Thus "communication" involves not only the expression of personal values and meanings by a speaker but also their interpretation by a listener. Such interpretation could transform a speaker's meaning or locate it in some way or associate/transfer/extend it.

The natural basis for such interpretation is of course the knowledge that one has about the speaker and his or her circumstances. In some cases one knows only that the person is a member of one's own culture, dresses thus and so, looks like this, has a certain nonverbal style of behavior, and is being met in a specific set of circumstances (e.g., an interview for a job, in a store, on a bus). At other times one has years and years of experience of the other person and a detailed comprehension of the ways in which he or she construes and describes experiences. In the latter case you have a very elaborate framework within which to differentiate and extend the meanings that a person may express by simple single utterances—based on, and done simply because of, the knowledge that *you* will be able to fill in the gaps as no one else could. In every case, talk expresses and exhibits one's ways of seeing the world. The degree to which such ways are understood depends on the listener's ability to fill in gaps and interpret meaning. A *relationship* provides information about the filling in of such gaps and thus represents a way of knowing another person, not just a way of relating to the other person.

This chapter has thus developed several themes suggested in Chapter 1 and anticipates four distinct types of social construction that are the basis for relational communication: (a) construction of the world by an individual; (b) partaking of cultural δοξα or received opinion and communal construction; (c) the causal happenstance of common constructions of experience by two individuals; (d) the active common development of sharing by two persons adapting their views to one another. Chapters 1 and 2 attended to the first three points, so it is this last process to which we devote our energies in the next chapter.

❧ An Appendix of Formal Statements

The above considerations can be summarized in a number of formal statements concerning the basic nature of the construction of meaning and its organization into a system that bears on the conduct of relationships. The ones listed here will be supplemented in Chapters 3, 4, and 5 as the argument develops.

Basic Suppositions

1. *Experience may be segmented or construed in more than one way by different perceivers or by the same perceiver at different times.* This idea has been basic to the present chapter's argument.
2. *A person's psychological activity is shaped and channeled by the ways in which he or she segments or construes experience.* As argued in the chapter, an individual's personal meanings are based on the ways in which the person segments reality and construes experience. Thus, in order to understand that person, an outsider has to develop some grasp of the ways in which the person does such segmentation and construction of experience.

Corollaries

Construction: A person gives personal meaning to experience by simultaneously identifying patterns-and-contrasts in the flow of phenomena. As noted in the chapter, the importance of contrasts is to be found in their value in defining what a pattern can be distinguished from.

Replication: A person's meaning for a phenomenon is based on construction of its replications. That is to say, personal meaning is essentially the process of anticipating how things will repeat themselves.

Serial Construction: Persons continually construct meaning in serial fashion as they revise their anticipations of the manner in which replications of a phenomenon will occur.

Aspiration to Validity: A person constructs meanings for experience that are judged valid according to a person's own standards of validity. While a person seeks to interpret experience in a useful and valid way, the person also sets the standards for deciding when an interpretation works, and such standards are as personal as are the interpretations themselves. Thus a person may decide alone that interpretations are no longer valid or may resist "demonstrations" by other people that his or her interpretations are "not valid."

Context: A person characteristically constructs meaning for a phenomenon in the context of other meanings and chooses for the moment that vantage point for constructing meaning that is most likely to extend understanding of other aspects of experience also.

Reflexive Metaconstruction: A person may reflect on and give meaning to the process of constructing meaning. In other words, a person can reflect on or think about the process of construing (i.e., may metaconstrue).

Organization: A person's meanings are organized into a system of hierarchical interrelationships and metaconstructions.

Commitment: A particular construction of meaning may be organized in the system in such a way that the individual feels personally committed to it, such that its disconfirmation or rejection by others is an especially aversive occurrence or its support is especially rewarding.

Fuzzy Form: Individuals express meaning in incomplete, multiple, or fuzzy forms and do not necessarily present meaning exhaustively or in the same way to every audience or on every occasion.

Consistency: One set of meanings may be inferentially inconsistent with another set of (the person's own) meanings.

Most of the above statements are merely formal encapsulations of the arguments presented in the chapter, but one or two have additional twists that take us further into the argument of the book. For example, the consistency corollary points out that individuals may become aware, through thought, behavior, or conversation with others, that their system contains dynamic tensions and inconsistencies that require resolution. The reflexive metaconstruction corollary likewise becomes important in the context of sociality, where two people discuss and compare their views of experience. The ability to reflect on and act on the reflections that are stimulated by conversation provides us with one means by which persons persuade and negotiate about their relationship. Such processes will now be explored in the following chapters.

3

One Mind Encounters Another

Imagine [a] Martian's astonishment after landing when he ob-
serves that earthlings *talk all the time* or otherwise traffic in
symbols: gossip, tell jokes, argue, make reports, deliver lectures,
listen to lectures, take notes, write books, read books, paint
pictures, look at pictures, stage plays, attend plays, tell stories,
listen to stories, cover blackboards with math symbols—and
even at night dream dreams that are a very tissue of symbols.
Earthlings in short seem to spend most of their time trafficking in
one kind of symbol or another, while the other creatures of earth—
more than two million species—*say not a word.* . . . [Yet] when the
Martian made enquiries about . . . possible connections between
man's peculiar symbol-mongering and his even more peculiar
behavior [in relationships] he was given a copy of *The Naked Ape.*

W. Percy (1975, pp. 12, 29, gendered language in the original)

OVERVIEW

The two relational partners who meet are two self-reflective individuals surrounded by various social and human contexts considered in
Chapters 1 and 2. The present chapter develops the exploration of the
temporal and linguistic contexts that affect the ways in which two
partners come to understand more about one another. As they try to
gain access to each other's personal meaning system, each person
looks first to explain behavior (i.e., explanation of other as object) and
second to construe another's system of meaning (i.e., understanding
other as person). The chapter discusses the roles of time in such interpretation and then shows that an everyday speaker's selection of everyday terms in everyday talk inevitably makes use of an inescapable

motivational language that, like metaphors, both extends and constrains our understanding of others. Lastly, I propose that relationships between people are formulated by the extent that each person
can develop an understanding of, or can (to his or her own satisfaction) construe the meaning system of, the other person—that is, the
chapter argues that limits on such understanding circumscribe relationships themselves. The theories of George Herbert Mead, George
Kelly, and Kenneth Burke are thus tied together to illuminate how
partners come to know each other as individuals and to differentiate
partners from the generalities of contexts where they are encountered.

N o two persons are ever psychologically identical even when
they belong to the same culture or use the same language.
Instead, minds are individuals' "property," even though they are
constructed using the tools and materials provided in advance by
society and in social interaction. When two minds encounter one
another they already know that each is a different mixed compo-
sition of constituents drawn from materials recognizable and us-
able more generally by others. Yet the externally visible features
of speech and behavior must at first be commonly available or the
two minds will not be able to communicate at all. This dry fact is
interesting to a relationship scholar looking for the ways in which
two minds connect, but in real life the fact presents a social
dilemma to two new relaters: How do they differentiate their
partner from everyone else and, more important, how do they
come to understand the partner as an individual?

The study of relationships thus brings us to a crossroads because
individuals obviously construct their own system of meaning using
culturally available symbols but can nevertheless participate in the
joint construction and use of meaning. The least interesting form of
psychological overlap (because it is the most common) is that provided voluminously by common cultural membership. The most
interesting relational questions focus on the social consequences
that eventuate as persons make assessments of overlap and connection between themselves.

The present chapter thus looks at previous discussion of cultural
and personal contexts from another side—as means of understanding the thinking of other individuals as individuals, not just
as specimens of their culture. By doing this, I hope to clarify how

minds from the same culture can meet in the interesting sense that provides the basis for voluntary personal relationships. We will be looking at a complex process through the analysis of its separate parts, but it is not a one-way process: I am splitting it up into "person expressing" and "one person understanding another" only for convenience of analysis at this point. Also for convenience, the chapter first looks at how we come to characterize someone as an object; it later goes on to the way in which we understand the person in terms of that person's own system of meaning. But I regard the two processes as very closely linked in the realities of everyday life.

❦ Temporal Contexts and Relationship Thinking

In Chapter 2, we considered some important contexts for a person's construction of the world as a whole. The present chapter extends to a subtler point, that knowledge about such contexts also provides a background for an individual to comprehend how other people know and construe the world, that is, as we come to know someone's personal meaning system, we (perhaps unconsciously) take account of the contexts noted in Chapter 2. Such an extension confronts us with some of the thinking of George Herbert Mead (1934/1967).

A Small Cup of Mead

The mention of G. H. Mead is usually enough to strike terror into otherwise alert and intelligent beings. Mead's published works are difficult reading, largely because his legacy of ideas was handed down through editions of notes taken by students at his lectures. As most teachers and students know, this kind of translation can render brilliant thoughts into nonsense, yet Mead's concepts were inherently very profound and difficult in any case. The trick is to summarize Mead's ideas in a form that, while leaving out most of their subtlety, makes clear some of his basic principles and shows their relevance to my developing arguments about relationships.

Mead was generally concerned with the relations between society, self, and mind, specifically with the way in which society "gets into the individual." His answer was that we are "talked into humanity" and vice versa—a very radical view in his day. Such vocal admission tickets are continually presented as we interact with and through the significant symbols of the society, culture, subcultures, families, and dyadic relational cultures to which we belong. Through interaction with symbols that have meaning to ourselves and to others, we gain access to the codes and ideas of the culture, and we can use them for our own purposes.

Mead's key insight was that in order to do any of this, we have to know that such symbols are meaningful to others, too. Our use of symbols is perpetually recontextualized by that knowledge and by our recognition that other people use meaning in some of their own personal ways. We come to know such plurality of meanings through (among other things) conversation, discussions of common experience, and the comparison of our pasts (Katovich & Couch, 1992). In talking, we compare and share experiences, and we do so through common symbols that have personal meaning to us yet can be unpacked and interpreted by other people.

Mead stressed a pragmatic approach to social behavior: He saw knowledge as related to action, or in George Kelly's terms, he saw meaning as formed and enacted in behavior (see Chapter 2). Mead would probably have endorsed Kelly's view that behavior is an experiment that ventures a view of the world and tests personally meaningful hypotheses about it.

Mead also emphasized process. For Mead, the real world is not timeless, that is, not filled with ideal events in an abstract sense. It is instead composed of things occurring constantly in the flow of time. Likewise, the human self is characterized in part by its ability to reflect about time, past and future as well as the present. When individuals suffer memory loss they change as persons in important ways.

Nor do people have relationships in an abstract or timeless sense; they have real interactions with other living beings here, now, yesterday, and tomorrow in real chairs, cars, and cafeterias. The things that bother or excite them today will affect their interactions, their choices of conversational topics, their views of themselves, and their assessment of their partners' responses, yet all these considerations may be mere traces in memory or even gone forever by tomorrow. Thus interactions today will be molded by different influences from those that affect tomorrow as well as by some similar ones. All the same, a jointly constructed past is an important moderator of present action in relationships. No general law of relationships that fails to account for that fact could properly encompass what it is that the real people actually do. The temporal context for relational events affects their meaning.

For Mead, the constant passage of time gives rise to events for which a person requires adaptive preparations. But, more than this, the relationship between an individual and society as a whole (or between an individual and specific others) is a ceaseless process of adjustment. The adjustment involves the interaction between individuals and a community of other minds acting as a framework for the interpretation of personal meaning. Our ability to continually reflect on or adjust to the other person in an interaction (e.g., by seeing self as an object for that other person or by taking account of that other person's responses as we communicate) is also a perpetually unfinished task.

Mead's emphasis on the importance of events and experience taking place "at a time" and "in a place" is one that is particularly useful for thinking about relationships. For instance, Werner, Brown, Altman, and Staples (1992) analyzed the importance of having places to meet with friends. As an example they reported the social disruption to a Nubian community when the community was rehoused in buildings that disrupted their ancient patterns of meeting "over the fence." In seeking to understand relationships, Werner et al. (1993) further advocated exploration of the physical environment and social context as integral to relationship processes, and not merely as scenic contexts in which such processes occur. Would you be more likely to meet friends for a chat in a bar/restaurant or in a funeral home, on their deck/patio or in a schoolroom, in your house or in a busy office? Equally, people relate not only *in* contexts but *on* contexts. The environment is occasionally arranged in a way that celebrates relationships, a simple instance being the placement of wedding photographs—that is, photographs of a particular event in time—in prominent places around the home rather than in a drawer— thus celebrating the perpetual extension of the event through time. As this example indicates, contexts may remind people of relational history, which then influences interactions in the here-and-now.

Stripping Temporal Variation From Real Lives

By contrast with Mead, researchers who (implicitly in their method or explicitly in their theory) treat general truths about disembodied relational interactions as if they were timeless events, run a risk of ignoring important influences of time and place on behavior. Such disembodiment trivializes the personal and pressing meaning of such circumstances in relationships (Gergen, 1990). In real life, relational events are interpreted in temporal context and convey meaning about a partner's mind in that context. By contrast, research on social exchange, for instance, typically looks for the generalized role of rewards and costs as factors in behavior, without contextualizing each exchange in the personal moment or the place where it occurs (e.g., Foa & Foa, 1974; or La Gaipa, 1977). This extraction from context implicitly attributes greater constancy to a "reward" or to an "exchange" itself than it might actually have in the lives of the subjects on a particular occasion or in a particular set of circumstances. As such, it strips away an important element of the meaning that is attributed in real life to the event as a guide to understanding the mind of another person.

How much is a dollar worth? A dollar is a dollar, right? Well, actually no. Today at the Student Memorial Union, it was worth three Cadbury's Creme eggs, but yesterday it was worth two (they are having a sale today). It was also worth a bus ride or a gallon of unleaded gasoline. Two days before the U.K. Conservative party's election victory in 1992, a dollar would buy you 49 British pence, but the day after that it was worth 57, and today you could amass 65 pence for every buck. It's all a matter of context and the influence of context on the relevant target. The item itself has no absolute true value. Its value is rooted in whatever it is that people do with it at a particular time and in a particular context.

Why bring this up? Well, how much is a kiss worth (and what information does it convey)? How valuable, how rewarding, is a statement of commitment (and what does it tell us about the other person's mind)? How much value is there in the state of being married (and what does it mean)? If something as apparently simple as the value of a hard currency can vary from day to day, why should not the value of a kiss also take on different value according to the time and personal context of meaning in which the kiss occurs? Well, of course it does, depending on whether the kiss is from a lover, a relative at a wedding, or Judas Iscariot. However, let us go further. A kiss from the same lover can vary in value, on a first meeting, after 6 months of separation, after a fight, and as a ritual on waking in the morning. In each case, the value depends on the meaning attached to the kiss *at the time* and *in context*. Therefore relationship researchers should be very cautious about generalizing, except in a completely superficial way, about the exchange value of a kiss as distinct from the exchange value of information or money, as some have sought to do (e.g., Foa & Foa, 1974). No exchange variable has an inherent and inviolably perpetual meaning. The personal meanings attached to an exchange variable in context are the most important things to attend to. Researchers should not just say that personal meaning matters (Kelley, 1983), but they should actually also measure personal meaning in context on each occasion. Fluctuations in the value of a social relational commodity are an integral part of the symbolic meaning of the commodity, not a deviation from such meaning, and that was Mead's point.

Such a focus on time also means a focus on the experiences of social actors in other ways. For example, when authors (e.g., Baxter, 1990; Hinde, 1981; Rawlins, 1992) write of dialectics (or the tensions created by the simultaneous experiencing of one thing, such as a need for *privacy*, and its contrast, such as the *openness* required in a developing relationship), they often stress the fact that the dialectics do not just spring out of an abstract vacuum. Dialectics are essentially based on *praxis* in time—the practical doing of social behavior on an occasion. Dialectics are practical dilemmas and are not free-floating ideas that have no reality for the people trying to manage them in a particular moment. Dialectic tensions arise in situations or contexts in time, not just as disembodied experiences. Likewise, dialectical terms are the subject of reflective thinking or reformulation of experience across time (Baxter, 1990). Ultimately such dialectics are practical dilemmas for people because people interact with one another in time. Dialectics, too, contextualize the interpretation of behavior.

Putting Temporal Factors Back Into Relationships

Contextualization in time also becomes important to relationships in several other ways when we look at the process of comprehending other minds.

The Role of Time Frame and Life Cycle in Relationships. Time influences relational choices and people's behavior in relationships in one simple way: *Decisions about relationships occur in a time frame and a life cycle.* For example, young adults are most active in seeking life-partners during the years from about 16 to 26 in Western culture (Bailey, 1988); persons in committed heterosexual relationships are faced with make-or-break decisions about whether to turn them into a marriage after about 15 to 18 months (Levinger, 1979); students typically make important relational decisions a few weeks before the end of a semester (Hill, Rubin, & Peplau, 1976); people have expectations about the "appropriate time" in the development of a relationship at which different degrees of sexual activity are acceptable (Christopher & Cate, 1985). As a different sort of example, relationships often contain a temporal averaging assumption, that in developed relationships you do not repay partners immediately but balance things out over the life of the relationship (cf. Mills & Clark, 1982). Even more poignant is parents' expectation that their dedication to their infant children will eventually be repaid by those same children as adults when the parents are less able to look after themselves during old age.

These examples briefly confirm that time affects relational behavior in important ways that should be neither discounted nor ignored, nor labeled by research as merely technical reliability issues. Time influences actual conduct of relationships by allowing cultural and social forces (symbols, beliefs) to affect individual behavior by providing a reference standard for relational behavior. The notion of competence in relationships, for instance, very often implicitly assumes the notion of timeliness in response (e.g., answering a question immediately rather than leaving a 4-minute gap) or timeliness in behavior relative to the partner's action (e.g., responding to a greeting immediately rather than ignoring it, or not interrupting when someone else is speaking; Spitzberg & Cupach, 1985).

The Role of Variation in Behavior in Relationships. A second influence of time on relationships is exhibited in the *variation in ongoing behavior.* In Chapter 2, I discussed such variability only in terms of its implications for people's coping with the world. Let us now extend that. Imagine now that this variability is not generally in your own experience of life as a whole but specifically in your experience of the behavior or utterances of your relational partner. Our relational partners are variable and somewhat inconsistent across time, just as we are. Likewise, they have doubts, mood swings, moments of anxiety and overconfidence, regret, uncertainty, or vacillation. Thus the task for a person observing a relational partner is not simply to detect a "reliable" feature of the other person but also to detect the unreliabilities across time and to interpret them also—in other words, to know something of the person's range and individual boundaries. The film actor David Niven (1974) once wrote that Errol Flynn was completely reliable; you could absolutely count on the fact that he would *always* let you down! To make such a joke about a friend, a person has to recognize specific cases of behavior and interpret them as a pattern with meaning in the ways discussed in Chapter 2.

The general pattern that an observer attributes to another's behavior becomes a context for interpreting specific instances as the basis for understanding another's behavior and the mind behind it. A truly deep understanding of another's mind comes only from the ability to recognize and "place" inconsistent performance in the context of a previously attributed general pattern. Such constructions are necessary for relationships to be conducted well by people actually doing relating in the variable circumstances of everyday life. Thus Mead's point about time and context has this second relevance to relationships: Time allows us to pattern and organize information.

Time as a Transformer of Relational Experience. The third relevance of time is that it *changes, matures, and mellows our interpretation of events and people.* As reflective thinkers, humans can (and obviously do) rethink the past and reorganize plans for the future. In the context of relationships, Harvey, Orbuch, and Weber (1992) showed that persons devote enormous personal and relational energy to editing past experience so as to reformulate interpretations of those past experiences. An ally can be reinterpreted as having undermined me (Jones & Burdette, 1994). Another's treatment of me can be seen as indicating deeper affection than I first appreciated. As several researchers into uncertainty reduction theory have shown, later information (e.g., "I am having an affair") can destabilize existing expectations and increase uncertainty as well as reduce it (Berger, 1988; Planalp & Honeycutt, 1985). The point is, however, that such destabilization is a transformer of the organization of one's personal knowledge about the other person.

Moreover, many real life emotions are labels for reflection and reformulation of experience over time, whether focused on the past or the future (Duck, 1992a). Regret, remorse, disappointment, anxiety, hope, forgiveness, and expectation, for instance, are all feelings that relate one time point to another (e.g., "disappointment" describes the observation that hopes created for some event when it was in the future were not in fact realized when the event materialized in the present). Beliefs about the future trajectory of a relationship or the likely outcome of a romance are also time-based, and are *essentially* time-based, experiences of formulation and reformulation.

Finally, although researchers of attachment have yet to demonstrate completely convincing continuities between infant experiences and adult relational conduct (Bartholomew, 1993; Stafford & Byers, 1993), there is now good evidence that mothers' present recall of their own childhood definitely affects the ways in which they bring up their own children (Putallaz, Costanzo, & Klein, 1993). This suggests that recently explored parallels between reports of childhood parenting and present adult romantic experience might also be a result of a person reformulating memory of childhood in ways consistent with present experience of adult relationships (Adler, 1929). But just as adults can construct their childhood in order to make sense of present experience (Stafford & Byers, 1993), so too can they use present feelings about self to construct memories of childhood (Handel, 1993).

Any form of rumination therefore is an indication of the transformative processes noted in the previous chapter: Humans reflect in order to develop new workable explanations that make more sense of things or to learn, that is, in order to find meaning in past events that can be useful in the future. A key point, then, is that such meaning both is detected as a pattern and also forms a context for future interpretation of specific acts (cf. Chapter 2).

If these time contexts for a person's experience of relationships are so influential, then a full understanding of relational processes will eventually incorporate the effects of these contexts. My key point, however, is that such influences are also *present as knowledge for the persons interpreting someone else's behavior in relationships*. Mead urged us to attend to the effects of time on behavior, so he also reminded us of the effects of time on minds, on our understanding of other minds, and on the doing of social behavior in general. We should heed his lesson.

❦ Language Contexts and Relational Thinking

Earlier I noted that Mead recognized the importance of language and common use of symbols in communication with partners. Indeed his thesis depends on the recognition of the importance of communication as a basis for connecting thought and action. Talk in turn has roots in the ways in which we think about and use language to describe and interpret others' behavior. Thus language, talk, communication, self, society, and mind were all closely intertwined for Mead as they are in this book. So we need a closer look at language from this angle.

The present argument now develops by incorporating the thinking of Kenneth Burke, a rhetorical theorist, drama and literary critic, and observer of human social life. Burke attempted to explain the systematic themes running through literature, art, and human life as a whole. He did this via analysis of language and the use of symbols, which at first seem to have little to do with relationships or with the behavior of people in relationship. But the analysis has quite a lot to do with both: If one can detect some general truths about language that, like a metaphor, both extend and circumscribe our ways of understanding relationships or other people, then such truths ought to appear in our theories of relationships. Burke's work is relevant to the activities of relationship partners as they try to understand one another, because we typically use language to think, to describe, to attribute, and to converse with others. Burke's work also illuminates the activities of researchers as they likewise try to understand, characterize, describe, or write about their subjects' affect, behavior, and cognition in relationships (Dixson & Duck, 1993). Unfortunately Burke's writing, though full of remarkably penetrating insights, is usually just about as obscure as Mead's.

Burke contributes two main thoughts to the present line of argument: (a) He argued that English is structured in a way that typically frames us to think of motives in particular ways, and (b) he proposed that persuasion does not operate (as Aristotle and practically everyone else since then had assumed) through one person compelling another to take a different view of a topic from before. For Burke, persuasion occurs when one person makes another feel that the two of them share an understanding of something or take substantially similar approaches to something. For Burke, persuasion is the act of creating a sense of substantial similarity of values between a speaker and a listener, such that the listener identifies with the speaker and has a flashbulb sense of understanding as a result—a new way of looking at an old issue. Through identification, the meaning framework of another person becomes transparent, and the person becomes understandable because the hearer finds a way to fit the person's thinking into the hearer's own ways of thinking.

Burke, somewhat characteristically, used two forbidding terms for these processes: *identification* (as above) and *consubstantiality*, that is, the realization that you share some substantial commonalities with another person. The two processes are fundamental to social influence. Listen to political speeches and you will rapidly hear how speakers try to create some fundamental identity with their audience: "We Americans/Republicans/Democrats/Conservatives/members of the business community believe in the same values and this is why . . . ." (The speaker then goes on to name his or her own values and plans.) Such identification is a basis for sharing or consubstantiality of ideals and values—or, in the terms I have used hitherto, a sharing of meaning systems by an overlap of minds. My point is that such persuasion works in relational talk just as it works in other forms of address (see Chapter 4), and is always inevitably and inextricably a part of everyday conversations.

The Rhetoric of Motives

Burke, like many researchers on attribution after him, was aware that a central problem for human beings is the explanation of other people's behavior. In contrast to those researchers who looked for motives in other people, Burke was interested in the way in which language itself automatically leads perceivers to think in motivational terms about others' behavior—rather as metaphors continue to steer us into thinking about phenomena in a very channeled way. For Burke, action words surreptitiously contain a motivational or purposive implication that is hard to steer around. The implication predisposes ("extends") word-users first to think in terms of "motives" and then to start to look for, unearth, find, describe, and apply such motives. In other words, if we name something, the thing immediately feels to us as if it exists. I feel, so I must *have* feelings; I say you are an introvert, so the introversion must be inside you rather than in my claims about you. By contrast, for Burke, the description of others' behavior in motivational terms is a consequence not of *their* motives as such, but of *our* system of language. Intriguingly, George Kelly also felt that most motivational descriptions came *from the perceiver's styles of thought* rather than existing in the behaver's behavior. For example, Kelly (1969a) noted that:

> Each person seeks to communicate his [or her] distress in terms that make sense to him [or her] but not necessarily in terms that make sense to others or to the person complained about. . . . [S]o with all motivational terms—they lose their descriptive value when one becomes intimate with what is going on in the world of another person. (p. 58)

The Grammar of Motives

If we want to "explain" or account for something, what elements can we use to do it? Classic attribution theory (Kelley, 1967) offers three terms: the Person, the Situation, and Transient features. Burke, however, went deeper in several ways. First, he noted that there are more than three features to which we could attend in an explanation or account of anything involving people: (1) what was done (*act*), (2) who did it (*agent*—this corresponds to Person in attribution theory), (3) where it was done (*scene*—corresponds to situation in attribution theory), (4) how it was done (*agency*), (5) for what goal it was done (*purpose*). These five terms are collectively known as Burke's "dramatistic pentad." (He later added a sixth term, *attitude* or "incipient motive," essentially a term meaning the same as "extension," as I have used the term. Once we begin to describe a person's action, we can hardly resist a sequence of other terms for actions implied by the very choice of words to characterize the first action.) Formally defined, *act* is any verb that has connotations of consciousness or purpose; *scene* is the situation in which the act occurs; *agent* is the person performing the act; *agency* is the instrument(s) used by the agent to perform the act; *purpose* is the intent apparently behind the act or the ultimate goal sought by the agent (Burke, 1945/1969).

Burke made three other observations: (1) The choice of terms to emphasize is not determined or dictated by the behavior being explained but is chosen by the observer/explainer as a vantage point for explaining or accounting for anything (if I call you an introvert, it is because it helps me to explain your behavior, not because you *are* an introvert). (2) The selection of a single explanatory term is in fact rare. More often two or three terms are taken together and associated by implication. That is, the selection of a particular term is very often automatically, unconsciously, inevitably paired with the selection of another term or contrasted with another term, in the same inferential way in which metaphor leads us on to some new frame of reference. Thus we often pick "who-where" (or person-situation, in attribution theory terms) as a connected pair of terms and make them jointly the basis of our account, rather than either one alone. (3) In fact, many of the implications that get drawn out from the pairing are not empirically derived but are determined by the structure of language itself. If I choose "who-where" as the basis of my explanation or account, then I will pick out those aspects of the person that fit the situation and I will ignore other aspects of the person that do not seem to fit, for example. On this hypothesis, the selection of terms to explain others' behavior is a specific example of the general point that I am making in this book, namely that a speaker's terms both represent a choice by the speaker and also constrain and circumscribe the speaker's subsequent opportunities for discourse. Terms tell about the speaker, not necessarily about the thing described by the speaker, and they represent visions and vantage points.

A Rhetoric of Inference

Burke made further points about this last important observation: Descriptive terms are most often juxtaposed in "ratios" to one another (usually pairs), and the ratios frame our ways of thinking. They are not inferentially neutral; in other words, the use of any particular pair of terms predisposes us to think of certain "logical" or inferential relationships between the terms or to exclude and disregard other possibilities. For example, in using an agent:scene ratio we would inevitably start to think of sorts of places as appropriate for sorts of agents—we can't help it since the original choice of frameworks ("agent:scene") predisposes us to think that way. Burke used several examples from literature, one being that "these Arabs Mohammed was born among are certainly a notable people.

Their country itself is notable; the fit habitation for such a race. . . . Such a country is fit for a swift-handed, deep-hearted race of men" (Carlyle, quoted in Burke, 1945/1969, pp. 7-8). It feels like a natural comparison to relate the inhabitants' characters directly to the characteristics of their scene or location, but in fact the comparison works through the processes discussed in Chapter 1: inference, extension, and "going beyond the given." A different sort of example is the agent:act ratio: "Nice people [agents] do nice things [acts]." In explaining what happened, then, we do not bother thinking about the scene where the acts occurred, because we have first got into our minds the thought that we are dealing with a particular sort of agent and that such agents would usually do particular sorts of acts. If "*this* person is a *nice* person," then it follows that the person's acts will be primarily nice and are explained largely by the niceness. "Friends [agents] don't let [act] friends drive drunk" is another example of the use of this ratio. By implicitly focusing the statement on a ratio framework that is agent-led, we start to think in terms of personal characteristics and so to think next of acts that are appropriate to those personal characteristics. For example, a person may rebuke another with a definition of *agent*, as in the claim that "friends do not behave like that, therefore you cannot really be my friend." Such a speaker may then use the claim as the basis for interpreting the other person's true lack of commitment to the relationship, declaring the relationship spoiled, and so bringing it to an end.

The same sort of principle operates in the scene:act ratio. The scene is set for particular sorts of acts by the original framework that is selected. For example, by defining situations as emergencies (scene), politicians justify taking unusual actions (acts). The familiar cry that "desperate times call for desperate measures" is a scene:act ratio that naturally leads us from the first term ([desperate] scene) to expect certain types of consequences ([desperate] acts) more or less inevitably. We do not think: "These are desperate times, so let's not follow up on the implications of that characteristic of the times" or "These are desperate times, but let's not bother about that here."

Burke's important insight is that the choice of terms for thinking about a topic is a choice made by the speaker in a particular rhetorical context. The choice drags with it other assumptions and terminologies that steer the speaker and the audience in particular directions, just as metaphor does. In fact this implication is largely what Burke meant by "attitude" or incipient action. Choice of terms leads directly to the framing of the rest of our thinking about the relevant problem, person, or behavior. Thus the perception and the interpretation of relational behavior are partly influenced by the scene:act or agent:act ratios that are chosen by the perceiver to begin thinking about the problem, person, or relationship.

For Burke, it is the structure of language that influences our way of thinking once the speaker chooses a particular framework for thought, and not just the structure of the "real world" that does it. For Burke, even our perception of cause and effect is directed by the structure of language and the mind, not by relationships intrinsic in the real world. An example of such framing is provided by Surra's (1987) article where people who had defined their relationship as "close and personal" (a scene) found that their relationship was driven by close, personal dyadic forces (agents) and not by situational ones. In a sense, this result is a circularity that Burke would claim is framed by language, and it does not inform us about anything else; once people choose to describe their situation as close and personal, then it would be ridiculous and inappropriate for them to explain those circumstances in other than dyadic, close, personal relational terms.

The above discussion therefore leads us to the point where we see personal "causes" as partly inferences based on language. But in relationships, a description of *interpersonal* causes requires the agreement of both partners on some level. Thus Burke's notion of consubstantiality is a very important one—but it requires us to rethink relational processes in terms of *inter*action about causes and *construction* of agreement about them. How do individuals form impressions that they agree about causes or understand one another?

Grouping Inferences and Framing

Any attempt to explain another's thoughts or behaviors begins from the outside and explains in terms of general categories or motives. Such initial attempts at understanding will be shaped by the fact that we think with language and that our language has inferences, scenes, frames built in, just as metaphors do. Linguistic form and social context both operate together to circumscribe and extend our thinking about other minds.

Such a point is essentially a new way of thinking about the issues raised in Chapters 1 and 2, concerning the vantage points of observers and the ways in which these starting points "set" observers' interpretations of subsequent events. In Chapter 1, I put the point in terms of the ways in which metaphors about relationships steer our thinking; in Chapter 2, I related the same basic idea to the choices that a person typically makes. Here I am relating the idea to the nature of language, its use in the conversations of everyday life, and the fact that as we get to know someone we work from broad categories to fine-tuned constructions of another's personal meaning system. In all cases the same psychological process is at work and it depends on the ease with which perceivers classify groups of events and "go beyond" the individuality of those events, whether by applying a group stereotype or by assuming similarity between self and another.

Although it may be helpful to recognize another as a member of a given class or group (e.g., a Victorian), it is almost never true that all members of a given class of people act in precisely the same way, or have identical characteristics, or especially that all or any people act invariantly across time and contexts. For example, not all Victorians were the same. Neither were all Edwardian English the same (though they were different from the Victorians). The day before Queen Victoria died, not everyone was restrained, conservative, prudish, and strict, with special coverings wrapped around their piano lest the sight of its naked wooden legs should act as a metaphor for other naked legs and provoke overexcitement. Nor on the day King Edward VII came to the throne after Queen Victoria, did everyone immediately turn into a happy laughing group of relaxed liberals strolling around the parks on Sunday afternoons having a great old time, as the stereotype suggests they did.

To recognize a person as a member of a given class or group is to know only a little about the person's qualities, although perceivers do not often so restrain themselves and often act as if they have personalized knowledge, not general knowledge (Billig, 1976). All the same, in the early days of an acquaintance, we do not know specific and important details that characterize the person individually. Although membership in the class provides some contextual evidence about a person, it rarely provides—at least initially—important specific and personal evidence that is the basis of a *personal* relationship. Indeed, it is also true that even though the bulk of a person's behavior is characteristic of that particular person, many examples of inconsistency can be observed over time—instances of originality, occasions of surprise, occurrences of change or difference. Thus social actors have large tasks in differentiating their experiences, friends, and acquaintances from one another. A major enterprise in encountering another individual mind is to map its range and variability and to differentiate that particular mind from the others that one has met (and from one's own). Research on personal relationships has so far failed to warrant such differentiation of partners, because we have focused on the equally important task of finding out the commonly held ways of reacting to and responding to others (such as general effects on attraction, or typical ways in which friendships develop). But knowing others in real life is a personal, contextualized business as well as a common, human one—just like finding out the particular value of a dollar or a kiss on a particular occasion.

To reframe the above point about stereotypes in the terms used by Burke, the less one knows about a person as an individual, the less likely that one has available good individualized "agent" explanations for the person's behavior that could identify variabilities and stylistic centers (i.e., the less likely one can explain the person's behavior in terms of the particular characteristics of that person's response to the specific situation). If you do not know individuals as individuals, then their behavior can rarely be accurately explained with individual insights; neither can one carefully apply particular knowledge of the way in which the "scene"/situation may be affecting that individual's behavior. In that case we must focus instead on general agent/person explanations such as implicit personality theories provide. A classic example is the fundamental attribution error (Ross, 1977) that shows that observers tend to generalize from a specific piece of behavior to the actor's disposition, which is essentially like saying, "I've seen what you did and I assume that all your other acts will be similar to or consistent with it." As another example, one might be more likely to use stereotypical descriptions of agents one does not know well (e.g., to say "All people in that class or group act that way. That is what they are like" or "In that scene/situation most people would act like this"). One can employ much more differentiated agent explanations when one knows someone better, and so has a larger store of knowledge about the way in which the person has behaved in comparable situations (scenes) before (Dixson & Duck, 1993).

The terms of Burke's pentad are therefore not equivalently available or applicable to all people, nor to the same person at different times in the relationship—another reaffirmation of the effects of time as a context for relational behavior and explanation. Researchers have sometimes erred—as have relational partners—in assuming that the same processes can be used to understand someone else at all times, irrespective of the roll of time and its influence on the interpretation of events.

The way in which observers extend their inferences about stereotyped others is another example of the process of "extension" discussed in Chapter 1. The extension prompted through stereotyping is essentially one that derives from perceptions of a "similarity" between an individual and a class. "Similarity" in a general sense is itself a pointer to several examples of extension in human relational behavior, but all extensions are instances of people seeking meaning and interpretation by going beyond what is directly in their perceptions. For example, on TV this morning I heard a distraught parent ask "What kind of person could do that to a little child?" Evidently by doing a certain act, one becomes "a kind of person" rather than a doer of a particularly nasty act. In terms of the previous arguments, the general character is attributed by an extension from an act to a disposition that sets a scene for relating to the other person in terms of the disposition. Thus the extension from an act to a disposition is a way of creating a subsequent scene:agent ratio.

As another example, Vanzetti, Notarius, and NeeSmith (1992) showed that some spouses tend to generalize their expectancies about one another and to make many dispositional judgments about their partner's behavior even when they witness only single occasions of a behavior. High-efficacy spouses (i.e., those who have high confidence about the dyad's ability to resolve relationship issues successfully) are more likely than low-efficacy spouses to make a positive attribution to dispositions in order to explain specific behaviors that they see as positive when they were expecting a negative behavior to be exhibited. Low-efficacy spouses make negative dispositional attributions whether or not they were expecting a negative behavior. In short, distressed spouses expect more negative and fewer positive behaviors from their partners than nondistressed spouses expect, even if the behaviors are intended by partners to generate positive feelings (Vanzetti et al., 1992). In the terms I am using here, a distressed person extends from specific instances of behavior to add a negative tinge and also to fit new behavior into the negative mold in advance. We could expect that a distressed spouse's account of behaviors, as compared to a nondistressed person, is much more often characterized by negative extensions, negative language, negative nonverbal communication, and general evidence of a primarily negative way of looking at the world and explaining or reacting to it behaviorally. Indeed a negative style of perception (or any other style) is really a tendency to see primarily (negative) similarities between things where other (nonnegative) people tend to see no similarities. To rephrase this in the terms I have been using in this chapter, the person contextualizes the other's behavior by perceiving a negative pattern in it, creates that as a scene for interpreting the agent, and then relates to the other in a way that confirms or tests or assumes this construction.

As a third example, Miell (1987) indicated that persons are much more likely to show a recency effect and "extend" from the last 3 days of their relational experience in describing its likely future than they are to be influenced by the distant past. She found that subjects extrapolated from their recent experiences as if these experiences now formed an inexorable pattern of behavior and that subjects did not recognize the fundamental truth that shows life is variable anyway! People are inclined to project to the future on the basis of some detected similarity or pattern in past experiences (Chapter 2). To rephrase this point in the terms of the present chapter, by projecting a future that is similar to the past, individuals can structure their relational experiences by creating a scene:act ratio.

Equally, enemies expect one another to act in hostile ways similar to those apparently witnessed before (Wiseman, 1989). Haters expect the hated person to continue doing similarly hateful things (Shoenewolf, 1991). People characterized in a particular way (as friends, shy people, unreliable types, paranoids, charmers, or whatever) are expected to continue to behave in ways similar to (consistent with) those that earned the label in the first place. Likewise, concepts of personality also lead to such thinking, and so does the label of disability. The same is true of first impressions or initial attraction; here one hopes to "set" the mind of the perceiver to think of all one's acts, qualities, and characteristics as being similar to or predictable from the first ones observed, with later acts being fitted neatly into the prearranged frameworks of positivity (i.e., we make the mistake noted earlier and do not realize how or that people change and we expect consistencies in others). Because I have already written about scene:act ratios and agent:act ratios, I do not really need to point out that all of these uses of reasoning from similarity are examples of the operation of such ratios.

These examples help to establish the role played by groupings based on a perceived similarity between persons and a category or between an act and a category of acts. Each case provides an instance that extension by way of a similarity plays a role in social understanding by enhancing the comprehension of others' behavior, style, and meaning system in terms of a general scene. Also presumably such extension creates other social effects because it encourages conversational consequences: A person will talk to another in the context of scenes created in the above way.

A Brief Recap

Before we go on, let me reshape these key points for the next step in the argument. Persons in relationships try to comprehend one another initially in general terms, and deal with the problem of understanding why a partner behaved in particular ways on a particular occasion. To do so, persons use a contextualized motivational terminology that is built into our language system and also make projections beyond the observable ("extensions"). The notion of intent is strongly built into the descriptive language that we use to account for other people's behavior and words, so it seems as if we are really understanding someone's psychology when we use the terms. A search for intent is a part of one's natural armory for assessing, and making a chart of, another person's mind. Because persons' views of the world can be constructed differently (Chapter 2), the task of comprehending someone else's mind is facilitated by the extent to which one can act extensively to comprehend the general framework of meaning in which they operate.

Crucially, my argument is that this is not where the process stops. As relationships proceed, so partners proceed to another way of knowing one another: knowing the other *in the other's own terms*, not in our terms. In other words, the comprehension of someone else's mind is a function not just of experience (in the sense of "amount of time") in a relationship with the person, nor of applying descriptions or attributions about the person's behavior. Comprehension depends on experience of (in the sense of "learning about") the way in which the person operates upon the world.

Thus, one's knowledge about another person's mind must be built on awareness of the choices that the person makes and the dimensions within which such choices are made. The observer's/relational partner's job in comprehending someone else's mind is to become aware of the contrasts that highlight the other person's main themes in his or her theories about the world. This task of construing the frames of reference within which someone else thinks is not at all the same problem as knowing how to explain to oneself the causes of a person's behavior in the limited sense in which attribution theory seeks to explain "causes." Whether or not people always articulate that this is how they are working, grasping another mind is partly the business of construing the terms and choices in which it operates, not just the terms by which it may be described from the outside. Rather, as Billig (1987) also argued, statements must be understood in the context of other choices and dilemmas that face the person.

Clearly such comprehension is facilitated by a personal and contextualized understanding of individuals' ways of behaving and thinking acquired through observation, talk, discussion, reflection, and interaction (Berger & Bradac, 1982). Comprehension is also extended by the degree to which one happens to share common ways of looking at things with another person or can extrapolate from single utterances to the broader frames of reference in which the other person works. Construction is also facilitated by influencing the other's thinking to become more similar to one's own.

The process of acquiring knowledge about the other person's mind and mental geography has been well studied (e.g., Berger, 1988; Berger & Bradac, 1982; Planalp & Garvin-Doxas, 1994). My point is that the process is relentlessly extensive throughout a relationship and is also multilayered as the above proposals imply. It is also probably a mixture of articulated and unarticulated knowledge. We all try to understand other people in sufficient depth to enable adequate and satisfying information, but not everyone does this for every relationship. Partners can and do seek and discover different aspects in others' meanings at different times and do not seek only a global understanding for all time. The development of this crucial relational point takes us back to the writings of George Kelly.

❦ Construing and Relating

Mead teaches us how various temporal contexts operate in real life to add meaning to otherwise ambiguous or uncertain events and interpretations. Burke shows us how an attempt to construe others' behavior naturally leads us to use a language that focuses us on motives. Kelly can be used to develop these lines of reasoning by showing how the extent of our construction of others, their motives, and ourselves directly influences our ability to relate to other people on different levels.

Webs of Construing

Clearly the mere juxtaposition of two persons' cognitive systems—even if they are consubstantial—does not automatically mean that the individuals are able to comprehend one another nor that they give the same weights and meaning to the phenomena that they interpret (Dixson & Duck, 1993). Such comprehension is established through (1) knowledge of one's own mind (if I do not follow ancient Greek advice to "Know thyself," then how can I see that someone else is similar to myself?); (2) knowledge of the other's mind; (3) a mixture of interaction (and the evidence it provides about the other's mind) and interpretation, as I have been arguing. While Mead emphasized the role of interaction with other minds (and within one's own mind, which Mead recognized as necessarily social in character, even when one talks to oneself!), Kelly focused on the interpretation of a person by an observing construer. Both positions come down to much the same thing in the end, given Kelly's strong insistence that behavior is an enactment of a person's interpretations, constructions, and hypotheses.

Particularly important here is that Kelly insisted that there are two levels of understanding other people, one that treats them as an object for us as observers (as above) and the other that tries to get inside their heads and understand how they see their own circumstances (see below). Kelly (1969a) noted that:

It would be a good idea to identify two levels of construing. The first would be concerned with events and with [persons] treated as events. By this I mean we would construe [persons'] behavior rather than their outlooks. Another person would be simply another moving object on our horizon. . . . But then suppose there is a second level of construing. This would be concerned with construing the constructions of other [people]. Instead of making *our* sense out of what others did, we would try to understand what sense *they* made out of what they did. Instead of putting together the events in their lives in the most scientifically parsimonious way, we would ask how they put things together, regardless of whether their schemes were parsimonious or not. (p. 203)

This observation punctuates a crucial juncture in the book's argument with very significant implications for the way in which we understand relationships and people's ability to conduct relationships with one another. Empathy or intersubjectivity depend on seeing the other person in his or her own terms; that is, intersubjectivity consists not in seeing how I would feel if your experience, X, were to happen to me but in seeing how you feel when X happens to you.

For Kelly, the ability of two persons to behave with one another socially is defined, limited, and circumscribed by their comprehension of one another's meaning system. To put it more accurately, the nature of a given person's relationship to someone else is defined in terms of the extent to which that person construes or understands the way the other thinks. Kelly (1955) put it thus: *To the extent that one person construes the construction processes of another person, he or she may play a role in social processes involving the other person.* The important words here are "play a role in social processes involving the other person" and "to the extent that" (Duck, 1982a, 1983), and the rest of the chapter unravels this significance.

Note particularly the importance of Kelly's implication that the degree of understanding of one person by another is not necessarily equivalent in both directions, a point usually overlooked in traditional accounts of relational processes. For this reason the dupe and the confidence trickster (who understand each other to different degrees) are really in different relationships to each other even though they are in the same physical encounter. The same asymmetry of understanding is true for most adults interacting with most children (and is also, interestingly, usually claimed by experimenters to be true of their interactions with subjects). Also one problem

for adolescents and parents is that adolescents begin to understand
the parents better than they did before, while the parents *think* they
still understand the adolescent just as well as they used to understand the child (Rawlins, 1992; Rawlins & Holl, 1988; Stafford &
Byers, 1993).

To the extent that other personal relationship researchers assume
that "a relationship" is always the same psychological context for
both partners, they miss this important point about the asymmetric
nature of relationships—whether they state the symmetry explicitly
or merely use methods that operate as if equivalence obtained (e.g.,
by treating the two partners' data as equivalent on questionnaires
or by transforming data mathematically—Duck, 1990).

Relating as Understanding the Organization of Meaning

For Kelly, then (and of course also for us), the sorts of "social
process" in which a person may "play a role" with someone else are
defined in terms of the construction of the other's meaning that are
true of a particular moment. This is a rather interesting idea in the
context of relationships and leads me to a set of radical propositions.
For one thing it suggests that the development of relationships would
be affected not by some growth of closeness or emotion, nor by the
acquisition of information, but by one person's organized (re)construc-
tion of the other and the social consequences of that (re)construction.

Kelly's suggestion places the emphasis not on the content of *what*
one knows about the other person, as most other theorists do, nor
on *how much* information one can gather for oneself about the other
person from a variety of sources (Berger & Bradac, 1982). Emphasized instead are the social consequences of *organizing and filling out
one's construction* of the other person's psychological frameworks
and values—the extent to which one grasps the system or organization of the other's knowledge as well as its content; the framework
of operation and choice as much as the choices made; the things
distinguished from the chosen item, as well as the chosen item itself.
Such understanding has social consequences of great magnitude,
and it is this that affects social behavior. For example, given the
above, self-disclosure would be most significant in relationship
development when it contributes to a perceiver's construction of the
discloser's experience (= thinking) as a whole, rather than just when

it reveals the events that have happened to the discloser. An intimate self-disclosure that revealed little new about the *organization* of the discloser's thoughts or implied nothing new about the discloser's identity or experience (such as, by contrast, "I was raped when I was an adolescent" would do) would have comparatively little effect that would change the sorts of social roles that one could play with the other person. It would merely add to what one already knew in old roles, so would not have any organizational effect on understanding of the other nor on the consequent relationship between partners.

The determination of someone else's frames of reference is not a simple identification of the terms that he or she uses. Nor is it an imposition of one's own frames of comprehension upon someone else's behavior. Instead, the comprehension of someone else's mind in social relationships partly requires an organizational solution. That is to say, the relational problem is to determine how the other person organizes values and meanings, what it is that the person contrasts with what, what is excluded from what in the process of creating a personal meaning system (Chapter 2). (Indeed, in a comparable way, dating performs the same function of distinguishing what is suitable from what is not.) A person organizes meaning by the systematic elimination of alternative possibilities and the systematic contrasting of the remaining possibilities with other things. Kenneth Burke (1985, p. 20) put it into the aphorism, "Every way of seeing is a way of not seeing."

Relational Interdependence

The above analysis offers a chance to reconsider and test new propositions about the ways in which relationship interdependence develops. For instance, this is not an Aristotelian model of change in relationships where, for example, one person self-discloses to another and so "causes" change in the relationship, or moves the relationship semi-automatically to a new level or stage, or presents another person with an array of physical cues that "cause attraction," or says something delightfully strategic that "causes" the other to go out on a date. The above model can be combined with Burke's approach to show that the creation of a sense of identification, consubstantiality, or commonality creates a metamorphosis in both partners by transforming the nature of the social process in which they play a part with one another. On the above model, it is the act of construing some commonality between the partners that creates relational change, not the commonality itself (see Chapter 4). The psychological and social effect of the construing is to alter the partners' comprehension of the relationship between them. It is such alteration that constitutes relational transformation.

The above approach also offers a new view of the interdependence implicit in relational power: Relational power resides in the person who, for the moment, comprehends the other "better" or to the greater extent. To such a person lie open greater numbers of roles in social processes with the comprehended other. The more one grasps the thought processes of one's partner, the more one is enabled to adjust one's own behavior to the other in advance, to predict, or prevent, or anticipate the other person's responses. Such an hypothesis is quite readily testable in terms of the extent to which powerful people can "read" others on specific occasions.

The above analysis first suggests that everyday interaction and conversations in relationships provide not only amounts of information and context, but also organizational knowledge of others' articulated frameworks of thought and dimensions of construction. More importantly, it affirms that qualitatively different webs and organizations of psychological knowledge are simultaneously possible between two persons. Not only can two individuals construe one another asymmetrically or at different levels in general, but even in the same relationship or the same interaction, the degrees of understanding of one another could be different for the two persons involved. Such differences could exist even if in some respects the persons have very similar ways of thinking, because similarity at a global level does not necessarily mean identical activity on any particular occasion. Nor does it mean that "similarity" is a single all-encompassing description or a necessarily permanent state of relationship between two minds (Acitelli, Douvan, & Veroff, 1993). Once more, time and variability are relevant matters to consider.

Interdependence between two persons is thus not a behavioral achievement in the sense that two people have impact on one another, nor even a cognitive interdependence in the sense that one person's thought processes cause a change in the other and vice versa (Berscheid & Peplau, 1983, p. 12). Far less is interdependence an outcome of transactive exchanges. It is not enough to give a person what the person needs and take something in return; it is important instead to understand the framework for the need and so to understand what it is like to have such a need (Kelly, 1969a). Accordingly, interdependence is a fundamental social and psychological achievement based on more than the identification of another's thought content or behavioral connectedness with oneself. Such interdependence is not explicable in terms of a simple billiard ball model where one person's thoughts strike and move another's, nor where one person's behavior causes another to bounce behaviorally into a side pocket. It is more the relationship of engineer to a machine. An engineer acts in a given way in relation to a machine because of knowledge of its internal connections and organization and awareness that movement of one part affects the movement of other parts and so creates functional change in the whole machine. Likewise, I do not drive my car only by pushing levers and buttons but also by knowing what the buttons and levers do.

❦ Summary and Conclusions

The chapter has argued that a critical problem for would-be relaters is to comprehend the meaning system of the other person from the inside as distinct from attributing causes for behavior from the outside. However, to construe a meaning *system* pragmatically one has to first locate its general features from the outside and then comprehend the ways in which these are modified by various contexts. There are many contexts for understanding the behavior and the thinking of other people: for example, time, our system of language, and the tendency to seek patterns, commonalities, or consistencies in variable events and people. The critical importance of those points lies in the fact that the social roles that are open to individuals to play with one another are radically affected by their construction of one another's personal system of meaning. Construing the other person's meaning system is thus a significant modifier of relationships not because degree of understanding affects the amount of one's information about the other person, but because one's construction affects one's organization of that knowledge and hence one's ability to relate to the other person.

The chapter has considered the effects of different contexts of behavior that assist in the comprehension of others' meaning systems over time (and, by implication, over the development of a relationship). Important in initial encounters is the discovery of some form of similarity between the other person's actions or thoughts and those of others. Equally important is a perceived connection between the person's acts and other interpretable patterns, since the latter carry a broader range of already understood implications. The perception of similarity alone, while useful in finding the ballpark, is not enough. The ability to locate such similarity between the partner and other groups of persons provides a basis for inferences, assimilations, and quick-and-dirty outlining of the bases of the other person's behavior. These inferences allow an observer to generate outline constructions of the person's meaning system. Ultimately more powerful than this sort of guesswork, however, are the social consequences of the belief in similarity between the mind of another person and one's own. This belief matters for the same reason— psychological similarity *between self and other* permits extension of understanding. The reason is because psychological similarity between self and other implies that the other person is interpretable in terms that one already understands: the terms of one's own meaning system.

❦ An Appendix of Formal Statements

As in the case of the previous chapter, the above reasoning can also be expressed as formal statements with implications for the rest of the argument.

> *Range: Meanings are formed in relation to a particular range of experiences but may be extended to others as a result of reflection or interaction.* Such a claim is based on the ideas developed in Chapter 1 in relation to metaphor, but is now also extended as a result of the discussion of the role of time.

> *Personal Modification: A person's meanings for a phenomenon can be modified personally as a result of new construction, through thoughtful reflection, and as a result of some apparent change in the phenomenon across time.*

Interpersonal Modification: A person can be prompted to metaconstructions by construing the meanings of other people and their ramifications for his or her own system. That is to say, a person can be stimulated to reflect on his or her own meanings for a phenomenon by discussing it with other people and so being confronted with alternative meanings for it.

Sociality: Persons' roles in social processes with one another are defined by the extent to which they are able to comprehend one another's meanings and the organization of these meanings. As indicated in the chapter, the form and nature of the relationship are circumscribed by the extent of such comprehensions. As also indicated, two persons can comprehend one another's meanings (systems) to different extents and so in a key sense are in different psychological relationships even in the same physical encounter. For each person the relationship is based on comprehension, whether explicit or implicit, of the other's constructions of "experience."

These latter corollaries largely concern the influences that transform understanding in relationships, but they also carry some implications for the understanding of similarity (or any mental relationship) between people and it is to such a topic that we now turn.

4

Two Minds Together in Social Context
Guides to Personal Meaning

One's not half of two; it's two are half of one.

e. e. cummings

Friendship arises out of mere Companionship when two or more of the companions discover that they have in common some insight or interest or even taste which others do not share and which, till that moment, each believed to be his [or her] own unique treasure (or burden). The typical expression of opening Friendship would be something like, "What? You too? I thought I was the only one."

C. S. Lewis (1960, p. 97)

OVERVIEW

Individuals embarking on relationships attempt first to understand one another in ways considered in Chapter 3, yet also try to build up a construction of each other's meaning system more particularly in its own terms. As the persons become enmeshed in a relationship, so mutual exploration begins to include items drawn from the partners' common experience together in their relationship. The present chapter is about the ways in which two people construe one another's personal meaning systems at several different levels, how this construction process influences their ability to understand one another, how understanding affects their relation to one another, and how these processes together inaugurate the creation of shared meaning for their relationship; for example, beyond agreements about particular topics or similar evaluations of specific events, there is a realization by both partners that they construe large parts of experience in comparable ways, including the relationship itself. A belief in similarity is one way of connecting two realms of meaning (in this case, two minds) and permits reasonable inference from one realm to the other as a guide to parts as yet unseen. Beliefs about connections between minds, however, also generate social action, particularly talk. Taking the view that psychological similarity is an example of a social process and not as a purely cognitive state, the chapter proposes a model of the serial construction of meaning. This model suggests that initial commonalities are successively related to revised constructions of another's system of meaning and that a final goal of relating partners is shared meaning.

Obviously nobody believes that similarity is all that two people experience in a relationship. How can you live on this planet and not realize that disagreement, uncommonalities, dissimilarities, differences, compromises, and negotiation are the order of the day—even if you have not read Chapter 2's discussion of constructive alternativism? My concern in this chapter is with the effects of psychological similarity as a social instrument in such a background where disagreement, et cetera, are also common experiences. It has long been known that, whatever their experience of life's inconsistencies, human beings claim to prefer harmony, consistency, balance, congruence, or similarity (e.g., Festinger, 1954; Heider, 1958; Newcomb, 1971; to say nothing of Aristotle, Plato, and Cicero more than 2,000 years ago). It is that human preference that is noted in the argument here. The resolution of differences and the negotiation of dissimilarities are examples of the social effects of a preference for similarity, so when I write about similarity I shall often leave readers to fill in for themselves the fact that I assume that a search for similarity is often prompted by a discovery of difference and a wish to resolve it, even by agreeing to tolerate the difference or reconstrue the meaning of the difference (e.g., Wood, Dendy, Dordek, Germany, & Varallo, 1994). For instance, dissimilarity may be given the meaning that it ensures autonomy, enhances personal integrity, or evidences relational openness and mutual tolerance—just as much as it may be taken as a disconfirmation of self, or a creator of division (Wood et al., 1994). Dissimilarity has no absolute meaning but rather the meaning that it is given by relational partners in social processes. Indeed, difference can imply novelty and stimulation (McCarthy & Duck, 1976) or self-expansion (Aron & Aron, 1986) and is partly presumed in successful relationships—unless the other person is different from self, opportunities for growth and development of self are clearly going to be restricted (Murstein, 1971).

My main focus is accordingly on social processes that happen when individuals construct similarities between them in the two senses of *construct:* to create; and to compile, especially in the mind. In fact, I am proposing a general argument about the construction of meaning and the relationship between two minds by the persons involved, and I use similarity only as one well-studied example of that relationship.

❦ Psychological Similarity

The workings of psychological similarity have exercised relationship theorists for some time and have been as remarkable for the confusion that they have generated as much as for anything else (see, e.g., Bochner, 1991; Byrne, 1971; Duck, 1977; Duck & Barnes, 1992; Sunnafrank, 1991). A recent issue of *Communication Monographs* (Burgoon, 1992) had several articles devoted entirely to the subject of similarity, and the whole topic is still by no means as dead as some commentators have said they wish it were (e.g., Bochner, 1991). The present chapter comes right out and assumes that similarity does affect relationships but that it does so in several ways that have previously been run together or not distinguished. For one thing, similarity on a particular topic obviously increases understanding or the ability to comprehend and communicate with others quite directly in relation to that particular topic. More than this, however, it contemporaneously provides a basis for inferences about the other person. More than this, it also provides a good foundation for the two persons to accommodate to each other, using that particular similarity as a framework for negotiating—hence negotiators and intermediaries usually start by looking for common ground.

Because talk and behavior only *sample* a person's meaning system, it would probably take forever to assemble a complete picture of someone else's meaning system, especially since meaning construction is an ever-unfinished business. Partners do not need a full picture of each other, however—they need only a workable one. Therefore relational partners are able to use similarity to their advantage to save themselves time and effort. First, the establishment of similarity of other to self in a particular area cuts down the need to attend to each particular behavior or utterance with the same vigilant intensity (see Chapter 2), though the variabilities of behavior or mood and deviation from the pattern still command attention when necessary. Second, the tendency to extend or infer beyond the given evidence allows partners to construct projective models of one another's meaning system without actually observing its every nut and bolt. Chapter 3 began to look at some ways in which these processes work when one person sees another as a perceptual object and extends from the immediately observable behavior to imagine or set "a pattern" that is meaningful and interpretable. The present chapter examines some of the ways in which an assumption of psychological similarity (as an example) makes use of an existing system (one's own meaning system) and relates it directly to the other person's. The assumption of similarity permits a person to fill in gaps in a model of the other's meaning system. It facilitates the assumption that those gaps will be occupied by elements of meaning like those that occupy a similar position in one's own system.

A final element of similarity's role is that similarity very often (depending on the exact topics) offers consensual validation (Byrne, 1971; Duck, 1991), given that we all know that others will often see things differently from ourselves. This common knowledge faces us with a challenge to find out just when similarities are significant; when the similarity is genuine, it implicitly validates the two persons' independent judgments about that topic. Constructed psychological similarity is thus also a mutual *validation:* The fact that another person has, in the uncertain world discussed in Chapter 2, made similar choices is implicit support for the choices one has made oneself.

Because social relating is a continual process of checking, balancing, and adjusting to others, as well as a continual process of transformation, the influence of similarity is never finished. As relationships extend in time, whether they increase in intimacy or not (Allan, 1993), there are not only new instances of similarity to seek, but new levels of the organization of another person's meaning to check. The ebbs and flows of comprehension postulated in Chapter 1 are continually checked by reference to any new level of understanding that a belief in a particular similarity sustains or develops.

In the present chapter, I make a crucial distinction between two sorts of topics that relational partners could discuss from a basis of similarity or dissimilarity: (a) elements *exterior* to the relationship (e.g., past events that happened to each person separately, or views formed before the two persons ever met, or attitudes about topics that have little to do with the relationship directly, such as political views); and (b) elements *interior* to the relationship, such as similarity of beliefs about the relationship, similarity of constructive or destructive conflict behaviors, and things that could not be objects of perception were it not for the existence of the relationship—such as the relationship future, how the relationship should be managed, or how work, time, and leisure should be distributed within it. The present chapter thus moves us toward an emergent association between minds: similarity (and understanding) relative to common experiences within the relationship itself.

To develop these points we need to look at several aspects of similarity and to pick apart what it is, why it works, and why it matters.

❦ What Is It? The Many Faces of Psychological Similarity

Researchers have tended generally to relate their measures of psychological similarity not to social but rather to individual cognitive processes. Only recently, for example, has it been proposed (Burleson & Denton, 1992) that similarity of nonverbal behavior and social skills could have the consequence of making relational interactions more pleasurable for both persons and hence perpetuate their desires for continued interaction. Instead, by treating similarity as a drily mental comparison without a human voice or social accompaniments, research has left out the social power of the construction and management of similarity in everyday talk. Likewise, in treating disagreement and dissimilarity as simple negative experiences, we run the risk of overlooking the ways in which they are managed as a dark side of relationships in the context of the lighter side (Duck, 1994d) or the ways in which they are given an ultimately positive spin through discussion (Wood et al., 1994).

Furthermore, we need to reaffirm the important difference between simply being similar to someone else and acknowledging the fact. In assuming or recognizing similarity between self and other, two persons perforce engage in several important psychological and consequent social processes and not just in a single process of individual reaction to a psychological state of affairs. Assumption of similarity requires a model of another person's system of thought, but also recognizes that the other person also has a model of oneself. Early interactions in a developing relationship are likely to concern discussion and elaboration of similarities that are coincident in the two persons' prior histories, attitudes, or experiences before the relationship. As a relationship develops so it becomes important in addition for the partners to display, compare, and negotiate ways of dealing with their common experience in the relationship itself. Thus the blend of similarities is increasingly likely to incorporate new domains of experience: attitudes toward and psychological reactions about the relationship, one's partner, and the common experience of belonging to it, in addition to other sorts of mutual exploration.

Elements of Similarity

For the above reasons, I believe that psychological similarity is an issue that gets right to the essence of relationships, once it is properly understood and placed in context; properly differentiated from the notion of understanding, with which it has often been confounded (see Acitelli et al., 1993; White, 1985, for a discussion); and properly related to the ongoing social contexts for the unfinished business of relating that I have outlined in preceding chapters.

As will become clearer, "psychological similarity" has been used for many different types of connection between minds and people, ranging from similarity of attitudes, values, judgments, personality variables, and outlooks to equivalent evaluations of experience and events (Bochner, Krueger, & Chmielewski, 1982). Authors have mingled their terms (treating *similarity, reciprocity,* and *agreement,* for example, as essentially interchangeable; cf. Bochner et al., 1982); sometimes studying assumed similarity, perceived reciprocity, mutuality, projection, or perceived similarity rather than "actual similarity" (Dymond, 1954; Kenny, 1988; Kenny & Acitelli, 1989; Levinger & Breedlove, 1966; see Acitelli et al., 1993, for a review); sometimes seeing too little difference between "understanding" and "perceived similarity" (Acitelli et al., 1993, refer to both of these as "perceptual congruence variables," for example), or too little difference between empathy and other intersubjective processes (Ickes, Tooke, Stinson, Baker, & Bissonnette, 1988); and sometimes failing to recognize the different salience of perceptual focus for similarity at different points in a relationship's evolution (Duck, 1973, 1977). Especially important have been the tendency not to differentiate explicitly between similarity about interior and exterior aspects of the relationship and the tendency not to place the similarities in the context of time.

Some Clarifications and Distinctions. Among other things, the present chapter presents several reasons why it is important to *distinguish understanding from similarity.* As proposed in Chapter 3, one can be similar to someone else without understanding the person (e.g., my son Ben and I speak some of the same words), or one can understand someone without being psychologically similar (e.g., I can understand more of what Ben means than he understands of what I mean). Over time in a relationship, the two different intersubjective experiences of similarity and understanding may come to coincide to a greater and greater extent (Blankenship, Hnat, Hess, & Brown, 1984), but they are not necessarily the same things. The extent that research differentiates or confounds these convergent processes will depend on the aspects of the relationship of the two persons that are the focus of research attention.

At *different points in a relationship's life* psychological similarity could be more or less relevant (e.g., right now it doesn't bother me that Ben and I are not similar, but when he is adult, I might find it bothersome). It would also be useful to differentiate those similarities that lay the groundwork for superficial social relationships from those that actually promote relationships that become close and personal (Duck, 1977), while also recognizing that increasing intimacy is neither the desired nor the achieved goal for most relationships (Allan, 1993).

Certain sorts of similarity (e.g., common cultural membership, being on the same wavelength) either are assumed when people interact or else are denied, with nonengagement or rejection being the result

(Rodin, 1982; Rosenbaum, 1986). Equally, several studies have shown that the effects of similarity are modified (enhanced, reduced) by its rarity. The experience of finding someone who shares one's uncommonly held attitudes (e.g., the belief that the world is really flat) has a more powerful effect on attraction than the experience of finding one's commonly held attitudes shared (Byrne, Nelson, & Reeves, 1966). Also, similarity has more of an effect on attraction when it occurs in respect to important attitudes than to attitudes rated less important by the person (Lea & Duck, 1982).

Early research has shown that similarity of *different aspects of self* is progressively important as relationships develop (Duck & Craig, 1978). Equally, people can be similar on some aspects or hierarchical layers of personality at some times in relationships and not others (Kerckhoff & Davis, 1962). Some research shows that initial similarity is frequently reinterpreted and reevaluated as meaning something different in later acquaintance (Duck, 1975), or when a relationship is dissolving (Weber, 1983). Finally, partners can be affected by broad similarity at some points and by fine-grained or by less easily accessible similarity at others (Neimeyer & Neimeyer, 1985), and the pattern of interrelationships between similarity variables can shift across time (Neimeyer & Mitchell, 1988). Thus what is an important similarity at one time point of relationships might not be important at another. For example, the realization that you and I are both similar in that we come from Bristol, U.K., could be important information as a trigger for us to continue talking at the start of a relationship but won't, on its own, do much to keep a marriage together. Equally, the influence of some sorts of similarity may be felt most on some types of relationships rather than on others. It would be surprising if pairs of same-sex friends at work, for example, did not need to be similar in some of their attitudes about business organizations, but it might well be unimportant whether they are of similar race or sexual orientation or love style. On the other hand, for a romantic couple to be successful, some similarity in sexual beliefs and values would probably be important, but similarity of attitudes about organizations may never need to be considered at all.

Loose Use of Terms: Similarity of What? A second loose use of the term *similarity* stems from older research that tended to look at

similarity of specific beliefs, attitudes, or personality traits without embedding them in the large organized social contexts in
which they are operative (Day, 1961; Izard, 1963). By contrast,
Monsour (1994) considers the ways in which perceptual schemas
influence perception of similarities and affect their evaluation. He
argues that an individual's general schema for a particular type of
relationship (such as friendship) might encourage the person to
see certain types of differences as healthy or stimulating elements
of the relationship. In other words, similarity, like information,
takes a part of its meaning from the context in which it is found.
Likewise, other authors (e.g., Sillars, 1985; White, 1985) have cau-
tioned that researchers must be careful to restrict their discussion
to the specific referent measured in their work, because some
elements of perceptual similarity are multidimensional (Bochner
et al., 1982), and that transfer effects of similarity measured in one
way cannot be safely assumed for another measure, especially at
different points in a relationship (Duck, 1977).

For another thing, similarity and dissimilarity can coexist simultaneously between two people, making the statement that they "are
similar" too sweeping and in need of proper qualification to a
domain of experience and to a temporal context (Duck, 1977; Sillars,
1985; White, 1985). On the one hand, people often manage the
tension between coexistent similarities and dissimilarities fairly
well, recognizing that even two intimates are never going to agree
about everything (Wood et al., 1994) or about every aspect of a
complex topic where they have basic general agreement. It is important, I believe, to differentiate types and extents of similarity, not
only with respect to particular topics but also within topics (e.g., we
may agree that war is wrong but disagree about the means of
eliminating it). On the other hand, people do tend to get carried
away, whether they are ordinary folks just beginning to create a
relationship or scholarly researchers studying such ordinary folks
(or both). Rather than saying "We are similar in the strictly limited
sense that we both come from Bristol in the United Kingdom, and like
cheese," we say only "Oh, we *are* similar." If we, as researchers, allow
ourselves to test for similarity in a few limited cognitive domains
(e.g., a handful of factors on a personality test; Izard, 1963) and then
write easily about two people "*being* cognitively similar," as if they
were perpetual cognitive Siamese twins, we have ourselves fallen

into the same trap. We have generalized too far on the basis of a single instance (or a few instances) of similarity.

Why Bother With These Distinctions? The reason all of this matters is that, in real life, the above distinctions are socially important. Similarity in one domain does not at all necessitate similarity in other domains, and everyone knows that fact at the bottom of their hearts, even if the top of their hearts blissfully hopes for something else. Many hopeful relaters soon discover to their eventual dismay and disappointment as they develop their relationship through time that specific psychological similarities discovered in early conversations wash out (Sunnafrank, 1991, 1992). Equally likely is that such topical similarities do not generalize to broader similarities of meaning that are relevant to relationship management, though many do (Duck & Allison, 1978).

It is obviously possible for someone to utter statements that suggest similarity to or difference from a listener in one domain but not in another. It is obviously also possible for a hearer to infer similarity from a statement when such similarity is not directly stated. This inferential process is largely bypassed in work on similarity in the traditional style in social psychology and communication studies (Duck & Barnes, 1992), where persons are typically presented with unambiguous statements made by other people on attitude scales or personality profiles. Yet in their real lives subjects (a) may not detect the same sorts of similarities as those that are selectively presented to them in experiments; (b) may not attribute the similarities with the same meanings as those expected by the researchers; and so (c) may jump beyond those similarities idiosyncratically in forming impressions or reactions (Aronson & Worchel, 1966). There is both ancient and modern research showing that people do insist on leaping ahead of themselves and perceiving or assuming similarity between themselves when the objective observer just can't see it (e.g., Acitelli et al., 1993; Crohan, 1992; Levinger & Breedlove, 1966; Sillars, 1985).

It is a subtly interesting point that the existence of one instance of similarity exterior to a relationship easily suggests to an observing mind the greater likelihood of others that would be interior to the relationship. Similarity breeds promiscuous extension. Humans observe a topical psychological similarity and are very likely to make all sorts of hopeful assumptions that it will lead to a good relation-ship (Monsour, 1994). Dating agencies make their money from this misguided human hope, and ultimately that hope is the underlying assumption behind the belief that the right chemistry (i.e., the right mix of similarities and personality characteristics) is the basis for a good relationship—as if behavior subsequent to the first mixing of the "chemicals" has no effect at all (Duck & Sants, 1983). Writers of personal ads also make use of this assumptive tendency and use cue words like "slim," "easy-going," or "theater and music lover" not merely as descriptors but also as ideas to set up images in readers' minds ("extension" again!) and thus to imply satisfying relation-ships. This book has already urged that such leaping ahead is a natural process of extension that gives initial detection or assump-tion of similarity some of its social power.

Meaning Systems as Multilayered

Kelly (1955, 1969b, 1970) proposed that it is similarity of meaning that matters in defining psychological similarity and not similarity of beliefs, attitudes, and so forth, alone. Kelly (1970, p. 20), in correcting the original statement in his 1955 book, put it thus: "To the extent that one person employs a construction of [an] experience which is similar to that employed by another, his [or her] processes are psychologically similar to those of the other person [in respect of that experience]." Psychological similarity does not depend on two people just behaving similarly, nor saying the same words, nor "having" the same experiences, understood to mean *experience=events* (Duck, 1982a; Duck & Condra, 1989). Nor is it just endorsing the same attitudes or values, if such basic endorsements are taken as the whole story. Rather psychological similarity consists in the way in which the two people similarly construe and give fully organized personal meaning to events (i.e., *experience=subjective interpretation*). Such constructs can rarely be understood only from individual utterances or specific behaviors alone, but rather from the organization of meaning and the larger personal contexts in which individual be-haviors and utterances occur. To comprehend such organization and depth takes time and social action between relational partners.

Just as utterances can take different forms, so a person can be described at many levels. For instance, I can simultaneously experience a person as tall, physically attractive, intelligent, anxious, oppressed by memories of childhood, unsuccessful, a smoker, conservative, a good parent, irascible, a teetotaller, unlikely to support X in a faculty meeting, very funny, and someone I like more than I used to. On different occasions, different elements will be at the forefront; for example, "irascible" and "unlikely to support X in a faculty meeting" are likely to come to the surface when I am in tense faculty meetings with the person, but "good parent" and "very funny" are more likely to surface when I am attending the person's family barbecue with friends. At other times the apparent "logical" conflicts between some of these properties will be a problem for me as my context for perceiving this other person is modified (e.g., "intelligent" and "a smoker" might come to the forefront if the conversation turns to health). At yet other times these "logical conflicts" (as I see them) may have no psychological force at all but can peacefully coexist at the back of my mind (e.g., when I am on vacation with other friends). Thus different aspects of the other, different elements of our similarities and differences, and different weights given to such similarities and differences in sundry contexts will play into the enactment of our social lives across time.

A person's meaning system can thus be understood at various levels of psychological organization (e.g., into groups of "attitudes" or clusters of values or global styles of behavior, or even different subsystems of personal constructs [Hinkle, 1970]—a point recently extended by Neimeyer & Mitchell, 1988). Therefore, psychological similarity between persons likewise can be assessed and established, whether simultaneously or sequentially, at different levels of psychological organization. Since this is so, both the research study and the real life exploration of global "psychological similarity" per se become less important than exploration of similarity at multiple levels of psychological organization (Duck, 1973; Duck & Craig, 1978; Neimeyer & Mitchell, 1988; Neimeyer & Neimeyer, 1985). Two people can be similar at some level of personality organization (e.g., both being extroverts) without actually being similar in terms of every specific belief, preference, value, or personality subsystem at other levels (Acitelli et al., 1993; Duck, 1973). In the actual conduct of social life, the hierarchical and complex nature of persons will always present partners with problems of refining comprehension. The fine points of similarity are eventually likely to count for more than global comparability (Duck & Craig, 1978). This is especially likely when it comes to working out a fully operational relationship replete with specific behaviors, focused rituals, and particular activities.

Similarity, then, is not simple nor absolute in its character, much less in its effects. Meaning systems are displayed at different levels of organization on different occasions or by different means of expression in different interactions. As a result, in the normal conduct of a relationship, one can suddenly perceive similarity to (or difference from) someone else at one time and place, in reference to one sort of content, even if one has not assumed it before. Therefore, construction of meaning, understanding, similarity, or consubstantiality with the other person is a process that is a perpetually unfolding and changing part of the unfinished business of relating. Psychological similarity might thus better be seen as a continuous, active process of construction, not a simple state. It faces individuals with a continual task—the unfinished business of construing the evolving ways in which another person understands the world, in relation to one's own evolving view of the world.

Similarity as a Research Topic

Given the previous discussion, it is very important how similarity is assessed in research seeking to clarify its role in relating. At first, this appears not to be a theoretical issue at all but merely a methodological one. In fact it is a theoretical issue (Duck, 1977). If the investigator believes that similarity has an effect whether or not the two persons perceive it and are aware of it, then a measure that assesses "inaccessible" similarity will be fine (e.g., similarity of galvanic skin response patterns, or similarity of total scores on a personality test, or similarity of unconscious drives, or similarity of personality structure as measured by complex statistical means or computer modeling). If, on the other hand, the investigator believes that point-by-point similarity on specific issues is what is likely to matter in the conduct of everyday relationships, then the comparison of answers to specific questions or the use of specific tests of particular attitudes is the appropriate measure. There is a subtle but important social difference in "theorettes" (Chapter 1) between a measurement of similarity that could equally be used by subjects in real life (e.g., a global assessment of whether person A is as introverted as Person

B is) and a measurement that is too complex to be so accessible in real life (e.g., a measurement based on a specific battery of questions that are used to create 18 dimensions of personality that are then compiled through a statistical procedure into difference score totals; Hogan & Mankin, 1970). The present chapter urges reference to a measure's implicit representation of the social processes of "meaning construction" whenever reviewers are deciding the contribution of that measurement to our understanding of similarity in relationships.

"Similarity" or "dissimilarity" is not some sort of abstract entity floating about ethereally in social interaction but is something that is a real interpersonal process. Once one sees it that way, (dis)similarity becomes important not for itself but only and especially when the partners assume, realize, or establish that it exists between them. For one thing, once perceived, the (dis)similarity can be discussed between them as a topic in its own right—and that creates another layer of meaning to it derived from the shared experience of discussing (un)likeness(es). For this reason the psychological force of "similarity" is likely to come from the recognition of sharing rather than from its unrecognized "pure" existence at one time point of measurement. For this reason one needs to focus not only on how people use similarity to infer meanings but why they talk about it or reveal it in talk over time and further construct meaning from it. In other words we need to explore how similarity is (1) a foundation for relationships and how it is also (2) built and constructed by the people during a relationship as they seek to understand each other.

❦ One Way It Works: Similarity as a Rhetorical Instrument

The Roman orator Marcus Tullius Cicero, some 2,000 years ago, claimed that similarity was one of the great "loci" or "places" of argument on which cases could be built to persuade others. Similarity between things or concepts is itself persuasive: The fact of similarity persuades us to treat one thing as we treat another that we see as being like it. Cicero claimed that similarity worked by "intrinsic natural means." By intrinsic, he meant that similarity was a persuasive tool inherent in the material itself (as distinct, for example, from testimony adduced by an authority from outside). Similarity suggests to the observing mind an easy way to grasp a second set of circumstances with a sense of basic understanding. Similarity, like metaphor, pulls listeners' thinking toward those other aspects of the two cases that are not necessarily identical, but which can be seen to have some usefully evocative relationship. If the orator does the job well, then the audience will get carried along inexorably by the frames of reference that the speaker provides.

Likewise, similarity between two minds is persuasive. Similarity immediately connects two people but also stimulates inferences and extension (assumed similarity) by giving the persons a basis for expanding their discourse. One similarity between two persons immediately suggests—but only suggests—an extended, organized system of other similarities that the persons could explore usefully in the future conversations of the unfinished business of relating.

All the same, the initially captivating persuasiveness of similarity is, by necessity, only teasingly suggestive. Each instance of cognitive similarity invites a fuller exploration and yet poses a dilemma for people in their conduct of ordinary life. A specific instance of similarity of particular *experience=events* provides a safe guide to understanding another person only when it is contextualized in other information about the meaning system in which it is embedded (e.g., information about other related concepts, or information about previous behavior, or information about "motives"). For instance, even ingratiators can appear similar to a target other at first, but they are not necessarily truly similar. Therefore in real life, a listener sometimes has to do real social detective work in order to divine a speaker's underlying meaning structure. Such detective work, the relative skills of different detectives, and so on, are rarely if ever studied in the research on the effects of similarity, although second-guessing in general has been studied by Hewes and Planalp (1982). Yet relaters do this detective work and do it for a reason. When established under the right circumstances, psychological similarity offers a validation for one's own view of the world (Byrne, 1971; Monsour, 1994)

Similarity as a Constructive Perception

We should also note that in making judgments or constructions of similarity between self and other, individuals can do so too

inventively. For example, persons can construct entirely inappropriate views of others' roles, intentions, and behavior and can act on
those misconstructions in social interaction. As Duck et al. (1994)
have shown, lonely persons construct cognitive schemas for interaction that in some sense misrepresent the realities of interaction, at
least as judged by other observers. Likewise, an individual could
create an overgenerous assessment of similarity between self and
other and could act on it. However, the important points are that (1)
however "accurate" or "inaccurate" a person's judgments are, they
are nevertheless the judgments that are used by the person as a basis
for social action; and (2) such assumptions promote interest in
continuing a relationship with another person in order to diversify
and contextualize knowledge of that person. In effect I offer a reinterpretation of the effects of perceived similarity (Levinger & Breedlove,
1966), and the false consensus effect (Ross, 1977), if applied to
relationships, where people assume others are more like them than
the others actually are. This false consensus effect is usually explained as an attempt to reassure self of the appropriateness of one's
own views (McFarland & Miller, 1990). I offer a different explanation, namely that it is socially useful to make temporary assumptions
of "identification" and "consubstantiality" (Chapter 3) because they
prompt conversational explorations and so have social force.

For the same reason, differences in recognition of psychological
similarity might have other social force: If one person recognizes the
similarity and one does not, for instance, then they have different levels
of understanding of one another, and so that difference should affect
the two persons unequally. If both persons perceive that (dis)similarity
exists but one construes its significance for the closeness or the future
of their relationship differently from the other, then that again should
affect the relationship socially. For instance, if one person realizes that
the other is not as serious about the relationship as the person is, then
there are three obvious possible social outcomes: (1) break off the
relationship as a waste of time, (2) try to persuade the other person to
take as serious a view of it as one does oneself, (3) concede and make
the relationship a less serious relationship. Actually a fourth possibility
exists, too. If a person suddenly realizes from some word or behavior
that the other does see the relationship as equally important, then a
statement defining the relationship or a strong statement of commitment could well be the social result.

Thus the existence of "similarity" between two minds, even if such similarity were ever a permanent state for all time, is not important in itself, as a psychological state. It is important for its consequences socially because it provides chances for partners to identify, discuss, and explore the relationship between their minds and perhaps also to develop their organization of the relationship in terms of behavior and roles. "Being similar" and "knowing or believing that they are similar" are two different social phenomena for partners. The belief that something is shared is an important trigger for social relational effects. Such knowledge is contextualized by time, is accessed in talk, and is influential on the form of relationship flowing from it.

Thus we should be careful about assuming that similarity is a simple concept that would help partners to understand one another's minds easily. Similarity helps; but it needs also to be put in the context of other social processes and relational activities, especially talk.

Talk and the Detection of Similarity

Because the unraveling and understanding of others' meaning systems is a continually unfinished process, it necessarily prompts talk and interaction. Although psychological similarity probably stimulates talk in and of itself, the relational importance of psychological similarity becomes fully apparent only when seen in the context of the other social processes that I have emphasized: "extension," inference, variability of experience of life, talk, and meaning. When people talk together they likely discuss broader ranges of values and elaborate the extent to which they share larger areas of personal meaning (Monsour, 1994). Conversation has the ability to give context to information, clarify ambiguity, sort out dilemmas, and place topics in a framework of relational management and negotiation. Unfortunately, talk is rarely unambiguous. For example, "irony" requires that a message be heard by two different audiences or in two different ways, one way meaning something relatively direct and one more subtle than that (Booth, 1974). "Metaphor" requires that the literal meaning of a word or sentence be applied elsewhere as well as to the literal case. "Sarcasm" requires that the listener deduce, usually from the accompanying nonverbal behavior, that the face values of the speaker's words are to be read as actually negated (Zaidel & Mehrabian, 1969). There is a long list of such figures of speech, known collectively to rhetoricians as tropes. They each illustrate that social meaning cannot be deduced merely from intelligent analysis of the words themselves, but only by consideration of their social usage in conversational and relational contexts and from some ability to understand a speaker's likely intent or style. Because the tropes bring with them two possibilities of interpretation, each one depends for complete understanding on the listener's ability to comprehend what is not meant in the circumstances and so to grasp the speaker's meaning in context. For instance, irony works only if an audience appreciates that two different meanings can be read into the same words, depending on the vantage point that is adopted.

The variability and multiple meanings in behavior and talk also thus are not literary or abstract problems, but are real, breathing, social dilemmas for relating partners. In the real conduct of everyday life they present relaters with a more or less continuous, if usually low-level, monitoring task before each person can, on each occasion, respond appropriately to the other person. To the extent that one is similar in some respect to the other person, one enhances one's likely understanding of the other's behavior in that domain, and increased levels of similarity expand one's relationship range. The more levels on which one is similar to the other person, the greater the likelihood of understanding that person in different domains of experience and the greater ability of the listener to fill in the blanks in a knowledgeable way in order to "play a social role" effectively. The more adequately one construes the different layers of another person's mind, the more the relationship is also differentiated and the easier the communication becomes (Chapter 3).

Although similarity is based on a common set of meanings that are fundamental to the playing of basic social roles with other people, there is more to it. More complex understandings and more differentiated social roles and relationships are created through serial processes of extension and test, and of progressions through constructions of different aspects of the other person's mind.

❦ Why It Matters: Similarity Between Minds as an Example of the Social Process of Meaning Construction

The present section begins to rearrange the above topics to depict the progression through different levels of similarity as a functioning social process that tells us something about relationship development as the serial construction of another person's meaning system.

Similarity in Social Context

Berger (1993) has claimed that overlap of meaning or similarity of comprehension most often happens adventitiously and is not necessarily forged by mutual interaction. He is perfectly right. First, individuals can be "similar" for a variety of reasons, among them being the effects of common membership of a culture and its language system, which will make people more likely to construe many things in similar ways. For example, two native speakers of English will likely see the same things as "chairs" and will think about them in the same sorts of ways. Two people from the subculture of academe are likely to place the same sorts of values on such things as academic freedom, the life of the mind, and education (and also, incidentally, to think of "chairs" in at least one way different from everyone else). Berger is right so far. Yet it is important for the present argument to see how his approach can be usefully extended and developed.

Berger essentially emphasizes the sorts of commonalities that the early sociological and demographic researchers (e.g., Kerckhoff, 1974) demonstrated when they showed that assortative mating takes place. Classic research (Lewis & Spanier, 1973) showed that like tends to marry like, in terms of education, race, socioeconomic level, and so on, and that such homogamy—that is, the tendency for like to marry like—is the best predictor of marital stability. However, within such broad associations of class, individuals tend to make personal selections on grounds other than these assortative similarities (Duck, 1985). Thus, as it was sometimes put, the "field of desirables" (those whom people would choose or prefer) is contained within, and is smaller than, the "field of availables" or "field of eligibles" (those who constitute the whole range of the available or suitable choices). To put it metaphorically, the sort of food we would find delightful as a treat is contained within the class of all things that we would consider eating if we just had to survive.

Berger is right to argue that the majority of instances of commonality occur fortuitously. My contention, though, is that the most important cases for personal relationships (viz., the cases that promote comprehension of the deep structure of the organization of another person's meaning system) are those that are created by the two parties themselves in social process. Some commonality stems adventitiously from joint membership in a language culture, some from the limited imagination that comes with being human, some from membership in a cultural community that gives us a few prepackaged ways of looking at things as a benefit of membership. These are useful as a basis for a social relationship. However, the important forms of psychological understanding that lay the basis for personal relationships go beyond this and are based on deeper levels of psychological construction, to which we now turn.

A Model of the Serial Construction of Meaning

So far I have made two sorts of distinction: One, as above, distinguishes similarity across *specific topics* (as has been traditionally and implicitly measured in studies assessing the degree of similarity of particular attitudes or personality characteristics) from similarity of the *organizational structure of meaning*. I have offered the latter as a higher-order concept with much greater connection to the notion of understanding, or to the notion I discussed in Chapter 3 of comprehending Other in Other's own terms. The second distinction has concerned the nature and focus of the topics discussed: Where some research has focused on similarity of topics and issues exterior to the relationship (e.g., attitudes about work or politics; Byrne, 1971), other work has looked at similarity of behavior or cognition about the relationship itself (Acitelli et al., 1993). Yet other work (Ickes & Turner, 1983) has looked at similarity of, or the ability to read other's thoughts and feelings in, specific ongoing interaction (as distinct from general attitudes about the relationship as a whole).

I now want to weave these points of distinction into the fabric of the argument in a different way by pointing out the nature of some of the transformations that occur simultaneously as partners construct and develop their relationship. To comprehend the deeper levels of a person's psychology is simultaneously to gain access to more intimate information (Altman & Taylor, 1973) *and* to appreciate some of the structure of the person's thinking (else how could it be described as "deeper" levels?). Yet it is also important to recognize that partners move on to deeper comprehension of each other's system of meaning while also moving from exterior topics to those topics that are interior to the relationship. The relationship itself becomes an increasingly important topic to agree about, at the same time as the partners are reaching fuller understanding of each other's meaning system. To develop this point more completely and to emphasize the multiplicity of roles that similarity (as an example of cognitive relationship) plays in the process, I must now put some of this into a structure showing what I mean about the transformation in focus, empathy, and understanding that the above implies.

We can distinguish *commonality* from a number of other similar terms such as *mutuality, equivalence,* and *sharing.* The basic form of similarity is *commonality* of *experience=events,* called "common past" by Katovich and Couch (1992). In this case, the same events have occurred in the lives of the two persons, whether these be such things as the fact that they have each had children, turned 30, fished for trout in Montana, been to Europe, voted Democrat, or insisted on buying products that do not use CFCs. The persons have not expressed these commonalities until they declare them or believe/ realize that the commonalities exist. However, such sharing actually requires two other social processes: the process of declaration and the process of evaluation. *Declaration* (or self-disclosure) exposes the common experience or attitude and so creates a mutual past (Katovich & Couch, 1992), in the sense that now both persons have together taken part in the same conversation (about their common past). The mutuality is a joint realization that the two persons have the basic commonalities that were discussed in that conversation. Mutuality also permits the bidirectional transfer of feelings and thoughts about the common topic by the construction of a common frame of reference (Genero et al., 1992).

Evaluation is the assessment that each person makes of the common topic. Thus the mutuality may lead to a further reconstruction of one another by revealing that the two persons have an underlying equivalence of values that refers to and incorporates those commonalities. In short, they not only had the same things happen to them

	Undeclared	Declared
Nonevaluative	Commonality of experience=events	Mutuality
Evaluative	Equivalence of evaluation	Shared Meaning

Figure 4.1. Four Components of "Similarity"

NOTE: The *declaration* dimension distinguishes the fact that two persons may have common events in their backgrounds (commonality) and either may or may not know it. The *evaluative* dimension distinguishes the fact that "similarity" as normally construed, involves both the common facts and the common evaluation of the facts.

but appraised the *experiences=events* equivalently. Equivalence itself may then indicate that the persons share the same comprehension in respect of other, unrelated, domains of meaning within which they interpret, comprehend, and cherish these equivalences.

Figure 4.1 represents these different elements of similarity as a classic ANOVA 2 × 2 table, merely in effect noting the difference between the elements in terms of the two dimensions of declaration and evaluation. The evaluative dimension distinguishes the fact that similarity, as normally treated in research discussions, actually involves both the common facts and the common evaluation of the facts. The mere existence of commonality is one form of similarity, but our evaluations of that experience add another possible dimension to our similarity. Likewise, the declaration dimension distinguishes the fact that two persons may have common events in their backgrounds (commonality) and either may or may not know it. As the present chapter has indicated, both the declaration and the evaluation are important overlays to the simple fact of commonality.

Now consider not only the conceptual differences between these terms but also their place in the social process of the serial construction of their significance (Figure 4.2). Similarity (as one example of the focus of such a process) is serially construed and reconstrued in a process that acknowledges the original commonality and proceeds extensively from it toward a model of its meaning. Figure 4.2

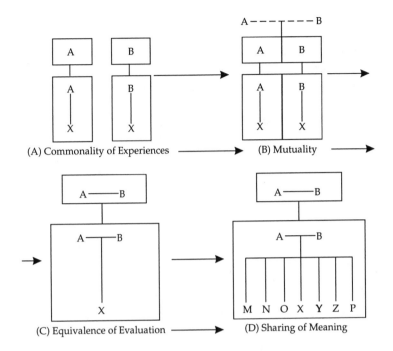

(A) Commonality of Experiences ⟶ (B) Mutuality ⟶

(C) Equivalence of Evaluation ⟶ (D) Sharing of Meaning

Figure 4.2. A General Model of the Serial Construction of Meaning

NOTE: In Figure 4.2 are represented schematically the progressively developing constructions of the two partners about each other in relation to topic X. In *commonality* the two persons A, B relate to topic X but do so independently of one another. In *mutuality* they now know that the same topic is in the experience of each of them (*experience=events*). In *equivalence* they both see how they evaluate X (*experience=subjective interpretation*). In *sharing* they see how they evaluate not only X but also several other topics, events, and experiences that contextualize their evaluation of X (i.e., they have a common organization for meaning surrounding topic X). The figure should not be taken to illustrate only the role of similarity in meaning. Rather it depicts the general process that continues with different foci during all the unfinished business of relating and it simply uses "similarity" as a convenient special instance.

represents the above as process in temporal terms where commonality precedes mutuality, mutuality precedes equivalence, and equivalence precedes sharing. In Figure 4.2 are represented schematically the progressively developing constructions of the two partners about each other in relation to topic X. In *commonality* the two persons, A and B, relate to topic X but do so independently of one another. In *mutuality* they now observe that the same topic is in the experience of each of them (*experience=events*). In *equivalence* they both comprehend how they evaluate X (*experience=subjective interpretation*). In *sharing* they see how they evaluate not only X but also several other topics, events, and experiences that contextualize their evaluation of X (i.e., they have a common organization for meaning surrounding topic X).

An overlay to the model in Figure 4.2 is that it may be applied to topics interior to the relationship as well as to those exterior to it. In the hierarchy of things that matter most, I would propose that sharing of meaning about the relationship is an exquisite realization with profound effects on the continual transformation of the relationship. The figure should not be taken therefore to depict one process, but it depicts the general process that continues with different foci during all the unfinished business of relating. Figure 4.2 could be construed in relation to dissimilarity or difference also; it is a model of progressive construction of the relationship between self's and other's experience, thinking, and meaning.

The model in Figure 4.2 therefore places (dis)similarity in the social transactive context of meaning construction. It provides a view of the social role of construction of meaning out of similarity (or out of anything else) and does not view it as an absolute, global, or undifferentiated mental relationship between two people. Also one begins to see the significance of taking note of the vantage point from which one views the existence of (dis)similarity. For an outsider (e.g., a researcher) to declare that it exists is to warrant a psychological relationship (i.e., mere commonality) that is in fact a different process from the case where the partners *construe* that commonality exists and deal with the implications of that construction. Such a difference is lost by measures of psychological similarity that implicitly or directly shortcut persons' beliefs about one another's psychological contents, as distinct from comparing the contents themselves.

The representation in Figure 4.2 thus suggests a process that models the changes in the relationship of Person A to Person B as they move through different levels of construction of a topic's meaning to each other. From Chapter 3's argument we deduce that partners' expanding and transforming construction of one another's meaning system will in turn affect and transform the ways in which they respond to and interact with one another (i.e., in Kelly's terms used in Chapter 3, the transformation of constructions of each other's meaning will affect and transform the social roles that they play with one another). Thus research on the full social meaning of *similarity as sharing* would in the future require four separate questions to be answered, not just the first of them: (1) Is there objectively assessable "similarity" located in the juxtaposition of the two persons' objective characteristics (i.e., commonality)? (2) Do both people know that the common element exists in each other's history (mutuality) (which is a state of knowledge "located" within the two persons' minds as a result of disclosure of commonality)? (3) Does each person know how the other person evaluates the phenomenon (equivalence) (a state of knowledge located at the level of metaperspectives about the other person's system of thought and also located in the assumptions contained in their talk)? (4) Does each person know the mental framework from which the commonality springs and in which it is organized (shared meaning)?

Beliefs About Similarity as Relational Forces

The above is a general model of meaning construction and it happens to take similarity as an example. Dissimilarity probably also provokes many of the same processes of inference, discussion, and negotiation or relational transformation, and it certainly conveys meaning and provokes necessary relational adjustment. Both similarity and dissimilarity can increase comprehension of another's meaning system. In reviewing the preceding discussion it is important to recall two points, one of them a reprise of Chapter 3, and one an earlier distinction that needs to be carefully reconsidered in relation to effects of (dis)similarity on relationships. First, Chapter 3 established the importance of noting possible asymmetries in two partners' comprehensions of each other and of anything else. The two partners in a relationship may understand one another to different degrees, or, in the present context, may assume or perceive similarity to different extents. In fact such asymmetry can be a relational force if one accepts not only that assumptions of (dis)similarity can be explored in ways that provoke talk, but also that the person who sees more potential in the relationship is likely to be encouraged to persuade the other to explore it also.

The second point is that one needs to distinguish the fact that the discussion so far has been focused largely on (dis)similarity of experience about things exterior to the relationship and in most cases prior to its creation. It is also important to consider how the two partners view (and understand each other's views of) events, behaviors, and feelings within the relationship.

In some respects, the beliefs that persons hold about their relationships could matter a lot more than the objectively determinable realities. Monsour, Betty, and Kurzweil (1993) found that perceived agreement and perceived understanding were greater influences on affection than actual agreement and understanding. In addition, Monsour et al., confirming a point made by Sillars (1985), found that persons used their own attitudes as a basis for predicting the attitudes of partners. Thus a shared reality is partly extrapolated from one's own system of thinking rather than from the true relationship between one's own mind and someone else's. All the same, when the beliefs of two friends do in fact start out being more similar than would happen by chance (Blankenship et al., 1984), so the assimilation of other, new elements into each other's belief system is likely to occur rather easily. Equally, the assumption that one person is similar to someone else could lead to social actions that are prompted by desires for fuller discovery and mutual disclosures that would develop the relationship. For example, Sprecher (1987) found that a couple's beliefs about their overall amounts of self-disclosure *given* and *received* were important in predicting long-term relational future. All the same, it was *perceptions* of degree of disclosure given by partners that were associated with affection.

In essence this argument suggests that the staple empirical constituents for most discussions of the effects of similarity on relationships misrepresent one important issue. They focus on the individual psychological level of analysis by looking at one person's evaluative reaction to instances of similarity. The element missing from much research is the social, *inter*individual consequences of similarity. These consequences are created by recognition of the existence of similarity and the appreciation or development of its significance. To use this notion one has to go to the other aspects of similarity discussed earlier. In doing this, one also goes up a level in the analysis when one looks not at "objective similarity," nor at one person's beliefs about similarity, but at one person's beliefs about the other person's mental structures. In Laing, Philipson, and Lee's (1966) terms we are dealing not with direct perspectives but with metaperspectives at this point: perspectives on perspectives, or A's view of what B thinks or knows. Ickes's work (Ickes, Robertson, Tooke, & Teng, 1986) on empathic accuracy is important here also. Ickes has explored partners' abilities to "read" one another in social interaction. From the point of view of the present perspective, this ability is an important component of meaning construction that represents a pathway between exterior factors and those that are deeply interior to the relationship.

Similarity, Meaning, and Social Action

Omitted from most discussion of assumed similarity and of interpersonal perception (which is rarely *inter*personal; rather it is perception *"of* persons"; Ickes & Gonzalez, n.d.) is consideration of what people *do* about them. The chapter has stressed the use of talk as a major, but not the only, source of information that expresses recognition of the relationship between two minds. I focus on talk because I assume explicitly that such recognitions themselves have social consequences on personal relationships exactly because people talk about them. In like manner, Acitelli (1988, 1993) has introduced the term *relationship awareness* to define "a person's thinking about interaction patterns, comparisons, or contrasts between himself or herself and the other partner in the relationship" (Acitelli, 1993, p. 151), and she has also strongly focused on the role of talk about relationships as a behavioral manifestation of such awareness (Acitelli, 1988). Acitelli's work on talk is a strong move to focus on the elements that I have termed *interior.* She has pioneered a crucial element of a previously ignored social process, therefore, and opened up the possibility of connecting one mind's thoughts about a relationship to relational outcomes through the social action of communication. Acitelli's work has so far focused on talking *about* the relationship, as distinct from talking *within the context of* a relationship, as I have been extending the point here (see also Ickes et al., 1988). Nevertheless, her work has now been pointed also to the exploration of the two relational partners' individual identities as reflected in such relationship awareness and indicated in relational talk. The present propositions build on this and assume that such work provides the necessary stepping-stone between an individual analysis and a dyadic analysis. Talk about similarity is the place where similarity slides over from being an individual, perceptual object and becomes a social, relational action grounded in mutuality and jointly constructed interaction.

❦ Summary and Conclusions

This chapter has offered five different ways in which similarity and assumed similarity affect relationships: (1) Similarity produces the persuasive "consubstantiality" that Burke wrote about (see Chapter 3) and so helps partners to accommodate to one another. (2) Similarity between one's own system and another at any point provides a basic topical understanding of the other person. (3) Similarity at one level provides a warrant for inference and extension to other levels of the other person's cognitive organization and so extends one's ability to construe the other person's meaning system. (4) Similarity offers an implicit validation for one's own way of thinking. (5) Similarity initiates social processes of discourse and comparison that lead to greater interdependence, intimacy, or closeness in relationships.

Psychological similarity is based on the common interpretation and construction of a range of events, not just on common endorsement of individual specific values, and not on having "similar" experiences. It involves a similar organization of different elements of meaning, not just a similarity of particular judgments on specific issues. Individuals can be similar in some psychological domains and not others. The trick (both for behaving social actors and for researchers) is to identify not only the specific but also the broader general ways in which two persons are "psychologically similar." Psychological similarity is essentially an organizational concept, and the task of relating partners is to comprehend the organization of one another's minds as well as their specific contents in particular topical domains.

Humans show a tendency to be persuaded by similarity. They also extend from one instance to an assumption of others, so a social problem for social actors is to establish the reality, extent, and meaning of the different possible levels of psychological similarity between themselves. This chapter argues that psychological similarity is not so much a state between two minds as a process that is continually under adjustment. Similarity inevitably ranges across specific topics exterior to the relationship, experiences within the ongoing flow of interaction, and conduct or evaluation of the relationship as a whole. These levels of comparison of thinking and evaluation between people must be distinguished.

The chapter presented a model of the Serial Construction of Meaning that further distinguished commonality, mutuality, equivalence, and sharing. It also showed how perceived and assumed similarity are different and yet both functional for relationships. Its final point was that talk provides the primary arena where the individual level of analysis of psychological similarity becomes a dyadic issue and partners most readily establish, transform, and construct the psychological relationship between their respective meaning systems.

The themes established in the chapter now lead us to a fuller consideration of talk in the uncovering of meaning.

❦ An Appendix of Formal Statements

Some of the arguments of the above chapter can be represented in the following formal statements.

Similarity: Two persons are psychologically similar to one another to the extent that they construct similar segmentations of particular "experiences" and characterize them with similar meanings. As argued in the present chapter and the preceding one, psychological similarity is founded on the similar construction of experience (*experience=subjective interpretation*), not on similarity of experience itself (*experience=events*).

Relational Force: Commonalities of experience assume relational force when recognized and acknowledged, usually in talk. As the chapter has urged, the mere existence of a commonality has no relational force until it comes into awareness as mutuality, equivalence, or shared meaning.

Relational Transformation: Changes in relationships are based directly or indirectly on changes in construction of another person's system of meaning. This corollary proposes that relationship changes are related to changes in understanding of another person, whether one comes to construe more of the other's system of personal meaning or comes to understand a particular part more thoroughly and fully.

Consubstantiality: Shared/negotiated meanings can be adapted or assimilated by individuals, dyads, or groups through talk. By bringing discussion of each other's meaning system into awareness, the partners facilitate the development of consubstantiality (Chapter 3) and generate possibilities for transformation of the relationship.

5

The Social Action of Relating
Talk and Meaning

What happens when people talk, when one person names something or says a sentence about something *and another person
understands?*

W. Percy (1975, p. 14, emphasis added)

OVERVIEW

The construing of another person's meaning system, especially concerning matters interior to the relationship, carries implications for
social action. In particular, the two partners in a relationship begin to
discuss their construction of the relationship and behaviors in it. For
this reason and others noted in the present chapter, information,
beliefs in similarity, and construction of the other person's meaning
system are neither absolute nor simply cumulative: They transform
and modify our relationships to others as individuals serially construe one another. Information, similarity, and knowledge are also
seething and variable as events and conversations develop and unfold. The present chapter explores the social dilemmas and relational
relevance of these facts of variability as persons seek to share meaning
in a context of alternative constructions of themselves and their
relationship. The present chapter illustrates the role of everyday talk
in accommodating alternative constructions, in providing a basis for
negotiating meaning, and in managing the form of the relationship.
The chapter also offers a composite model of social meaning as a way
of comprehending some of these processes in relationships.

Is relationship development simply a process of (or desire for) mutual discovery of selves at greater and greater informational depths? Yes and no. Obviously we do learn more about relational partners as the relationship unfolds, but that is a correlational claim! Besides, Chapter 4 added the notions that information can be "exterior" or "interior" to the relationship and in neither case is inert. Relationships involve construction, inference, and transformation in an extended social process involving talk. To represent the whole process of relating as a perceiver amassing more and more information is to pay too little attention to the role of dialogue in the expression of information, the modification of such expressions, the transformation of facts according to the purposes of the expresser, and the construction of shared meaning by listeners.

Traditional approaches assume that the meaning of information is absolute: Information is not seen as expressible in different forms according to dialogic principles, nor subject to variable interpretations by the listener in ways not necessarily foreseen by the speaker or researcher. In essence, such views assume that there cannot be two viable, correct construals of the same piece of information. We must now recognize the *relational* significance of alternative constructivism (Chapter 2), with the implication that two observers can take legitimate alternative views of "an event" (including especially a relational event—since it is hard to separate that particular class of events from the vantage point of the perceiver).

Two people in a relationship do quite often take different views of things (both exterior and interior things), and this fact indicates a parallel dilemma for relational partners and researchers alike. For relational partners it poses the problem of resolving or accommodating to the differences. For scholars, the recognition that two views on relational phenomena will always be possible and legitimate is a critical step that theorists need to take in this field (Duck, 1990). It is an issue that stands at the very heart of scholars' understanding of the nature of relationships. Those scholars who claim that we should gather data from both partners in a couple as a way of somehow strengthening our view of what is going on in a relationship (e.g., Noller & Guthrie, 1992) tend to perpetuate the absolutist mistake as to the nature of relational information. First, we need to know the theoretical interpretation that will be given to any discrepancy between two partners' views (Duck, 1990). Until we have theorized about the ways in which discrepancies are informative about a relationship's character, then we really do not gain anything by gathering sets of data from both partners.

The gathering of data from both members of a dyad is useful when and only when it is preceded by a clear model of communication that articulates the social consequences of the relational partners noticing that they are discrepant. In real life it is almost indisputable that divergences, dissimilarities, and discrepancies will lead either directly to talk about the issue or else indirectly to talk by way of some behavior that evokes remark. Therefore this chapter focuses on the transformative nature of communication in relationships and the ways in which the nature of talk itself indicates that relational (i.e., interior) meaning, like similarity, is a multilayered, unfinished, and protean concept. Meaning has components that are open to dispute in everyday talk, and these components may be perceived and detected differently by relationship partners—even in close relationships—especially across time. Thus the construction of meaning is an unfinished social analytical problem for partners in a relationship and should be characterized scientifically as an extended social process, not as a simple revelation.

❦ Some Views of Meaning Construction in Relational Life

Where is sharing (or similarity or intimacy or meaning) to be "located" (Cupach, 1991)?[1] Is it in a person's observable behavior or in the person's mind or in the dyad or somehow between the people? A focus on talk (or the practical semantic dilemmas faced by people relating in the real world) helps us to deal with this issue by extending the previous discussion of similarity and its serial construction. (Once again recall that I use similarity as a convenient example rather than as the only possible instance of the processes.) In traditional analyses of relational concepts like intimacy or closeness or similarity, these concepts are assumed to be located or fixed in the real world. Yet Acitelli and Duck (1987) questioned whether intimacy, for example, is best located as a stable characteristic of people or a long-term characteristic of relationships globally or a transient feature of interactions. Reis and Shaver (1988) offer a process model that likewise depicts intimacy as an emergent product of interaction rather than as an inherent property to be located in people or relationships. Likewise, Chapter 4 proposed that (dis)similarity is not a purely psychological state but instead is an emergent process that is a stimulus for social and communicative action in relationships. Thus the location of sharing and so on cannot be determined without looking at the role of talk and its force in producing relational meaning in reference to matters interior to the relationship.

The present chapter considers the degree to which various meanings of relational actions are located "between people" in the following sense. Mead proposed that the meaning of an action in a social setting arises in part from the response of the listener to the other person. "The act or adjustive response of the second organism gives to the gesture of the first organism the meaning that it has" (Mead, 1934/1967, p. 78). As far as two behaving persons are concerned, the conversational bargain is partly structured by the reactions of the person who speaks next. That is to say, my comments are given a social (in addition to my personal) meaning by the response of my hearer. My reaction to his or her response likewise frames the meaning of what is said to me as well as perhaps adding something to what I said previously: The other's response constructs the social meaning for both partners (Shotter, 1987). The two of us can transact such meaning either by staying within commonly available meaning frameworks or by creating new ones that we agree upon. Essentially a speaker will always have to persuade me that his or her comments mean something other than I take them to mean. Furthermore, my taking them one way rather than another either continues the flow of the conversation unremarkably along one of its possible paths or else occasions a change or interruption. For example, my reaction (or expected reaction) may occasion an explanation or an apology or an embarrassment or an affront or a new insight or a transformation in the implications of the relationship. For example, a famous seducer was once overheard saying to his female companion something that sounded ambiguous. Later, when asked if he had just propositioned his companion, he replied, "Well, if she had taken it as a proposition it would have been one, and my next words would have followed up on it. But she didn't, so it wasn't—and we just went on and talked about something else."

In everyday routine encounters, the reality of a relationship derives from *dyadic* transaction. The responses of the other person (and during the course of a whole encounter, the habitual responses of the two persons to each other over time) come to provide shape and definition of the relational meaning of interactions and social acts (Harris & Sadeghi, 1987; Masheter & Harris, 1986). An action always offers an amount of relational ambiguity and remains incompletely defined until the actor finds out how the partner responds (or until some possibility has been denied or negated in the clarifying way outlined in Chapter 2). Thus play is playful rather than serious because—and when—the two persons take one another's playful banter as being playful banter and not as being a serious or malicious personal attack.

If one distinguishes the social processes of meaning construction in the serial way depicted in Chapter 4, then these points become important for the same reason. Both similarity and meaning are created both from the individual actions or personal recognitions of individuals in their private information processing and from the social actions and social acknowledgments of partners in their open behavioral responses to one another. Normally one would expect that knowledge of the appropriateness of different forms of interactive response would be based largely on partners' previous experience and construction of one another, just as interpretation of another's behavior is influenced by experience of the person in relationship (Ickes, 1993). Thus the more one comprehends another person, the more one learns not only about the person's mind but also about the range of social actions that the person finds acceptable. In turn one can modify one's style of behavior in order to respond more appropriately to the person in the extended interactions of a relationship (see Chapter 3). For example, part of the signaling of appropriate ranges of behavior is carried out as a conversation proceeds and as the partners' mood and feelings are affected by the interaction. Appropriateness cannot be defined entirely from the things that can be said about the partners before the conversation occurs.

The above position points up an important issue lying behind what has been said so far. Some views of construction of meaning see it as an uncovering of components of a preexisting reality, and some see it as the creative manufacture of something by perceivers. Attention to the social action of talk allows us to combine these views constructively.

Realist and Relativist Views of Relational Phenomena

A realist position treats meaning as a given and feels able to focus (usually implicitly) on the general meanings that acts, behavior, and other people have in a culture. For instance, as noted in Chapter 2, it is taken as a given in discussions of relationships based in exchange theory that certain behaviors are rewarding and others are not. Equally, some scholars have sought to establish "the meaning" of accounts of negligence in relationships (Schonbach, 1992), of communication problems in committed relationships (Vangelisti, 1992), of attachment styles (Feeney & Noller, 1991), or of intimacy (Waring, Tillman, Frelick, Russell, & Weisz, 1980).

Is Meaning General or Personal? Other researchers look for the characteristic ways in which people as a whole construe the prototypical meaning of elements of relationships. Davis and Todd (1985), for instance, discussed Paradigm Case Formulations for terms like *friendship* and carefully expounded the components that are essential before people apply the label "friendship" to a relationship—such components as trust, spontaneity, enjoyment, or intimacy. Fehr's (1993) work on prototypes of love usefully seeks to predict the general classification of feelings and behavior by different groups of individuals. Fehr examined individuals' endorsements of certain general properties of love relationships by which they distinguish love from other sorts of relationships. Andersen (1993) also explored the social schemata that people as a whole use in instancing and defining key elements of relationships so that they can be reliably classified and distinguished. He pointed out that the schemata are by no means simple, involving both complex compounds derived from self and cultural values as well as several other knowledge bases.

Such work does a valuable service in classifying the general pool of social knowledge from which persons draw in their approach to relationships (e.g., in their decisions about the sorts of relationships in which they will become involved). Such research also makes clear that relationship feelings and behaviors are by no means simply idiosyncratic individual inventions, but invariably reflect or draw from agreed-upon cultural definitions.

On the other hand, such analysis does not identify the specifically individual meanings and weightings for such components that may make one member of a relationship (or of some cultural group) somewhat different from another (Duck, 1985). Nor does such analysis identify those elements that would help us understand why two specific persons from the same culture conduct and enact their relationship in their own particular idiosyncratic way (Baxter, 1992a). Finally, such work does not show us why certain elements of a particular schema or prototype would be privileged in some interactions as opposed to others. For example, why is loyalty in friendship prized in some discursive/rhetorical environments, while the selfless provision of services is valued in another environment, and openly expressed intimacy is paramount in still other rhetorical circumstances?

The realist model also lies behind some social-psychological research on interactive behaviors, such as self-disclosure in relationships. This research essentially assumes that the meaning of a self-disclosure generally can be assessed and applied across any set of circumstances. Davis and Sloan (1974), for example, rated the inherent intimacy of statements from nonintimate (such as, "How I react to praise and criticism of me") to very intimate (e.g., topics dealing with sex or shame or guilt, such as "My feelings about my sexual inadequacy"). Such work posits that the intimacy of the terms would be the same for virtually all people in virtually all cases and circumstances. Indeed such work is often quoted approvingly by other researchers who use such ratings as established measures of the intimacy of statements in relationships or as the basis for typologies of relational behavior (e.g., Hewstone, 1992). On this assumption, ratings of topic intimacy or typologies of intimate behavior are used to operationalize intimacy in empirical studies of respondents other than those from whom the statements were originally drawn. One can also create a picture of the ways in which intimacy of topic progresses as relationships themselves progress in intimacy (Davis, 1978).

Yet the intimacy (and the meaning) of statements often depends in large part on the situation in which they are uttered and the audience to whom they are addressed (Ginsburg, 1988; Montgomery, 1984). For example, statements about sexual practices are not always relationally intimate: They might be personally embarrassing or discomfiting, but when they are made to a physician they have little to do with relational intimacy in the usual sense. Likewise, statements about guilt or shame are not relationally intimate though they may be personally very difficult when they are made to an attorney preparing to defend one in court. Thus the quest for, and assumption of, the absolute level of intimacy inherent in given statements is only partly useful (Duck, 1992a, pp. 79-80). Culturally composed absolute meaning is most likely to be helpful when it is used precisely in those limited nonintimate situations where people meet for the first time and have little personal knowledge of one another. In such circumstances people do indeed rely on cultural rather than personal scripts so that they have some idea of the range of discussion topics that is appropriate (Argyle & Henderson, 1984)—a range that can differ from culture to culture (Althen, 1993). Indeed the search for absolute meaning of terms is most useful for such stereotypical moments as meetings between strangers or impersonal settings that have little direct mapping onto processes of real later development of personal relationships. Probably absolute meanings have almost nothing to do with the individually constructed relational practices and behaviors that occur in relationships sometimes depicted as close.

We should be cautious about giving primacy to cultural averages of meaning at the expense of meanings dyadically constructed within the relationship on particular occasions or instances of experience. Both, not one alone, are relevant to understanding relational activity. The central cultural core meanings must also be located in the particular dyadic, personal, and temporal contexts where they are adopted. By seeking only that core of meaning that has general application we can at best account for the generalities, like a weather forecast that deals with several local areas all together but may predict specific events in a given town incorrectly. By failing to account for the significance that a word, thing, sentence, utterance, act, event, or person can have within a specific individual's personal meaning system in particular temporal, personal, or physical contexts, we ignore the symbolic force of such entities for one or both partners. For instance, over the years I have acquired most of the recorded works of Ralph Vaughan Williams, the English composer. The *Fantasia on a Theme of Thomas Tallis* was the first piece of his music that I ever heard, and I have especially liked it for many years, often playing it in the background while I am writing. By complete coincidence, it happened to be playing when I turned on the car radio as I drove to the airport just after receiving news of my father's death. This gave the piece an extra symbolism for me, and now each time I play it, I think of my father. I would bet that each reader can think of his or her own examples of scents, places, noises, things, topics, and so on, that have similarly evocative symbolic weight and that could influence behavior, thought, and feelings about persons or relationships.

It is this very symbolic significance of phenomena that renders them important to people both personally and in relationships, and that invites attention to personal meaning. Partners create their own personally meaningful relationship symbols (cf. discussion of personal idioms and metaphors in Chapter 1). Partners also come, over time, to understand the symbols that matter to one another and how they matter. When symbols are shared by two partners in a relationship, particular forms of words or gestures or places have acquired personal meanings in the dyad (Baxter, 1987). Furthermore, the knowledge that significance is shared between partners likely enhances (or largely accounts for) its power to evoke and celebrate the relationship. In this sense, meanings are in people not just in things and words. Thus, to presume an absolute intimacy value for particular words or exchange resources, for example, is to fail to recognize the personal importance of the modifying force of couple culture in forging connectedness between two persons in personal relationships (Wood, 1982).

Where Is Meaning? Another aspect of the strict realist approach needs to be brought out so that one can best see its contribution in explaining specific behavior in relationships. In such an approach, the meaning of things is taken to be inherent in them. Observers simply recognize, expose, uncover, or discover meanings. This realist position derives ultimately from Platonic philosophy, which assumes that things take their meaning from the fact that they also partake of the essence of the Ideal Thing of which they are a particular instance (thus a chair is a chair because it partakes of "chairness"). This view seeks the essence of things as residing in the things themselves, while more recent views (such as relativity theory) make note of the activities of the actor or observer.

A relativist position assumes that meaning is in the eye of the beholder to some degree rather than inherent in the objects beheld.

Within this view, a thing means what it means because the observer thinks it does—and so acts toward it in a particular way. Nevertheless, because of immersion in a society and language system and experience of socialization, almost everyone will happen to agree about the central meaning of many terms. Such an agreement, however, is an empirical law rather than a natural law, and there can still be legitimate disagreements about the classification and interpretation of phenomena. Persons could change views about definitions, either as a result of something as whimsical as fashion (as when long hair became "in" in the 1960s to symbolize revolt or protest where previously, a hundred years before, it had symbolized convention and traditionalism) or as a result of some satisfactory demonstration of inconsistency with other previous perceptions (as when the terms *cruel and unusual punishment, pornography,* or *obscenity* are interpreted differently depending on who happens to be on the Supreme Court at the time).

In this view, the reports of two partners in a relationship will then naturally differ and lend credence to the claims of their really being in different relationships (Duck, 1990; Duck & Sants, 1983). Although the external situation (*scene* or *act* as discussed in Chapter 3) may in some sense be the same for both participants (*experience= events*), their internal (agent) representations of these acts or scenes may be vastly different (*experience=interpretation*). As already noted, evidence for this proposal can be found in research indicating how communication and interactions are punctuated differently by different participants, with each person noticing different elements as important or as the real instigators of a reaction that he or she has (Duck et al., 1991, 1994; Gottman, 1979). However, a further example is provided by the fact that an observer can punctuate or interpret things differently according to the extent of knowledge held about another person. For example, when one person comprehends the overall nature of the symbol system of the other person, he or she can distinguish and locate, relative to that system, any unusual aspects of it enacted at particular times (e.g., "He is usually mild mannered, but gets very rude to people he regards as fools when he is tired, just as he is now"). As a relationship develops, so that attribution of meaning (rather than of causes) is likely also to be modified by the listener's/observer's knowledge of the actor's personal psychological makeup (Chapter 4). One need only assume that a person can be simultaneously aware of the general cultural meaning of terms as well as the individualistic way in which a partner uses such terms in order to see that listeners face a choice when listening to a speaker. Given different levels of personal knowledge about a speaker, it is likely that a sentence has a particular average meaning (in the sense of cultural content), yet also can be interpreted differently by different observers (in the sense of personal meaning systems). Such a point again stresses the earlier one that although talk is the focus of attention here, it occurs in the context of a host of other cues to meaning in the normal run of relational life.

Detecting the Processes of Meaning

In the study of relationships, researchers could be learning more by asking not only "What is the typical/average meaning of this or that behavior or characteristic or act?" but also "How is the sharing of personal meaning developed between two people who know one another personally? How is meaning brought into being between people who are getting to know one another?" These latter questions refer us not to pieces of information, but to knowledge (i.e., the organized array in which pieces of information are related to each other and understood). In essence the additional question focuses us once more on a process of serial construction based on the notion that meaning is, in fact, a composite from many sources and processes. Yet it departs from other serial discovery or social penetration models (Altman & Taylor, 1973) by stressing the variability of such discovery in its dialogic and temporal contexts. The approach therefore accents the contribution made by the perceiver and by the disclosing target as well as by the temporal context.

The serial construction of meaning can now be seen to have three broad elements: (a) The *content component* refers to the meaning of the words as generally understood in a culture; (b) the *individual component* refers to the speaker's/listener's habitual modifications of cultural codes and individual adaptations of forms of cultural expression; and (c) the *context component* refers to an individual speaker's modifications of habitual or cultural codes in particular relational circumstances (cf. Montgomery, 1988).

It is important to be clear that I am not writing here about how any of these three things contributes to the *transfer* of meaning, but

I write about the *sharing* of meaning in the sense depicted in Chapter 4. The plumbing model of communication that lies behind the transfer metaphor would suggest that interaction is a simple pipeline between two heads and that thought or meaning is transported in some simple way from one head to another. That approach has been attacked very successfully by Berger (1993) and is no longer widely held. The pipeline model works only if the receiver of messages is not an interpretative being with personal meaning to attach to what is heard, but rather is a passive recipient into whose mental storage tanks others' meaning is simply deposited. Such a passive view of listeners pays no attention to either their own psychological processes or the history of the two partners in relationship (Stinson & Ickes, 1992). It essentially debases the influence of talk in social processes and even repudiates process as such.

Instead my proposal indicates that in everyday life, the decomposition of meaning occurs serially in the same way as one might decompose variance in an analysis of variance (ANOVA) by attributing certain elements or components to certain sources and processes or to their interaction. The full meaning of an utterance is composed of a combination of different solutions, depending on whether one is taking the viewpoint of (or looking at the contributory force of) one person or another, much as one might make one variable dependent and another criterion in a statistical analysis.

Meaning is centrally grounded on the typical mean meaning (as it were)—the large part created or derived from the population characteristics as a whole (in this case the culture). Meaning is, however, topped off or modified by the contribution of the two separate individuals; their relational context for interacting with one another; and the joint constructions manufactured, understood, and enacted between them. This view also assumes that the nature of communication between people is dependent on the extent to which each construes the other's meaning system and interprets the specific meaning created in specific circumstances against that construction. Again note that I am looking at social and serial construction of meaning (especially meaning of things interior to the relationship in the sense depicted in Chapter 4), and at the ways in which a listener can move from one component to another with greater ease as a relationship develops and as the listener likewise develops a greater ability to construe the agent more fully (cf. Chapter 3).

The *content component* of social meaning is basically an agreed core that can be checked against cultural reference points, such as is discoverable through searches of a dictionary, or in the import of a nonverbal communication system that is also culturally understood (Ginsburg, 1988; Keeley & Hart, 1994). The cultural rules that apply to meaning and the expression of ideas are thus applicable and appropriate as initial basic guides to indicate a person's meaning in this sense (e.g., Argyle & Henderson's, 1984, discussion of rules of relationships).

The *individual component* has two elements that are reflective of one another: the speaker component and the listener component. The speaker component is based on the individual personality characteristics of the speaker (the typical manner of perceiving communicative contexts), the speaker's style (the way the person sends messages in general), the person's intent (on specific occasions, as in work on message goals analysis; e.g., O'Keefe & Delia, 1982), the speaker's social position (gender, social class, ethnicity, etc.; Allan, 1993; Wood, 1993a), the extent of the speaker's knowledge of, and accommodation to the listener's meaning system (as when I talk to my son using childish terms), and the speaker's awareness of the above. The listener component is a reflection of the same things listed for the speaker: the individual personality characteristics of the listener, the listener's attributions of the speaker's intent, the extent of the listener's knowledge of the speaker's meaning system as a modifier of messages and communicative goals, and the listener's awareness of the above. In both speaker and listener components, personal variations of usage (derived from a general personal style or from momentary accommodations to circumstances) are essentially based on the core of social meaning but they also modify the interpretation of that meaning. Any style is a generalized framework circumscribing the manner in which a particular individual typically deals with certain types of experience and thus is an indication of organized personal meaning. Thus work focused on the speaker's style of communication (Norton, 1983) or on the adaptation of messages to audiences (McLaughlin, 1984) is essentially illustrating part of the speaker/listener elements of the full meaning ANOVA formula as it were, as is psychological work on language in social context (Giles & Coupland, 1991).

Lastly, the *context component* subsumes and goes beyond broadly shared social meanings for words. It stems from the relationship ambience, the place/environment, and the context of past interactions or relationship culture that help to clarify for partners that the general cultural content or personal style is not what is exclusively or primarily relied on in a given utterance (Hopper et al., 1981; Stinson & Ickes, 1992). Such interpretative modifications of the central core of social meaning rely upon partners' prior constructions of each other that allow a perceiver to interpret the actions or words in terms lodged centrally in personal knowledge of the other (Shotter, 1992). Such modification also entails the ability to recognize that any atypical statement simultaneously displaces, negates, or denies the habitual or expected response.

Such a decomposition of the different influences on construction of relational meaning should allow us to investigate not only specific utterances in context, but also the ways in which one relational partner learns about another in the serial construction of meaning and its organization. The approach is susceptible to an ANOVA style of analysis laid on top of the serial developmental processes of relating. Here one could partition the contribution of different elements to the final solution of the problems of meaning. Although I believe that researchers can do this (and indeed the proposal has some similarities to Kenny's, 1988, social relations model, which focuses on the contributions of different persons), I think it is exciting to see the ways in which relational partners proceed to understand one another through everyday talk.

In circumstances where the partners are not personally known to one another, a predictably greater contribution to the overall construction would be derived from content and context. On the other hand, individual (speaker and listener) components would be likely to contribute more if the parties know more about one another. As an instance of the relative effects of different sorts of meaning as persons adapt to new forms of relationships with one another—a marriage as distinct from a courtship, for instance (another way in which two persons get to know each other in context)—Crohan (1992) points out that previous research indicates the importance to couples of having a common language, especially insofar as is related to judging events and processes interior to relationships. Development of shared relational reality is possibly the most important process in relationship adjustment and satisfaction (Berger & Kellner, 1964). However, Crohan's work shows that:

similarity of beliefs, per se, is not as important to marital happiness in the first year of marriage as much as it is important that both husbands and wives hold certain [general assumptions] about . . . conflict. . . . Using discrepancy scores masks important differences in the content [and meaning] of beliefs [to the persons themselves]. (Crohan, 1992, p. 99)

This observation supports the point that construction of shared reality is more important than similarity itself, and hence the point that forms of similarity are not equivalent.

Thus the full meaning of A's behavior for person A and for person B could easily be different, either in gross terms or in fine nuances even though they are in the same physical encounter. Their ability to share meaning would depend on the extent to which each grasps the other's system of meaning and can use talk as a means of decoding the other's intent.

❦ Persuasion, Meaning, and Everyday Talk

Talk as Evidence About the Personal Meaning of a Relationship

Talk as a whole is action, not just picture painting and description. It does more than just convey attitudes and personal self-disclosures, it demonstrates and structures the way we think, and it illustrates our definition of ourselves and our beliefs. In Shotter's elegant phrase "in everything I say, I also make a claim to sincerity, justice, truthfulness, beauty, and so forth—a claim that will occasion a response" (Shotter, 1992, p. 29). More than this, even everyday talk also contains the speaker's views of the relationship between the speaker and the listener (Conville, 1975). For example, it subtly indicates liking, aloofness, superiority, hostility, and fear (Duck, 1992a). Such implicit assumptions about self, partner, and the relationship between them have been studied at the level of "immediacy" behaviors indicating closeness or inclusiveness (Mehrabian, 1971) and in other more complex ways (Duck, 1992a; Giles & Coupland, 1991). The present book has rejected the idea that talk is merely an inert channel for conveying information, untransformed, from one person to another.

When we focus specifically on everyday talk in relationships (as distinct from language as an abstract grammatical organization), we can see several ways in which it reveals not only a speaker's meaning in general, but particularly attitudes about others, including the relational partner (Watzlawick et al., 1967). Talk also conveys perceivers' views of other people at large, not only in its contents but also in its style, not only in what it says but also in what it omits (Daly, Vangelisti, & Daughton, 1987). Furthermore, when we talk to other people to perform the many daily routine, dull, boring, acts of our relational existence, we are still acting in a symbolic world that is largely a creation of the language we use to portray things to ourselves and others. Daily talk is not only a neutral medium or a simple expressive act but also an organizer of relational worlds in ways that sustain, maintain and perpetuate them (Duck, 1994c). Indeed, talk has consequences that make certain sorts of relational experiences possible in the first place (e.g., verbal arguments).

Everyday talk in relationships obviously occurs between people who have identities and histories (perhaps the two persons even have a joint history as a relational dyad), yet each piece of talk is shaped by and shapes those influences, as Bakhtin (1981, 1984) pointed out. Talk also continues to project those identities and histories and to extend their reality to the next encounter, thus presenting a rhetorical vision or an image of the other person and the relationship and offering its visions in different ways at different times (Potter & Wetherell, 1987).

Everyday talk is also an active, ongoing social process that constitutes views of many more things than at first appears—including the relationship between speaker and listener (Watzlawick et al., 1967) and the speaker's knowledge concerning what the partner knows. In so doing, talk provides the fodder for much declaration and advertising of the views about the relationship that structure experience for the speaker and listener both as individuals and as members of their relationship. Talk also offers material to strengthen partners' grasps of one another's meanings and offers opportunities to extend, or to go beyond them, at the same time as the relationship proceeds.

In everyday talk, exposure to richly loaded information is possible all the time. Look at all there is to talk about: (1) the ways in which each partner splits up the flow of experience, which can be a personal and individualistic way of so doing (and which may therefore need to be explained to the other person); (2) the choices that each partner makes in describing and anticipating the flow of

experience (which probably merit discussion in a relationship conversation); (3) the ways in which each partner constructs and recon-
structs memory of experience (which can be assessed by others only
if they talk about it); (4) the desire to set up an interpretation of
events that is workable (including one that is validated/shared
through discussion with others); (5) the role of imagination in
anticipating the future or memory in reviewing the past (since
experience is not limited to what is happening at the moment but to
the ways in which one can think about it or talk about other times
than the present); (6) a rhetorical representation of one's views about
experience in forms that can be heard and accepted by others. Talk
is not only transmission of information or an expressive act but is
also a decisively social and rhetorical behavior in a relational context
(Duck & Pond, 1989).

Everyday talk, more than perhaps has been realized, offers many
opportunities for revelation and self-disclosure (of course) but also
for realization of something relationally profound and important.
Not only may a partner's remark give one a flashing and intense
insight into some pain or triumph, but it could easily depict their
experience of being themselves and of being in the relationship, once a
listener attends carefully for signs of the structure of meaning in
which a remark may be made. Likewise, everyday talk is a practice
of social interaction whereby people become aware, in ephemeral
experience, of the profound meaning that some relationship partner
or value or linguistic expression has for them or the relationship
itself (Stromberg, personal communication, September 21, 1993).
Such experiences of sudden insight or epiphany work to anchor
and/or map the path of a relationship or a self. How many times
have we had a sudden flash of insight that has changed our ways of
looking at something but that hangs only on the peg of some casual
remark by another person—a remark that is a catalyst for us to
reformulate some aspect of ourselves or of a relationship in a way
we had not seen as possible before? These sorts of transformational
insights are the true turning points of relationships as well as of
persons and identities (Stromberg, 1985; personal communication
September 21, 1993). Such turning points occur in everyday talk in
relationships as persons traffic in rhetorical visions and negotiate
about their relationship.

Talk as a Basis for Negotiating Meaning

Although talk produces strictly relational side effects as well as
providing information and energizing the social actions mentioned
in previous chapters, it is also a fundamental basis for the organization of meaning in relationships. This includes the direct influences
of talk (e.g., where people ask each other out on dates, make proposals of marriage, have arguments, or talk about the relationship—
Acitelli, 1993; Baxter & Wilmot, 1985). It also includes the ways in
which talk about anything purveys incidental messages that permit
deductions or constructions relevant to relationships. Wood (1982,
1993b) regards talk as the main vehicle for relational behavior. She
stressed the role of everyday, casual talk, especially talk focused on
memory (for anything, not just for the relationship). She argued that:

> relational culture arises out of communication and becomes an in-
> creasingly central influence on individual partners' ways of knowing,
> being, and acting in relation to each other and the outside world.
> Communication constitutes and modifies human relationships in
> ways not recognized by work that sees communication as merely a
> transfer of factual information from one head into another, or as
> something essentially only instrumental in the conveyance of psycho-
> logical factors from A to B. It is through talk that persons define
> themselves and their relationships, and through talk that definitions
> once entered into are revised over the life of a relationship. (Wood,
> 1982, p. 75)

Wood (1993b) has also recently argued that the focus on significant (event) talk rather than on experiential (process) talk is a way
of overlooking the manner in which everyday talk composes and
sustains all sorts of relationships such as parent-child or friendship or
co-worker relationships. Duck (1990, p. 24) also claimed that many
"relationship events are perceived not in a direct way but in mediated
ways through memory, recall, dialogue, and conversation."

Talk therefore also offers the chance for interactants to construct
meaning together. Obviously the process of forging joint understanding is subsequent to, dependent on, but more than, several
other processes discussed previously (Chapter 4). It is based on an
individual's serial processing of information. It has several elements, one of which is the explicit interpretation of another person's
comments. Another could be the creation of some personal idi-

omatic code that is assimilated by partners. Another will obviously be the explicit negotiation of agreement (shared meaning) about behavioral performance in the relationship. The starting point for any joint agreement must be the individual meaning system that each person brings to a relationship and the subsequent interaction between it and the system brought by the Other. Partners can first make such comparisons between Self and Other only from their own starting vantage points as individual perceivers (Chapter 3), but in relationships they begin to understand the extent to which their individual perceptions overlap or could accommodate to one another.

The processes of mutual construction of mental overlap are extended and complex, making relationships also extended and complex processes in themselves. These processes involve more than just clarifying others' meaning and then working it into one's own understanding. In real life, cooperation, negotiated behaviors, and comprehension are not merely abstractions of which researchers write, but are actions that are achieved through interaction and talk (Berger & Kellner, 1964). Furthermore, such actions result in products (ideas, meanings, values) that, although shared in common, are also incorporated into individuals' cognitive frameworks separately so that these frameworks are thereby themselves altered (Shotter, 1992). Thus to talk of conjoint construction of meaning is to continue to consider a process that works at both the individual and dyadic levels. The process finds expression in both daily talk and relational routines in both the life of the relationship and the lives of the individuals separately.

Partners in conversation thus observe and traffic in at least three sorts of meaning simultaneously: (a) that which has been assembled by the two separate individuals, before their meeting, as a constructed personal view of the world and brought separately to the relationship (the two individuals' personal meaning systems); (b) that which is constructed by the two persons in the relationship as they listen to one another (e.g., their constructions of the other person and other's experience, their interpretation of other's meaning); (c) that developed over time by the two persons together as they traffic in and share their original and revised individual meanings. This latter piece of traffic is essentially a process whereby the persons accept into their own personal meaning system constructions that have been made together rather than separately. The persons therefore inevitably know that they share these meanings.

By trafficking in individual meaning to start with, partners reach, as it were, meaning deals or symbolic bargains between themselves. These deals function to negotiate between their two original and different ways of looking at life (e.g., the meanings that they construct between themselves for use only in that relationship, such as the personal idioms that I mentioned in Chapter 1). This latter construction must not only be agreed between the two but then assimilated by transforming each individual's own psychological system and meaning framework. The origin of the joint construction, however, is the dyad and the development within it of new ways of seeing, as a result of discussions. Such a process parallels the operation of metaphors (Chapter 1): Two different domains of meaning or ways of characterizing events are brought together, and the connection evokes a new way of conceptualizing one or other domain.

Talk as an Indicator of Relationship Features

How does talk, in addition to the above contributions that it makes, act for partners as an indicator of the sort of relationship that they have? I will develop some of Burke's points (Chapter 3) and argue that it creates a sense of consubstantiality and identification (a sense of "agreement" or "oneness of perspective"), not about exterior things but about interior ones. Various symbolic features of talk indicate to partners that they share a view of the relationship and identify with one another in that respect. Using that framework, we can begin by looking at the ways in which everyday talk helps to separate different levels of meaning or allows researchers to ask old questions in new ways as well as to pose some novel questions. Even if we focused on the content of everyday talk alone, there is much that can be analyzed in terms of its rhetorical and practical or psychological significance to people in relationships. For example, if people are conducting exchanges in social interactions, as theorists usually assume that they are, then how do they actually do it in talk? How/when is exchange directly done and how/when indirectly signaled? What cultural, relational, and personal assumptions are built into bargaining talk and how is bargaining conveyed by such indirect means as banter or playful teasing? Does choice of words have any impact on the way in which an exchange is transacted or interpreted, and/or does it modify images of what happened in the transaction? In short, does the kind of talk affect the way in which a transaction is really exchanged over and above other exchange behaviors? Does talk generate different notions of power in exchange by its style as well as the direct features that have been well studied? If people value commitment, as most theorists assume that they do, then how do they express it in talk? I do not mean just "What do people say commitment is?" nor "How do they tell a partner directly that they are committed?" Instead, I mean "What signals does everyday talk perhaps inadvertently contain that convey symbolic messages of relationship commitment?" For instance, any reference to a shared future—even a mundane one—implicitly voices some level of commitment (Spencer, 1994).

Never mind what people say to researchers about the nature of intimacy in the abstract (Waring et al., 1980), what do they say to one another to convey it either symbolically or directly in the social interactions of everyday talk? How about talk and power, talk and love, talk and attachment, talk and relationship disengagement? When people talk, they might not say directly that they are attached or in love or have power, yet there are facets to their talk that necessarily convey these ideas (Cody & McLaughlin, 1985; Giles & Coupland, 1991; McLaughlin, 1984). How do these concepts work in talk, how are they brought to life in talk? I do not, incidentally, enquire here about narratives about power (Holtzworth-Munroe, 1992), love (Hendrick & Hendrick, 1993), relationship disengagement (Cody, Kersten, Braaten, & Dickson, 1992), or attachment (Collins & Read, 1990). I am asking about the linguistic and discursive mechanisms and features that either characterize or symbolize the actual execution of those social activities. Even if they can happen without talk, do they normally so happen? One could sometimes be forgiven for thinking so as one leafs through great piles of research reports that focus on strategy selection rather than strategy enactment, or don't even mention how presumed social effects were actually effected or mediated conversationally.

Other aspects of talk also indicate the construction of conjoint meanings or else of symbols, since people do not only speak content, as it were, but they distribute the amounts of talk that they produce in relationships (Duck, 1987b). That is to say, they talk to different people in different amounts, as well as about different topical content. Some network members are spoken to often and some rarely—

and this variation means something in relational terms. Variability in talk defines something about the nature of the relationship between members. How much talk is there with different network members, and is it the same as the amount of interaction that is usually assessed abstractly in reports of network activity (Milardo, 1992)? Is the amount of talk with network members a good measure of involvement with one another (if that is actually a different thing) or not? Does it matter if the talk is face to face or on the telephone or electronic mail, and how does that modify the experience of a relationship? Ask anyone who has ever been in a long-distance relationship! Does it matter when I talk to a particular network member (e.g., do we learn anything significant about a relationship from finding out that talk in it typically occurs only at Christmas time? [Werner et al., 1993])? Does distribution of talk change as relationships change? That is, do people talk to different others in the network as they experience change in their primary dyad, rather as Milardo, Johnson, and Huston (1983) showed that persons in developing romantic relationships spend less time with network members as they get more committed to a partner? Baxter and Widenmann (1993) have indicated that people consider quite carefully whether to reveal to their networks their romantic involvement with a new partner before that relationship has stabilized, for example. Might people tend to talk to others to seek advice, for example, when a primary relationship is in trouble, and could the patterns of distribution of talk across the network add something useful to an outsider's knowledge about the status of the primary relationship (e.g., an indication of increased advice-seeking in the broader network might well mean that the person is having a problem in the primary relationship [Duck, 1985])?

There are also other symbolic elements of talk that should be of concern to relationship researchers (Davis, 1973), such as the tone or temper of the talk, and the ease of communication that relationship partners experience at different stages of relationships. Other aspects of structure and construction of talk, such as its presentation of attitudes, status, and power toward a conversational partner, or its demonstration of relational accommodation to the other person (Giles & Coupland, 1991), are also of relevance in moderating claims about the direct effects (on relationships) of discursive enactments of disclosure, exchange, intimacy, commitment, or power.

All of these considerations pose some questions for relationship researchers. In what ways does talk construct and embody individual intent and individual meaning (or even dyadic belief systems and dyadic conversational content and style) as well as it constructs relationships? However, there are other (and I think more important) reasons why the study of talk is an immediate source of valuable insights into the real conduct and trafficking of meaning in relationships, once one focuses not only on talk's content or distribution but also on why people talk and what happens symbolically or psychologically when they do. Even in a casual chat with friends, talk constructs versions of events and people and makes the speaker's approach to life available to others. When one sees the other person's rhetorical vision of a thing, one is able to recognize its (dis)similarity to one's own vision or to detect points of difference. It is this process of recognition and ability to depict the other's vision of the world that is the essence of the comprehension of meaning. (Indeed it is a powerful experience to understand another's meaning system even if the perceiver does not know or interact with the other. Therein perhaps lies some of the popularity and beguilement of the TV soap operas—where the characters seem to spend all day talking about relationships and hardly ever seem to work or do anything else!)

Thus persons symbolize their relationships with other people in many different ways through talking. That fact helps each person (and could help researchers) to discover something useful and important about the partner, the partner's vision, and the partners' attitudes towards one another. Talk provides them with evidence about the way in which another constructs the relationship and, more importantly, the frameworks of comprehension within which the other does so.

Talk as a Constructor of Shared Meaning

At another level, we can see that talk is also used to compare and construct shared meaning for a relationship. Shared relational histories and stories of the origin of a relationship ("our first meeting") are stories constructed between two persons and that encapsulate the jointness of their relationship in a symbolic fashion (Johnson, 1982). Such stories are often mistakenly treated merely as "factual records" of events (Surra, 1987) in the past of a relationship rather than important social and relational (re)constructions that serve significant constructive purposes for the relational partners, as I am arguing here. For example, the topics chosen as the essential features of a history are selected to present a rhetorical vision of the relationship and to characterize it in one of several possible ways that have to be negotiated between the partners. "Origin stories" for relationships are of some interest, not just for themselves, but for what they say about relational construction processes. These have to be constructed jointly by the two persons, and, as Duck and Miell (1986) noted, they can be different on different occasions. Thus two persons who initially might recall their first meeting in entirely different ways from one another could nevertheless come eventually to agree on a story that shares and transforms elements of both original stories without being an exact copy of either of them or a formulaic sum of the two. I strongly suspect that the joint creation of an origin story actually is a part of the creation of a relationship and is an achievement that serves the function of celebrating, rather than merely reporting, its creation. Origin stories start to emerge and be accepted by both partners as a part of the process of making the relationship, and they do not just simply demonstrate how it began. Likewise, reminiscences may be a safe way of discussing the state of a relationship, which is otherwise a taboo topic (Baxter & Wilmot, 1985), or is seen as pushy, presumptuous, or precipitate (Perri Druen, personal communication, April 1993).

Also, as a relationship emerges, it takes on a multiplex and differentiated character that means that partners have more evidence of both positive and negative features, any one of which a person could focus upon in suitable circumstances—just as discourse theorists suggest (Potter & Wetherell, 1987). Thus there is nothing odd about people emphasizing the negative side of partners when they leave a relationship, just as they emphasize the positive side when the relationship is going well. It just illustrates that relationship facts exist in the minds of the relationship partners and may (and do!) change (Berger & Kellner, 1964). Stories about those facts pick out features that the partners wish *at that particular rhetorical moment* to applaud or denigrate in the relationship itself.

Talk and Memory in Relationships

Finally, talk represents meaning for dyads by its tendency to include reference to the past and the future as well as the present. Harvey and his colleagues (Harvey et al., 1992) have illustrated this phenomenon neatly, in other theoretical terms, in their work on accounts. They suggested that a consequence of account-making is to end up with an altered identity that enables one to go forward after a tragic or traumatic event, having learned something useful for the future. Similarly, one spends time mulling over ended relationships in order to learn lessons and conduct one's future relationships in different ways (Harvey et al., 1992) or, as an outsider, in order to know how to treat other people after their relationships have ended (Duck, 1982b).

Historical accounts of relationships and relationship endings serve many purposes for people, such as saving face or accounting for the ending of a relationship (Duck, 1982b). Like other relationship histories, such histories are not always told the same way all the time but are characteristically modified according to the circumstances of the speaker. Weber (1983) noted that persons in broken relationships usually report feeling more negative about the relationship at its end than they report at its start, which is not surprising, but is psychologically interesting for what it implies. Metts, Cupach, and Bejlovec (1989) nicely illustrated the different tones that were given to accounts of ended romances depending on whether the partners had been friends before the romance or not. Redefinition of an ended romantic relationship is more positive if the two ex-lovers had been friends before they became lovers. In other words, the ability of partners to construct a theme of continued liking is greater when there is an identifiable history of previous friendship. The partners simply exclaim that they still like one another as persons but did not like the *form* of the relationship as lovers.

The above observations about the symbolic force of histories of relationships reflect the broader observation by some scholars of historiography who have pointed out that no history or (auto)biography is a simple dispassionate record of neutral facts. Instead any history is a story about a culture, organization, or person framed in a way that selects facts and relates them in terms which the culture, organization, or person feels are suitable (Burkitt, 1991) (and some commentators go on to say that it is usually related in the terms in which the dominant forces in the culture want people to think of it; Lacan, 1977). Relationship histories are likewise not necessarily neutral or dispassionate but embody something about the way in which the two partners see themselves, and, moreover, want to see themselves in relationship to one another or want to interpret their past and their relationship. Partners' editing of relationship stories or experience in talk allows partners to square up their different accounts or permits greater functional alignment of the two selves in the relationship (Berger & Kellner, 1964).

Edwards and Middleton (1988) noted that conjoint memory can be used to "locate" a person (frequently a child) in a family system. These authors' interesting work looks at the uses of joint memories in relation to family photograph albums to help the child to gain a sense of the identities and histories of other members of the family as well as of the child's own past (perhaps in relation to those persons). This is a particularly intriguing, but by no means unique, method by which persons create relational memory through conversation.

Finally, as couples talk and use memory, they also implicitly organize their relationship (and hence create meaning in it) and so also implicitly organize their roles and their relative power in it. Wegner, Raymond, and Erber's (1990) concept of "transactive memory" demonstrates that couples often arrange for one of them to store certain sorts of memories (e.g., acquaintances' addresses) while the other one remembers other sorts of things (e.g., directions to acquaintances' houses by car). Thus one partner will refer to the other for some sorts of information rather than knowing it personally— and vice versa. Wegner likens this to the way in which a computer "refers" to different directory paths for its information. In this sense, the management of memory within the relationship is transacted between the two partners through their talk to one another, although it is also similar to a division of the labor of memory or to a disjunctive memory (i.e., it is organized *non*overlap between people).

It would be interesting to extend to this notion of memory in relationships some of the rhetorical analyses that communication scholars apply to other organizational elements of discourse. For instance, much work analyzes the management of power through the rhetorical or social control aspects of history writing (Althusser,

1971). An extension of such ideas to relationships would allow researchers to discover the functional implications for relationships of the organizing of memorial duties. This organization is not as neutral as may be implied by Wegner's analysis to date. You could almost bet that the person with the power will arrange to remember the sorts of things that are the most powerful. Thus transactive memory has real, and so far unexplored, social implications for the relating partners' organization of other behaviors.

In all of the above cases, memory is transacted through talk yet carries significant implications for relational organization. In subtle ways when two partners reminisce or construct joint memories they essentially engage in Burkean persuasion of themselves and others. Burke's view of persuasion is thus consistent with the above outline and also carries extra implications that depict a role for persuasion in relationships by way of everyday talk. The study of memory in relationships is important because it is a place where and a means through which partners construct the agreed history of a relationship from the many possible views of relationships that are available to the partners (and, of course, remain available even after such joint construction). In other words, the social construction of memory is a particularly striking occasion when joint memories are forged and continually refined or revised, not just replayed on some dyadic relational tape player. It is one place where the meaning of events and behaviors (and people) becomes shared by two individuals by persuasive or rhetorical means involving presentation of a vision that is acknowledged and accepted by the other person.

❦ Summary and Conclusions

This chapter has proposed that different tissues of meaning are simultaneously available in encounters for detection and use in the task of building a picture of the other person's mind and its structure. To make this final part of the argument, the chapter focused on talk as a mechanism for relational negotiation of meaning. The chapter continued to develop the notion of serial construction of meaning outlined in Chapter 4 by indicating how such different levels of meaning could be constructed in talk. The chapter offered a decomposition model of meaning that attempts to relate different sources of meaning to one another by placing them in the context of serial social processes and indicating how talk plays different roles in each. The chapter also explored the role of everyday talk in the uncovering of the different aspects of meaning and laid out some of the contributions of talk to relational information-building and meaning-construction. Its broad case was that talk, being public dyadic behavior, not only displays personal meanings attached to the relationship (and so can signal to a partner a person's feelings about the relationship), but also engenders jointly constructed relational meanings that indicate and symbolize the relationship. The chapter finally pointed out the many different active contributions of everyday talk to the relationship enterprise, including reminiscing about the relationship and stories of its origin and history, through to the symbolic organization and construction of the relationship. The chapter concludes the argument that relationships are constituted and reified in talk. It presented talk's many roles in the serial construction of meaning and the creation of models of partners' meaning systems. It also indicated how talk offers a person chances to present his or her own personal meaning system to other people.

❦ An Appendix of Formal Statements

Relational Communication: Relational communication is communication based on the act of construing specific domains or general areas of shared or personal meaning and can be achieved verbally or nonverbally. The chapter has argued that the representation of a relationship occurs in the talk that the partners carry out and that communication in a relationship is based on the act of comprehending or construing the partner's meaning system in some general or particular way.

Relational Effects: Persons' meanings for relational acts are catalysts for change or stability and can themselves be construed within the relationship by the partners together. As indicated in various places in this chapter and previous chapters, it is the meaning that a person attributes to something that acts as the catalyst for change or reconstruction of relationships. As indicated in the reflexive metaconstruction corollary (Chapter 2), people can construe/reflect on/discuss/or think over their thoughts about a relationship or a person. However, this corollary goes further and indicates that partners together can think about or discuss one another's constructions of the relationship or each other. Such open discussion of constructions is a relational rather than a personal activity and has relational rather than simply personal effects. Such relational communication can disturb, alter, invalidate, refine, reinforce, or support particular ways of construing experience, whether personal ones or relational ones.

Relational Value: The relational value of one person's personal meaning depends on the ability of the partner to construe it. An element of a person's meaning system has no relational force unless the partner is able to construe and comprehend it in some way, usually in ways clarified by conversation. However, this does not require that the partner necessarily construes the system in the same way as the person construes it. Recall the notion of relational asymmetry developed in the book previously.

Relational Meaning: Negotiation of dyadic and relational meaning occurs through relational effects, relational value, and relational communication. In other words, the open discussion of the two partners' constructions of domains of meaning lays the foundations for meanings to be shared within the relationship and for them to take on a role within the relationship as well as for individual partners.

❧ Note

1. W. R. Cupach (personal communication, April, 1991). Question after talk at Normal, Illinois: Where Is Sharing Located?

6

Meaning and Research

The sociology of knowledge must be concerned not only with the great universes of meaning that history offers up for our inspection, but with the many little workshops in which living individuals keep hammering away at the construction and maintenance of these universes.

Berger and Kellner (1964, p. 24)

A living tradition does not give rise to a completely determined form of life, but to dilemmas, to different possibilities for living, among which one must choose.

Shotter (1992, p. 22)

OVERVIEW

This chapter applies the previous analysis to some specific topic areas in relationship research and shows how they can be approached differently using the construction of meaning as a central concept.

One major challenge arises from the previous reformulation of some of the questions and emphases of research on relationships: What difference does it make if we conceptualize relationships in the ways proposed here? In rising to this challenge I will indicate how some of the implications for the field are general framing issues rather than specific hypotheses, but such hypotheses are more directly dealt with in the formal statements of position at the end of some of the previous chapters. These statements create an overall system that forms the basis for the present chapter's meditations, and here I deal with some of the broader implications for specific areas of the field.

At present our theories of relationships actually work only in a very restricted set of environments, those that explicitly favor the theoretical principles being tested there by decontextualizing the thoughts of subjects from the practical realities and talk of daily life. I believe that we can place our theoretical quest in a number of triangulating coordinates and set the task within them. One group of coordinates is obviously the daily routine conduct of all that makes up the everyday experience of the reality of relationships. A second set of coordinates is the general effort to create meaning that characterizes human life, lived as it is amidst chronic uncertainty. A third coordinating referent is the clarification of the roles of talk in achieving the other two.

❦ Process and Meaning

The present state of research into social and personal relationships is both satisfying and unsatisfying (Duck, 1994b). It is exciting that the last 10 to 15 years of investigation have moved us away from one-shot cues about interpersonal attraction as a predominant theme and inexorably toward a fuller emphasis on the processes of relating. In fact, much of this progress is due less to spontaneous and isolated scholarly discovery of new ideas than to social and organizational changes that have created a field and given it a sense of tangible coherence, such as series of conferences, the field's *Journal of Social and Personal Relationships,* and its societies, such as the International Network on Personal Relationships. These organizational creations have exposed the scholars from a given discipline to the themes, assumptions, vantage points, and styles of other disciplines and have led to broader ways of thinking about personal relationships. This is itself a good example of the point that organization creates meaning from possible alternative constructions: "Extension" and "sharing of meaning" are beneficial!

However, it is still evident that much research on relationships is essentially (and often implicitly) concerned with the same issue as the original, and now dated, work on interpersonal attraction: the initial choice of partners. If one focuses on initial choice alone then one naturally omits all the social actions that have relevance when real life *conduct* of relationships is the focus of people's activities. A focus on attraction also mutes the dialogic possibility that the very feature that attracts us to a person to begin with could nevertheless come back to haunt us (Felmlee, 1993): What is initially exciting today could become irresponsible tomorrow; what is charmingly eccentric today could become an embarrassing irritation tomorrow; what is intriguingly stimulating today could be seen as unbearably erratic tomorrow.

The next few years are going to take us on to greater appreciation of dynamics of relationships. Of lesser interest will be the preexisting characteristics of individuals or the contextual or individual conditions that prompt hopeful inaugural encounters and optimistic first dates. We should continue to develop our understanding of initial attraction, but pay greater attention to the manner in which attraction is conveyed and managed in talk. For example, we should attend to the management and process issues that surround the "consolidation" of relationships from a first encounter to a second encounter, a very surprising omission from present research on attraction (Sprecher & Duck, in press). How do people negotiate the business of turning a first date into a second date? What do they say? What strategies are employed? What cues are central? What talk is used? How is it done? We must move beyond accounts of relationship development that simply slide over the mechanisms of such processes.

Another issue of dynamics develops an earlier prediction (Duck, 1988, p. 85) that relationship texts will soon mercifully toss out their overweightedness toward initial attraction and will instead fill their pages with discussion of relationship management and maintenance (see Canary & Stafford, 1994; Dindia & Canary, 1993). I'd still bet on that for a few years, but the new version will be to deal with the transformation of relationships from one encounter to the next— through meaning and talk. We will do this not in the old boring way where we see relationship development as a progression through real or imagined stages. Instead we will attend to the interior conversational mechanisms and dyadic memory processes by which relational metamorphoses and transfigurations of meaning occur (Honeycutt, 1993). What changes occur within the talk in relationships such as to change them from casual to close relationships

(Conville, 1988)? Planalp and Benson (1992) and Planalp (1993) have looked at the differences in the talk of acquaintances and friends, while Planalp and Garvin-Doxas (1994) have proposed an approach to dynamic change from one relationship status to another. These ideas need follow-up. In effect we will begin asking how individual and dyadic symbolic acrobatics bring a relationship into being and then constantly refine, redefine, and modify what the relationship means, such that it eventually becomes recognizable as a different type.

Along with these intriguing dynamic issues about talk, we need to ask what the partners mean to one another and how their selves change during relationship evolution (i.e., how their individuality is reconstructed and transformed in the relationship). For example, Spencer (1994) explored the use of self-disclosure in the development of adolescent identities and demonstrated how topics and styles of conversation modified the relationship between adolescent and parent. They also provide opportunities for similar studies of power and control, autonomy, and independence. Similar studies of the conversations of other sorts of relational dyads would clarify some of the presently mysterious workings of power in the actual dynamics of real relationships.

Furthermore, all of the study of relationships needs to be placed more strongly within the social contexts that surround dyadic relating (Allan, 1993; Duck, 1993a, 1993b). We have been remiss and lethargic in our efforts to understand how external influences channel relational behaviors (Baxter, 1993a; Klein & Milardo, 1993; Wood, 1993a)—for example, how the reactions of others to one's personal circumstances affect relationships, as when we become ill or unemployed, or are caught having an affair, or fall in love and wonder whether to tell other people about it (Baxter & Widenmann, 1993). Such tasks are far more complex than the challenges we have hitherto set ourselves as a field and will take much time and energy to accomplish, but are also exciting ones for us to wrestle with if we really want to understand functioning relationships.

Another line of development would be to resolve the dissatisfying aspect of the present state of affairs, which has a charming simplicity to some of its attempts to attack relational issues. Mostly, such efforts center on an individual level (or a disguised individual level) of analysis and dismiss as unproblematic not only the talk between the two relaters but also broader aspects of relational conduct.

Research on commitment, intimacy, or love is often concerned only with the way in which one person feels about these things rather than with how each of these topics is constructed and constituted in talk. Research on relational information acquisition or schemata or MOPs (memory organization packets; Honeycutt, 1993) is concerned with the ways in which an individual organizes or collects information and not with how information is managed and used between people in the conduct of conversations in relationships. Research on relational attribution is invariably focused on the ways in which one person thinks about another rather than on how the two of them communicate—or agree—about their attributions. Of course such things are important and clearly in need of investigation (Fletcher & Fitness, 1993), but we also need to extend and contextualize them by checking how they are enacted in praxis. It is not enough to gather data from two persons in a couple (for reasons discussed in earlier chapters); instead and in addition, we must explore the ways in which people confront and manage the fact that prima facie legitimate alternative constructions of events can coexist.

Let's look at some concrete examples of how existing research can be developed to follow up on these points.

❦ New Lamps for Old: Another Look at Familiar Topics

This section revisits some famous old relationship topics and gives them a reinterpretation in the proposed new terms, as instances of symbol and meaning sharing that occur in talk. In doing so, I provide one answer to the question: "What difference does the advocated viewpoint make?" The subsequent section then raises some general issues about the field as a whole in the same terms.

Sharing and Exchanging

Metaphor, other ways of sharing meaning, and exchange have been proposed in this book as instances of the basic human interpersonal characteristics that create sociality as well as examples of the tendency to extend and "go beyond the given." Their common character is their extension and their inherent incorporation of different sorts of vantage points simultaneously. The exposure of alternative vantage points implicit in these activities helps us to comprehend more fully their connection to personal meaning and relationships. It also reinterprets their fundamental driving forces by claiming the centrality of the human quest to generate meaning and to place it in the context of talk with other human beings.

The present argument has placed the ultimate relative significance of human activities and their relational consequences within a framework based on personal meaning and the construction of meaning in talk. In that context I have already proposed that a person's own system of meaning is what makes a reward rewarding, whatever the generally accepted view of reward may be. Because people are socialized into cultures that in large part indicate for them what is rewarding, it happens that in many cases people agree on the rewardingness or costliness of certain things. However, these generally agreed-on things are guides and not prescriptions, and in any case it is the personally meaningful items that are most important for personal relationships. Generally agreed-on meanings are, rather, only a first crude layer of meaning that may be shared with a stranger—a meaning layer that is likely to work at a general level of probabilistic prediction about possible relational success. Future studies involving assessment of exchanges should incorporate some contemporaneous assessment of personal meaning as decomposed in Chapter 5 and should begin to explore the fuller layers of such meaning as relationships develop. If exchange theories work, then they should be able to work more powerfully when general meaning is pitted against the richer personal meanings that lie within symbolic rewards.

Exchanges take some of their power from the symbolic character with which partners imbue them. As relationships develop and acquire more and more personally and dyadically constructed significance, so the specific symbolism of particular acts becomes more complex or layered within the dyad in context. For example, Baxter (1987) reports a respondent having a bamboo flute that he could not really play. His friend could not only play it but could spin it round on his finger! The person commented that the flute came to be an important indicator within the relationship because it signified trust when the first person lent it to the second and he returned it without being asked. The flute itself was inconsequential and of little value, but the act of lending and retrieving it came to be relationally significant. Furthermore, Montgomery (1988) noted that individuals progress from culturally shared meanings to unique and idiosyncratic ones. This latter effect differentiates developed relationships from developing ones. For example, Baxter (1987) reported that one of her couples occasionally pretended to be dogs and would remind one another of this nonverbally in larger groups as a way to signal the uniqueness of their relationship and its ability to exclude others.

One implication is that the value of specific exchanges for a developed dyad cannot be easily predicted on the basis of common cultural meaning. The personal significance of acts and items tends to diverge from the common or culturally agreed values for these items and so become less predictive of relationship behavior as the relationship itself evolves. It is specifically in the prediction of reactions of strangers to one another that a general rewards-and-costs analysis might be most useful, or else in those cases where close partners are asked to contemplate nonclose things or depersonalized relational contexts such as their reactions to imagined (and so personally unmeaningful) scenarios.

It is also the personal meaning of rewards that makes the difference between communal relationships and exchange relationships (Mills & Clark, 1982), not the mere length of time over which the exchange balance is calculated nor the objective type of relationships that are considered. Of course, in past research the issue of type of relationship has been inevitably confounded with the changed and different nature of personal meaning that inexorably takes place as relationships transform (not merely move) from one form to another. Secondly, exchanges of rewards and costs indicate values, meanings, and priorities of a person on a general level as much as they indicate specific exchange of commodities such as love and information. A person exchanges love because love matters personally at the time or answers information with money because that is what the exchange means to him or her in the present circumstances. A person's contribution to an exchange is not prefigured, but in practice it helps to define the nature of the exchange. An exchange response declares the way in which the exchange and the relationship are constructed in the person's mind as well as how the relationship is presented to others. For example, to respond to a gift by paying its price is to indicate that the giver bought it on one's behalf, but to respond with profuse thanks is to indicate that it was bought as a mark of esteem. Since the analysis of the person's meaning viewpoint is never operationally separate in research from the analysis of the exchanges in which the person takes part, the confusion between the viewing mind and the objective facts, too, has never previously been separable—that is, research has assumed that all viewers will see the exchange in the same way, and this assumption removes the chance to define exchanges in terms of what they mean personally to the participants. Third, exchanges also are implicitly illustrative of ways of extending a particular relational form into the future in that they point to the likely type of relational meaning that one person will have to another into the future (compare and contrast the proposals by Huesmann & Levinger, 1976, that looked at future exchange projections). For example, to decline to be reimbursed for a purchase made on another's behalf is to change the character of the relationship from a service relationship to a friendly one and also incidentally to oblige the other person to reciprocate *in that form* in due course also.

As another instance of the difference made here by a focus on vantage points of meaning, consider the claim by exchange theorists (e.g., Levinger, 1979) that relationships fall apart or are threatened when an alternative attractive relational partner appears. Despite its feeling of familiarity, there is one additional implicit concept that has to be imported to make the claim work, and it adds a reinterpretation along the lines I am proposing here. An alternative becomes an alternative only when someone opens an eye afresh and allows the alternative to become one. Alternatives cannot be denoted as such without knowledge of the meaning of the alternatives from the viewpoint of the person. The meaning of an alternative thus necessarily changes before it becomes available as an alternative. The world is always populated with alternative partners in an objective sense. We do not see them as alternatives, nor do we treat them as available, until we become dissatisfied with what we have (i.e., until the meaning of participating in an alternative relationship changes for us). The availability of an alternative is thus a purely subjective thing, not an objective one that can be defined in absolute terms. In the language of the previous argument, the availability of an alternative is created by a prior shift in personal meaning.

Thus every actual exchange of goods or services or objects, and so forth, is also an exchange of symbols or metaphors or meanings in the sense that the exchange of goods, etc., means something to the exchangers. For example, each exchange item has implicit meaning within the culture as a whole (thus exchange of wrapped birthday presents would make as much sense in the United States as would exchange of sea shells in the Trobriand Islands, but a simple transposition of cultural contexts could make each gift look inappropriately foolish).

Yet exchanges are also symbolic within the culture of each relationship. Although exchanges of love are probably equally acceptable in most close dyads, the exact form of an exchange (as well as the particular activity that counts as an instance of affection) is probably dependent on the ways in which the partners construe specific acts and behavior. For instance, a person providing a partner with breakfast in bed may be regarded as loving in one relationship and irritating in another, where the act may seem to evoke undesirable overtones about whose role it normally is to do routine food preparation work. Equally, one could give a partner breakfast in bed in a way that implied the recipient was a lazy person who expected to be waited on hand and foot. Thus the symbolic meaning of an exchange is greater than and other than the exchange itself. In quantifying only the objective exchange (i.e., in studying only the common cultural meanings for a resource rather than also its personal meaning to the participants), researchers miss other elements of meaning explored in the social process of the decomposition of meaning outlined in Chapter 5. Acts of exchange necessarily imply something about A's construction of B (and B's of A) and are presumably taken as signs of this in at least three ways: (1) by B within B's thought framework (what B personally thinks A is up to and what the act means to B); (2) by A within A's thought framework (what A thinks A is up to and what the act means to A and what A presumes it will mean to B); and (3) by any outside observer within his or her thought framework (what outsiders without inside knowledge of the relationship think is going on or what it means to them) (the viewpoint usually privileged in social scientific work at the expense of the other two). Only when (1) and (2) match up (and are recognized to match up as a result of the processes depicted in Chapter 4) does the act have character as a relationship symbol collaboratively defined and understood.

Exchange is thus not just the transfer of goods and services but the engagement of symbols and the meanings of people through such things as goods and services. To the extent that any study reduces exchanges to brute acts (and hence to common, average, cultural rather than personal meaning) it ignores the personal. Thus the debate between strict exchange theory and communal exchange theory (Mills & Clark, 1982) is essentially misplaced because it takes insufficient account of the different meanings that attach to pure exchange relationships with strangers and communal ones with friends. The difference is that the two are interpreted differently (or given different personal meaning by the partners) a priori, and thus meaning and relationship type are perpetually confounded in the research.

While we thus need to contextualize specific interaction outcomes in their symbolic, social, and cultural contexts (Montgomery, 1988), we should also take account of the role of choice in the provision of context. When I go to the supermarket (or to the supermarket of life), I do not just exchange cash for goods but I choose those goods, I deliberate about those choices, I review my needs, I consider available options, act on or react to impulses not in response to prior calculation. I may also discuss the choices with Joanna together since *our* needs were different when she was pregnant with our second child (who turned out to be Gabriel even as I desperately tried, unsuccessfully, to finish this book before he showed up). This context of choice is important and shapes the meaning of choices just as it shapes the exchanges in personal relationships. People choose to emphasize specific sorts of exchange as a result of the meaning that they attribute to the exchange *in the context of other choices that could be picked instead.* Exchanges are not absolute nor abstract. By carrying them out in a context of other choices, people take account of the exchanges' dilemma in personal terms, not just in terms of the broad common ground (Billig, 1987).

According to the present proposal, a relationship is never constructed only by different levels of exchange—except insofar as the meaning of those exchanges is universal and not personal—even though different sorts of resources can be differentiated and arranged in ordinal relationships (Foa & Foa, 1974). The difference in the level and type of exchange items comes from the symbolic meaning that is attached to them through the viewpoint taken of them within the social, relational, and individual context of their enactments (see Chapters 1 and 2). Changes in relationship form are made instead by the serial realization that different levels of exchange should be warranted—that is, by a prior transformation of the meaning of exchange (see Chapter 4). Likewise, relational interdependence is not created by interaction patterns alone but rather by beliefs and mental attitudes about those patterns. (Indeed the construction of patterns is itself a mental act—cf. Chapter 2.) Hence the measurement of personal meanings attached to exchange and to interdependence in specific circumstances should be more predictive of relationship outcomes than mere analysis of existence and type of exchange and interdependence themselves, if that analysis relies only on the general meaning of exchange and interdependence. In this way, relational acts have impact on relationships not only directly or in a mathematically and scientifically certain way as determined from an observer's perspective. Rather they work only through the medium of each perceiver's interpretation of their relational force. In everyday relationships a perceiver's interpretation is usually transformed by talking.

From that perspective, the development of relationships is not simply the increase of information about someone (Altman & Taylor, 1973) nor just the reduction of uncertainty (Berger & Bradac, 1982), although these are indisputably important processes. Information will have effects only when it changes a person's metaperspective on the relationship or partner and so affects one person's social behavior with one another. If talk adds factual information without also changing the perceiver's ability to structure and organize a view of the other person, then it will likely have almost no effect that changes relationship experience. Reinterpretation is a reorganization of meaning, after all.

Self-Disclosure

I have said quite a lot about self-disclosure as I have gone along, so it should be clear why I believe that the meaning of a disclosure is not necessarily the same for speaker and listener, as has all too often been assumed. Perhaps because of implicit awareness of this fact, persons who wish to make a disclosure make strategic preparations to manipulate context so that the listener's response becomes somewhat more predictable. Miell and Duck (1986) have shown that people lead up slowly to the disclosure on intimate topics in real encounters, first testing the ground by mentioning the topic in a joking or slighting way in order to see the general reaction of the listener to the topic as a whole. If the response is safe (i.e., if it appears that the listener is not hostile to the topic), then the speaker will go ahead and make a self-disclosing statement about the topic. Thus the risk of intimacy that is often discussed in research reports about self-disclosure, and is sometimes seen to give self-disclosure its intimate meaning and force, is in fact strategically reduced beforehand by manipulation of *the meaning of the situation* where the disclosure is about to be made.

Furthermore, Miell (1984) reasoned that other meanings can be constructed for apparently self-disclosing statements. Self-disclosure can be used in order to interrogate other people! Miell argued that people are aware that a norm of reciprocity exists in respect of disclosure and that if a person discloses to us we are implicitly pressured to disclose in return. Given such knowledge, then, it is possible to ask another person questions in a very subtle manner. Miell showed that speakers would declare their own experience with a topic and then sit back and wait for the listener to feel the pressure of a norm to reciprocate equally disclosing information.

Equally, Spencer (1993) has noted that self-disclosure has other more complex meanings than those that researchers assume. In many circumstances, especially in mentor or parent-child relationships, the disclosure often has an educative purpose. The disclosure is not intended to tell the listener about the speaker's personal life nor to increase relational intimacy so much as to provide guidance based on the speaker's experience. For example, Spencer (1993) found that parents would declare to adolescents statements of the form: "When I was your age I used to feel terribly shy too, but I overcame it by . . . ."

In these cases, the meaning of the act of disclosure is rather similar to the advice-giving strategies used by teachers (Glidewell, Tucker, Todt, & Cox, 1982). In the latter study, inexperienced teachers told stories about problems they had encountered, yet they did not ask directly for advice about how to solve those problems. Experienced teachers did not respond with advice as such either, but instead told stories about situations where they had solved a similar problem. Thus the disclosure of both predicaments and possible solutions was handled indirectly without one side having to lose face by a direct request for help or a direct acknowledgment of the one-down position of being advised. These examples again suggest that the meaning of a situation is a guide to the interpretation and understanding of what people do in it, more so than is the absolute value of the behavior per se. In the everyday discourses of life, then, the revelation of a speaker's feelings may be oblique to self-disclosure in the traditional sense. The nature of a disclosure takes its meaning from the speaker's purposes in the encounter, and the response of the listener to that meaning.

Finally, in everyday life, statements that would be rated as disclosures may in fact be used to share broad experiences rather than literal and specific content. For example, my wife Joanna recently told me about a friend she had during teenage years and some of the unconventional things that they did. Joanna disclosed many memories and feelings about the friend during this conversation. It was also clear to me, however, that these details were essentially irrelevant to her purposes. The point of describing them was to convey to me the significance of the friend in forming Joanna's view of herself as a teenager and *that* was what was really being disclosed. The fuller experience—not the specific details or emotions—was the essence of the act of disclosure that had meaning to her and to me.

In all of the above instances, some drawn from research and some from life, there is evidence that an utterance can be designated as a true self-disclosure in the sense assumed in research only after careful consideration of the relational and interactional context in which it occurs. The literal meaning of the utterance itself is therefore less important for relational research than the social meaning and significance of the fact of its utterance. This can be determined only after careful consideration of the interpersonal meaning that it has for the relationship rather than only from the personal significance or literal meaning of the statement. Such contexts are provided by several types of components discussed in Chapter 5.

Love and Attachment Styles

The extensive work on love attitudes (e.g., Hendrick & Hendrick, 1986) uncovers the same general process discussed above. In preferring a style of approach to love, or a style at a particular time, subjects essentially attribute meanings in systematic ways guided by their personal system of meaning. For instance, if people are in love then they tend to view things through rose-colored glasses (Hendrick & Hendrick, 1988).

Nevertheless, when subjects are asked to provide responses about love in the structured circumstances of a study, they tend to report experience in a shape that is somewhat different from the shape that they give in unstructured accounts. Hendrick and Hendrick (1993) offered the proposal that the different structures were partly a function of the rhetorical situation in which subjects find themselves in the two cases. Extending this point, Duck (1991, 1992a) proposed that the reports about the type of love felt in the same relationship will be modified by the nature of the rhetorical situation in which the reporter is found. Heavy-breathing couples in the throes of passion are likely to report erotic love attitudes to any investigator with the courage and meanness to interrupt them. Couples discussing a proposal of marriage are more likely to report pragmatic feelings about their love. In other words, the rhetorical situation for evoking thoughts about love will help the respondents to focus on some constituents of the whole complex experience in one set of circumstances and others in other circumstances. Likewise, Duck (1986, 1992a) speculated that as lovers' relationships develop from a heady and erotic start through to an organized lifetime partnership, so the partners will change the profile of their love attitude scores in a way that reflects the change in meaning of the relationship as a whole—and hence in the appropriateness of certain kinds of statements about it.

A further hypothesis is that the expression of a person's attitudes to love can be likened to the ANOVA decomposition of meaning in Chapter 5: It is composed of a gender element (e.g., there are findings on sex differences; Hendrick, Hendrick, Foote, & Slapion-Foote, 1984), of a personal stylistic element (as found in studies of persons' characteristic styles; Hendrick & Hendrick, 1986), of various local situational elements as proposed above, and of the larger situational element provided by the person's construction of the likely course of the relationship.

Another approach to romantic relationships, the approach from attachment (Hazan & Shaver, 1987), is susceptible to the same sorts of analysis. *Attachment style*, as for any style of behavior, is essentially an organized system of meaning relating the organization of memory and the coherence of discourse or mind. A style characterizes itself by denoting certain sorts of elements of experience or people as pivotal and then organizing the specific meanings attached to these pivotal events and relationships, especially those concerned with key figures early in perceptual life (Duck, in press-a). The style represents the person's extrapolation from past experiences, through organized personal meaning systems, to expectations for future action. It can be conceptualized as a working model of a person's experience at the hands of others in particular sorts of circumstances that reflect the circumstances giving rise to the pattern (Bowlby, 1988). In other words, a working model of relationships is simply an extension or projection to future relationship forms on the basis of the subjective and personal meanings attached to prior experience. In a sense, this process of generalization is indicated by any use of the term *style*. A style is a consistency detected by some perceiver, whether self or other observer. If attachment styles (Hazan & Shaver, 1987), for example, are based on working models of relationships (Bowlby, 1988), then they may be instances of a patterned perception of the past (childhood relationships with others) leading to a patterned way of anticipating the future (adults' relationships with others). What this means is, in effect, not that people have only a working *model* of relationships but that they have a *working* model (Duck, 1993c). The perceivers apply the model in their real relational lives, and the model contextualizes information that they receive from relational partners. Attachment is thus an example and subset of the general tendency for humans to put meaning on things for themselves and to react to the meanings that are evoked for them in similar (or extensive) circumstances as previously discussed. Even style may vary as events are interpreted, but it is more likely that the notion of style attaches to a consistency of perceptual experience that shapes the experiencer's ways of recalling or responding to events—that is, the ways of putting personal meaning on them.

The important element represented in an attachment style is the meaning generated for self by one's treatment at others' hands. Such meaning is often argued to be encapsulated into one's system at an early age and then continues to exert an important effect on later life, though not a deterministic one, in circumstances having reference to one's treatment of or by others (Bartholomew, 1993). Having developed a pattern in which we tend to see certain sorts of people in certain ways, we are inclined to incorporate new information in a way that reflects the bias of the hypothesis and so reflects to other people the meaning that we think we have. Thus in this way attachment theory may be related to early research on impression formation and person perception.

The present approach is broader than attachment theory alone because it views attachment processes as a part of personal meaning as a whole, and therefore addresses a broader range of relationship issues. In other words, the existence of attachment styles exemplifies the broader tendency for people to attach meaning stylistically to all sorts of domains of experience. My approach can also account for the effects of prior experiences of relationships other than parent-child or romantic without violating Bowlby's original claims. For example, Dunn (1992) developed the interesting observation that siblings learn important lessons about their value to others not only from direct, but also from indirect, experience. As they observe their parents treating their sibling(s), so children can pick up an image of their comparative worth to other people, who is favored, and whether all receive equal treatment. They can also gain vicarious knowledge about such social experiences as sharing, equality, cooperation, and competition. These experiences may or may not have relevance to later adult romantic relationships but could certainly have relevance to other sorts of relationships in which no romantic element is involved. For instance, Socha (1991) showed that one way in which children learn about compliance is from observing their parents do it. In other words, a meaning structure about compliance is made available to children by parents and may be assimilated largely by exposure effects (Zajonc, 1980). As with other perception and experience, incoming information is assimilated into, and yet transforms, the perceiver's outlook, or else confirms the outlook already operative.

In brief, I propose that developmental experiences operate through the activity of a child's own meaning system, which is composed partly of the child's own perception and partly of the child's assimilation of interpretations of experiences provided by others. The whole composes the child's own system of meaning. It is this that affects later relationships of all sorts, and the principles exposed by current work on attachment are therefore not inconsistent with my present proposal. Of course the child's meaning system develops partly through language and partly through relationships to other people (Fogel, 1993). Thus, to pick up on points made in Chapters 2 and 3, it is inconceivable that over the length of infancy or childhood the child is not going to be exposed to variable behavior from each parent (What parent is ever completely consistent for, say, 10 years of real life at a stretch?) and also to differences between the two parents (Duck, 1994a). It is not these inconsistencies themselves (nor any consistencies, for that matter) that will lead to a given attachment style, but whatever it is that a child makes of such variabilities and perceived consistencies in relationships to itself. Likewise, over the length of childhood it is implausible to imply that the child retains such a unitary and purposeful view of self and its attachment figures that the meaning of self and those figures remains invariant. Researchers into attachment clearly should be looking at the ways in which children represent their attachments in talk at different times and ages, at the ways in which attachment figures talk to them, and at the ways in which such things are reflected in the meanings that children give for attachment, self, and attachment figures—rather as researchers have already explored children's changing views on the nature of friendship over the course of childhood (Duck, 1993b).

❦ A Look Ahead: Future Research Topics

Once we entertain seriously the importance of studying how talk both manifests and manages—by defining, focusing, and extending—meanings in relationships, then we are led to attend to practical relational issues that historically have been of little concern to scholars (Wood, 1993b): problems, hassles, and hurts whose meanings must be constructed in ways that allow practical outcomes, such as the continuance or dissolution of the relationship. If the relationship is to continue despite such matters, then social action has to be creatively managed to reroute the relationship around its obstacles, but if the road block is impassable then at least one of the partners has to do something to let the relationship die, even if it is only by consciously ignoring the relationship.

Relationships and Real Life

Theorists must therefore incorporate the dark side into relationships along with the bright side, while also recognizing that these terms, and this dichotomy, are really far too simple (Duck, 1994d). I have suggested that analysis of personal meaning provides such an integrative force that puts bright and dark back together. Because the interplay between "bright" and "dark" together constructs the meaning of a relationship (and the positive or the negative in isolation do not), the meaning of a positive or negative individual act is derived not from its generation of a reward or a cost alone, but from its place in a pattern of activity. In reality our relationships are not all joyous sunlight and satisfying rewards but are also (and sometimes simultaneously) places of occasional pain and anguish. There is nothing odd or strikingly original about this observation; we all know it but write theories as if we do not. In reality, people spend plenty of time managing, defining, and making sense out of both relational pleasures and the pains—and they do so quite often in and through talk that is not necessarily premised in the supposition that the relationship is about to end. Equally, relaters are doing more than merely adding rewards and subtracting costs: They are working out how to deal with them in a meaningful way. Costs are not just cognitive or emotional costs but also carry the additional costs of their own management, such that a cost analysis becomes an infinite regression.

The often manic portrayal of relationships as lyrical havens of whole happiness (Argyle, 1987) or paradisiacal committed centers of closeness and contentment (Kelley, 1983) simply tell us about no more than some—probably not even half—of a much more complex picture. The actual praxis of the interminable complexities of relating; the nonidealized, real life of relationships; and the talkative daily enactment of relationship maintenance are all out there waiting to be explained. This has to be done in a way that richly and realistically accounts for the meaningful actions of daily life before we go around congratulating ourselves too easily (and far too heartily) that a science of relationships is about to bring about a new Golden Age. For example, on the blackest extreme of the dark-side continuum, the consequences for relational praxis are even more acute. People have to handle enemies, not merely be aware of them. One has to undo their deeds, raise a shield to counter their comments, defuse their interpersonal grenades, spike their hostile public gunnery, and plan to execute revenge raids (Wiseman, 1989, in press). An enemy is not a simple source of negative evaluation nor a cognitive ghost pressing one's emotional buttons; an enemy represents a living challenge to one's system of personal meaning and to the management of one's identity. It is, further, a challenge about which people do something.

Cupach and Spitzberg (1994) have demonstrated that much else in the dark side of relationships has been overlooked in recent nonclinical theories of relating (cf. Gottman, 1991). This fact is of interest in itself but is also important because the bright side exists in praxis too and both require management separately and together (Duck, 1994d). Inevitably relationships encompass irritations with partners, the binds that go with the bonds (Wiseman, 1986), and some of the downright mean-spiritedness that humans cook up to embroil each other as we "always hurt the one we love." It is relatively easy to come up with quite long lists of relational negativities that are all too rarely studied and almost never incorporated into theory in any substantial or integrative way (e.g., revenge, teasing, needling; Duck, 1994d; Duck & Wood, in press; Wood & Duck, 1994). Yet the dark side constitutes not only a meaningful set of relationship experiences for people but also a set of relational activities that arise during the constant work on other relationship activities. For instance, daily hassles, minor conflicts, duties of loyalty, and helping others with tasks, are all small examples of the binds of relationships that can happen at any time in ordinary life (or of the ways in which what is "bright" at Time 1 can seem "dark" at Time 2). These problems do not necessarily cause the end of the relationship: They are the seeds that come with the grapes, but they still must be dealt with. At the other extreme, enemies, hatred, regret about relationship interactions or discussions, disappointment in partners or in relationship goals, betrayal, relational sabotage, needlings, unkindness in relating, letting down, missing specific people (a subset of loneliness?), are all experiences that people also have in relationships.

Such topics do not become less important to people in relationships just because academic researchers hardly ever study them (although of course many clinicians do). It may, of course, turn out that these things can be simply accounted for in terms of existing theory, but since they have not been systematically investigated, one does not know with certainty or even with confidence. It seems more likely that such relational dark facts will be hard to explain in existing theory, just as many bright ones are, precisely because their existence cuts right to one of the major points of this book: Such facts exist not in the mind alone but in the praxis of daily life. As such, these aspects of relating present organizational and management problems for people and relational binds are not just curious individualistic cognitive phantasms that have no connection to the enactment of real life. All relationships have binds and obligations that come with them as part of their nature: For instance, a person gives up some autonomy and independence in order to be a member of any relationship (Baxter, 1993a). Such sacrifices for a relationship take many forms but they do not lead to relational dissolution; they lead to a need to manage and continue the relationship—a difference that depends on the meaning attributed to the obligation or cost in relational context. For example, obligations or costs may require one to manage one's time differently, to forgo some enjoyable activity in order to help a friend, or put effort into helping a partner, for some obvious examples. Even in the case of parents and children there are many forms of felt obligation that structure the relationship and balance out the obvious rewards yet do not lead to the severing of the bond (Stafford & Byers, 1993; Stein, 1993)—precisely because of what the bond means.

One might be tempted to explore such occurrences in terms of rewards and costs. Yet the existence of the costs within a relationship that nevertheless continues raises important issues not solvable in terms of comparison levels alone, if indeed one's culture is one in which the whole idea of relationships based on costs and rewards makes some sense (as it does not in the Orient, for example; Yum, 1988). Obviously one neither has nor exercises the choice about staying in such relationships that is sometimes implied in formulations that see the existence of a relationship as due to one's balancing of rewards and costs (Rusbult & Buunk, 1993). Nor is the effect of such costs on satisfaction of much interest, since satisfaction is likely to be unrelated to continuance of a number of relationships (e.g., parent-child, work, or neighbor relations). The real issue is not one of relational outcomes as a product of costs and rewards but is rather the process of management of the relationship to which one finds that one belongs. How do people in relationships think and talk about what have been counted costs, dissatisfactions, and so on, in ways that nevertheless enable continued participation in the relationship?

Interpersonal conflict provides an apposite example. Conflicts are often tolerated because they are seen as an inevitable consequence of relationships, yet may also provide a good example of a case where the generalized "going beyond" meaning of the activity has been given insufficient attention in the research on its relational effects. Hocker and Wilmot (1989) note that the researchers' classification of communications into a stylistic category (such as conflict styles) often is seen as putting them into an absolute category. However, a conflict style is truly dependent on the viewer's vantage point and is not an invariant personality style but is reactive to situations. Yet measuring instruments all too often fall into the traps I have earlier discussed, where they assume general-meaning consistency across contexts, relationships, and conflict situations as well as within the particular conflict situation.

Before one understands a conflict, one needs to know about the meanings of behaviors that lead up to conflicts as well as the conflict itself within the relationship (Cloven & Roloff, 1993; Witteman, 1988). For these reasons there is merit in focusing on the patterns of communication and behavior that, in normal situations, bring the individual up to a conflict in certain circumstances or relationships and not others. Such patterns indicate how the person defines the meaning of particular behaviors within particular situations and in relation to particular others—and the transformation of those meanings within the dynamics of the situation (which also explains why some conflict is good for a relationship and leads to satisfying resolution of problems because it is seen as constructive, if argumentative, dialogue; Hocker & Wilmot, 1989). Moreover, when one uses the above approach to look at what "bad" conflict means to the persons involved, it seems plausible that a major element is the diminishing of self's view of life that is presented by having another person challenge it. If this hypothesis proves to be correct, then the focus on the literal content of conflictive exchange will need supplementing by attention to the personal meaning of the conflict for the partners. But once again, we would be seeing the negative effects of conflict as provoked not by the events but by the meaning of the events to the person.

The Conduct of Diverse Relationships

Equally there are scores of nonvoluntary relationships that people conduct every day and about whose existence or on whose outcomes reward-cost computations have little influence (Stafford & Byers, 1993). For instance, relationships with in-laws, relationships with elderly parents, collegial relationships at work, and so on have little of the freedoms of choice made in the sophomoric romantic selections that are the most frequent source of data about so-called close relationships. It may be a choice to put a baby in a dumpster, to place granny in a home, or to commit suicide, but such choices have a different sort of meaning from those where a sophomore is offered a choice between a silhouette with large buttocks and one with small ones in an experiment on interpersonal attraction (Beck, Ward-Hull, & McLear, 1976). Relationships where one has considerable and continuous choice about one's membership are different from those where personal threats, family norms, endemic poverty, or cultural expectations influence one's freedom to leave (Duck, 1993a). In the latter case, the issue has to do with practical management of the relationship and one's identity, not with the continued existence of a relationship.

In similar fashion, it is also possible to list large numbers of types of relationships evident in normal life that have properties that present similar challenges to existing theories. The problem comes when such theories are based only on rewards and costs analysis, or when they assume linearity of growth in commitment over time, viewed as simple cognitive calculating problems (Duck & Wood, in press; Wood & Duck, in press). There is very little investigation, for example, of the similarities and differences between the conduct of heterosexual and homosexual relationships. To study gay and lesbian relationships will almost certainly require a consideration of social forces and contexts such as roles, norms, and expectations that are almost never incorporated into purely social cognitive explanations of other sorts of relationships (Allan, 1993). Yet why would researchers not attend to the relevance of social forces and contexts in all relationships? Why take one vantage point for some relationships and another for others? Why give one sort of meaning to some relationships and another sort to others? All relationships are conducted against a backdrop of such roles, norms, and social guides (Duck, 1993b). To focus research on the cognitive processes alone is to miss the opportunity to give cognitive processes their due and proper weight.

Likewise, the actual conduct of relationships in populations challenged by physical and emotional constraints is also given too little attention, because theorists assume that such palpable impediments as physical disability or psychological disturbance or even the social upheavals of reconfigured families can be explained by the same principles of cognitive calculations of exchange and reward/cost ratios (cf. and contrast Lyons, in press). Can these real behavioral dilemmas be explained in the same terms as the cognitive and often imaginative activities of college sophomores? It is all very well to ask students to think about relationships or imagine how they might respond if they were to pretend that they were themselves divorced, minority, physically challenged people having long-term relationships in their fifties. If scholars rely on such sources to do that, however, then they and their readers must preface statements about their findings with truly humble and fastidious restrictions. Such exactness will require us to stop seeing all relationships as the calculated products of attitudinal and cognitive arithmetic and to note that all relationships are activities enacted completely in contextualized daily lives that for some people have real doors, actual toilets, substantial appreciable constraints, interpersonal discomforts, stereotyped responsive behaviors, behavioral reactions to stigmas, and normative realities that are simply not reducible to dispassionate cognitive arithmetic. The relational restraints of poverty are not products of cognitive algorithms alone: They stink and stick to your boots.

As another telling example, work on relationships in minority populations has only a few outposts in the incompletely charted research prairies. Yet the usual models, which represent relationships as almost entirely the result of internal psychological activities of individuals, need to confront some social facts. Relationships between members of minority populations in a majority culture have to manage many social constraints and effects of difference that would seem to make the real life conduct of such relationships distinct from that of relationships more routinely studied and especially challenging (Gaines, in press). The little available research on such issues clarifies the fact that there are social constraints on behavior in these relationships and alludes to the role of social forces in the conduct of intimacy that are too often overlooked in models based exclusively on individual psychodynamics alone. In addition, because those psychodynamics reflect patterns, family styles, and identity processes derivative of middle-class white heterosexual culture (Wood & Duck, in press), they are likely to fail to account for dyads within an extended kin structure organized along matriarchal lines, as often occurs in African American families. Theories often assume a structure that is not in fact practiced as it is assumed (e.g., theories assuming power differences in couples do not speak to single-parent families or to the fact that a child may have experienced a different family power structure before the parents were divorced and the family became a step family; Coleman & Ganong, in press). All the same, such issues are not special ones that apply only to some types of relationships, though they may be different in degree. All relationships have such social contexts for their conduct; fuller understanding of these is simply something that has to both be done and be built into theory (Duck, 1993a; Klein & Milardo, 1993; Milardo & Wellman, 1992).

❣ Some Final Personal Meaning

I have to admit to recognizing a certain spirality to some of the logic in this book. As each chapter has unfolded, it has occasionally been necessary to revisit earlier concepts from a different angle or to expose and evaluate other facets of a concept already explored from certain angles, but I did warn readers that it would be like a car trip! To some extent this spirality itself demonstrates that relationships are perhaps not the linear developments that we often assume them to be and that "cutting" the phenomena in order to explain them always means cutting from some angle while leaving other approaches unexplored. In other respects the spirality emphasizes stylistically a point I have wanted to make throughout: Every description, every theory, and every method contains a vantage point, and the vantage point is an important component of the way things "look," including relationships and books.

I have many times been struck by the consistencies and constructive overlaps between different vantage points of psychological, communicational, sociological, and other relational research. These connections seem to me to be more important than the differences and to indicate general styles of human response to experience that can be pulled together into a general proposition. As we have moved along I have tried to display some underlying patterns drawn from the literatures of those different disciplines and to tie some pieces of the overlaps together.

It is not that I subscribe to a School of Universal Oneness. Rather, I believe the processes of human enquiry manifest themselves in different ways in different places while also having a substantial underlying similarity. They are all drenched in meaning. Where one discipline or investigator perceives meaning in one place in one way and another in another, both are doing the same thing: Both are constructing meaning within an overall framework in which the pieces of meaning are organized. Likewise, readers defining the meaning of a book are doing essentially the same thing as those other human beings who write books and do science or make speeches. Each is interpreting the world in a way consonant with his or her preexisting systems for the organization of meaning. Each is also attempting to extend from his or her own meaning to the other guy's and so construct the recognitions, acknowledgments, and realizations of shared meaning that are the basis of relationships, of sociality, and of society itself. Relationships themselves and the natures of relationships are profoundly contoured by the extent to which one person can construct the vantage point of another person—which is where we came in.

Incidentally, today Ben and I went through our usual ritual of pointing and blankness. But after a few moments' thought he pointed at my finger and said "La." I think we are getting somewhere. . . .

Now, listener, I have told my dream to thee.
See if thou canst interpret it to me.
Put by the curtains; look within my veil;
Turn up my metaphors; and do not fail
There (if thou seekest them) such things to find
As will be helpful to an honest mind.

—From Bunyan's *A Pilgrim's Progress*
(also used as the final narration in a work
set to music by Ralph Vaughan Williams as
"A Bunyan Sequence")

References

Acitelli, L. K. (1988). When spouses talk to each other about their relation-ship. *Journal of Social and Personal Relationships, 5,* 185-199.

Acitelli, L. K. (1992). Gender differences in relationship awareness and marital satisfaction among young married couples. *Personality and Social Psychology Bulletin, 18,* 102-110.

Acitelli, L. K. (1993). You, me, and us: Perspectives on relationship awareness. In S. W. Duck (Ed.), *Individuals in relationships* (Understanding Relationship Processes Series, Vol. 1, pp. 144-174). Newbury Park, CA: Sage.

Acitelli, L. K., Douvan, E., & Veroff, J. (1993). Perceptions of conflict in the first year of marriage: How important are similarity and understanding? *Journal of Social and Personal Relationships, 10,* 5-19.

Acitelli, L. K., & Duck, S. W. (1987). Intimacy as the proverbial elephant. In D. Perlman & S. W. Duck (Eds.), *Intimate relationships: Development, dynamics and deterioration* (pp. 297-308). Newbury Park, CA: Sage.

Adler, A. (1929). *What your life should mean to you.* New York: Bantam.

Allan, G. A. (1989). *Friendship.* Hemel Hempstead, UK: Harvester Wheatsheaf.

Allan, G. A. (1993). Social structure and relationships. In S. W. Duck (Ed.), *Social contexts and relationships* (Understanding Relationship Processes Series, Vol. 3, pp. 1-25). Newbury Park, CA: Sage.

Althen, G. (1993). *Manual for foreign students, scholars and advisors.* University of Iowa Office of International Education, Iowa City.

Althusser, L. (1971). *Lenin and philosophy and other essays.* London: New Left Books.

Altman, I., & Taylor, D. (1973). *Social penetration: The development of interpersonal relationships.* New York: Holt, Rinehart & Winston.

Andersen, P. (1993). Cognitive schemata in personal relationships. In S. W. Duck (Ed.), *Individuals in relationships* (Understanding Relationship Processes Series, Vol. 1, pp. 1-29). Newbury Park, CA: Sage.

Argyle, M. (1987). *The psychology of happiness.* Harmondsworth, UK: Penguin.

Argyle, M., & Henderson, M. (1984). The rules of friendship. *Journal of Social and Personal Relationships, 1,* 211-237.

Aron, A., & Aron, E. N. (1986). *Love and expansion of the self: Understanding attraction and satisfaction.* New York: Hemisphere.

Aronson, E., & Worchel, P. (1966). Similarity versus liking as determinants of interpersonal attractiveness. *Psychonomic Science, 5,* 157-158.

Bailey, B. (1988). *From front porch to back seat: Courtship in twentieth century America.* Baltimore, MD: Johns Hopkins University Press.

Bakhtin, M. (1981). *The dialogic imagination: Four essays by M. M. Bakhtin* (M. Holquist, Ed.; C. Emerson & M. Holquist, Trans.). Austin: University of Texas Press.

Bakhtin, M. (1984). *Problems of Dostoevsky's poetics* (C. Emerson, Ed. and Trans.). Minneapolis: University of Minnesota Press. (Original work published 1929)

Bartholomew, K. (1993). From childhood to adult relationships: Attachment theory and research. In S. W. Duck (Ed.), *Learning about relationships* (Understanding Relationship Processes Series, Vol. 2, pp. 30-62). Newbury Park, CA: Sage.

Bartlett, F. (1932). *Remembering.* Cambridge: Cambridge University Press.

Bavelas, J. (1990). *Equivocal communication.* Newbury Park, CA: Sage.

Baxter, L. A. (1987). Symbols of relationship identity in relationship cultures. *Journal of Social and Personal Relationships, 4,* 261-279.

Baxter, L. A. (1990). Dialectical contradictions in relationship development. *Journal of Social and Personal Relationships, 7,* 69-88.

Baxter, L. A. (1992a). Root metaphors in accounts of developing romantic relationships. *Journal of Social and Personal Relationships, 9,* 253-275.

Baxter, L. A. (1992b). Forms and functions of intimate play in personal relationships. *Human Communication Research, 18,* 336-363.

Baxter, L. A. (1993a). The social side of personal relationships: A dialectical perspective. In S. W. Duck (Ed.), *Social contexts and relationships* (Understanding Relationship Processes Series, Vol. 3, pp. 139-165). Newbury Park, CA: Sage.

Baxter, L. A. (1993b). Thinking dialogically about communication in personal relationships. In R. L. Conville (Ed.), *Structures of interpretation* (pp. 23-38). Norwood, NJ: Ablex.

Baxter, L. A., & Bullis, C. (1986). Turning points in developing romantic relationships. *Human Communication Research, 12,* 469-493.

Baxter, L. A., & Widenmann, S. (1993). Revealing and not revealing the status of romantic relationships to social networks. *Journal of Social and Personal Relationships, 10,* 321-338.

Baxter, L. A., & Wilmot, W. (1985). Taboo topics in close relationships. *Journal of Social and Personal Relationships, 2,* 253-269.

Beck, S. B, Ward-Hull, C. I., & McLear, P. M. (1976). Variables related to women's somatic preferences for the male and female body. *Journal of Personality and Social Psychology, 34,* 200-210.

Bell, R. A., Buerkel-Rothfuss, N., & Gore, K. (1987). "Did you bring the yarmulke for the cabbage patch kid?" The idiomatic communication of young lovers. *Human Communication Research, 14,* 47-67.

Bennett, J. (in press). *Time and relationships.* New York: Guilford.

Berg, J. H., & McQuinn, R. D. (1986). Attraction and exchange in continuing and non-continuing dating relationships. *Journal of Personality and Social Psychology, 50,* 942-952.

Berger, C. R. (1988). Uncertainty and information exchange in developing relationships. In S. W. Duck, D. F. Hay, S. E. Hobfoll, W. Ickes, & B. Montgomery (Eds.), *Handbook of personal relationships: Theory, research and interventions* (pp. 239-256). New York & Chichester: John Wiley.

Berger, C. R. (1993). Goals, plans and mutual understanding in personal relationships. In S. W. Duck (Ed.), *Individuals in relationships* (Understanding Relationship Processes Series, Vol. 1, pp. 30-59). Newbury Park, CA: Sage.

Berger, C. R., & Bradac, J. (1982). *Language and social knowledge.* London: Arnold.

Berger, P., & Kellner, H. (1964). Marriage and the construction of reality: An exercise in the microsociology of knowledge. *Diogenes, 46,* 1-24.

Bernard, A. C., Adelman, M. B., & Schroeder, J. (1991). Two views on the consumption of mating and dating. In R. H. Holman & M. R. Solomon (Eds.), *Advances in consumer research* (Vol. 18, pp. 532-537). Provo, UT: Association for Consumer Research.

Bernard, J. (1972). *The future of marriage.* New York: World Publications.

Berscheid, E. S., & Peplau, L. A. (1983). The emerging science of relationships. In H. H. Kelley, E. Berscheid, A. Christensen, J. H. Harvey, T. L. Huston, B. Levinger, E. M. McClintock, L. A. Peplau, & D. R. Peterson (Eds.), *Close relationships* (pp. 1-23). San Francisco: Freeman.

Berscheid, E., Snyder, M., & Omoto, A. (1989). Issues in studying close relationships: Conceptualizing and measuring closeness. In C. Hendrick (Ed.), *Close relationships* (pp. 63-91). Newbury Park, CA: Sage.

Billig, M. (1976). *Fascists.* London: Academic Press.

Billig, M. (1987). *Arguing and thinking: A rhetorical approach to social psychology.* Cambridge: Cambridge University Press.

Billig, M. (1991). *Ideology and opinions.* London: Sage.

Billig, M., Condor, S., Edwards, D., Gane, M., Middleton, D., & Radley, A. (1988). *Ideological dilemmas: A social psychology of everyday thinking.* London: Sage.

Blankenship, V., Hnat, S., Hess, T., & Brown, D. R. (1984). Reciprocal interaction and similarity of personality attributes. *Journal of Social and Personal Relationships, 1,* 415-432.

Bochner, A. P. (1984). The functions of human communication in interpersonal bonding. In C. Arnold & J. Bowers (Eds.), *Handbook of rhetorical and communication theory* (pp. 544-621). Boston: Allyn & Bacon.

Bochner, A. P. (1991). On the paradigm that would not die. In J. Anderson (Ed.), *Communication yearbook 14* (pp. 484-491). Newbury Park, CA: Sage.

Bochner, A. P., Krueger, D. L., & Chmielewski, T. L. (1982). Interpersonal perceptions and marital adjustment. *Journal of Communication, 32,* 135-147.

Bolger, N., & Kelleher, S. (1993). Daily life in relationships. In S. W. Duck (Ed.), *Social contexts and relationships* (Understanding Relationship Processes Series, Vol. 3, pp. 100-109). Newbury Park, CA: Sage.

Booth, W. C. (1974). *The rhetoric of irony.* Chicago: University of Chicago Press.

Bowlby, J. (1988). *A secure base: Parent-child attachment and healthy human development.* New York: Basic Books.

Burgoon, J. K. (Ed.). (1992). A Chautauqua on similarity. *Communication Monographs, 59.*

Burke, K. (1969). *A grammar of motives.* Berkeley: University of California Press. (Original work published 1945)

Burke, K. (1985). Commentary. In B. L. Brock, K. L. Burke, P. G. Burgess, & H. W. Simons (Eds.), Dramatism as ontology or epistemology: A symposium [Special issue]. *Communication Quarterly, 33,* 17-33.

Burkitt, I. (1991). *Social selves: Theories of the social formation of personality.* London: Sage.

Burleson, B. R., & Denton, W. H. (1992). A new look at similarity and attraction in marriage: Similarities in social-cognitive and communication skills as predictors of attraction and satisfaction. *Communication Monographs, 59,* 268-287.

Byrne, D. (1971). *The attraction paradigm.* New York: Academic Press.

Byrne, D., Nelson, D., & Reeves, K. (1966). The effects of consensual validation and invalidation on attraction as a function of verifiability. *Journal of Experimental Social Psychology, 2,* 98-107.

Canary, D. J., & Stafford, L. (Eds.). (1994). *Communication and relationship maintenance.* New York: Academic Press.

Christensen, A., Sullaway, M., & King, C. (1983). Systematic error in behavioral reports of dyadic interaction: Egocentric bias and content effects. *Behavioral Assessment, 5,* 129-142.

Christopher, F. S., & Cate, R. M. (1985). Premarital sexual pathways and relationship development. *Journal of Social and Personal Relationships, 2,* 271-288.

Cloven, D., & Roloff, M. (1993). Sense-making activities and interpersonal conflict II: The effect of communicative intentions on internal dialogue. *Western Journal of Communication, 57,* 309-329.

Cody, M. J., Kersten, L., Braaten, D. O., & Dickson, R. (1992). Coping with relational dissolutions: Attributions, account credibility, and plans for resolving conflicts. In J. H. Harvey, T. L. Orbuch, & A. L. Weber (Eds.), *Attributions, accounts and close relationships* (pp. 93-115). New York: Springer.

Cody, M. J., & McLaughlin, M. L. (1985). The situation as a construct in communication research. In M. L. Knapp & G. R. Miller (Eds.), *Handbook of interpersonal communication* (pp. 263-312). Beverly Hills, CA: Sage.

Coleman, M., & Ganong, L. (in press). Family reconfiguration following divorce. In S. W. Duck & J. T. Wood (Eds.), *Relationship challenges* (Understanding Relationship Processes Series, Vol. 5). Thousand Oaks, CA: Sage.

Collins, N. L., & Read, S. J. (1990). Adult attachment, working models, and relationship quality in dating couples. *Journal of Personality and Social Psychology, 58,* 644-663.

Conville, R. (1975). Linguistic non-immediacy and attribution of communicators' attitudes. *Psychological Reports, 36,* 951-957.

Conville, R. (1988). Relational transitions: An inquiry into their structure and functions. *Journal of Social and Personal Relationships, 5,* 423-437.

Crohan, S. (1992). Marital happiness and spousal consensus on beliefs about marital conflict: A longitudinal investigation. *Journal of Social and Personal Relationships, 9,* 89-102.

Cupach, W. R., & Spitzberg, B. H. (1994). *The dark side of interpersonal communication.* Hillsdale, NJ: Lawrence Erlbaum.

Daly, J. A., Vangelisti, A., & Daughton, S. (1987). The nature and correlates of conversational sensitivity. *Human Communication Research, 14,* 167-202.

Davis, J. D. (1978). When boy meets girl: Sex roles and the negotiation of intimacy in an acquaintance exercise. *Journal of Personality and Social Psychology, 36,* 684-692.

Davis, J. D., & Sloan, M. (1974). The basis of interviewee matching of interviewer self-disclosure. *British Journal of Social and Clinical Psychology, 13,* 359-367.

Davis, K. E., & Todd, M. J. (1985). Assessing friendship: Prototypes, paradigm cases and relationship description. In S. W. Duck & D. Perlman (Eds.), *Understanding personal relationships* (pp. 17-38). London: Sage.

Davis, M. S. (1973). *Intimate relationships.* London & New York: Free Press.

Day, B. R. (1961). A comparison of personality needs of courtship couples and same-sex friends. *Sociology and Social Research, 45,* 435-440.

Dindia, K. (1994). The intrapersonal-interpersonal dialectical process of self-disclosure. In S. W. Duck (Ed.), *Dynamics of relationships* (Understanding Relationship Processes Series, Vol. 4, pp. 27-57). Thousand Oaks, CA: Sage.

Dindia, K., & Canary, D. J. (1993). Definitions and theoretical perspectives on maintaining relationships. *Journal of Social and Personal Relationships, 10,* 163-174.

Dixson, M., & Duck, S. W. (1993). Understanding relationship processes: Uncovering the human search for meaning. In S. W. Duck (Ed.), *Individuals in relationships* (Understanding Relationship Processes Series, Vol. 1, pp. 175-206). Newbury Park, CA: Sage.

Duck, S. W. (1973). *Personal relationships and personal constructs: A study of friendship formation.* Chichester: John Wiley.

Duck, S. W. (1975). Attitude similarity and interpersonal attraction: Right answers and wrong reasons. *British Journal of Social and Clinical Psychology, 14,* 311-312.

Duck, S. W. (1977). *The study of acquaintance.* Farnborough, UK: Teakfields/ Saxon House.

Duck, S. W. (1980). Personal relationships research in the 1980s: Towards an understanding of complex human sociality. *Western Journal of Speech Communication, 44,* 114-119.

Duck, S. W. (1982a). The commonality corollary: Two individuals in search of agreement. In J. Mancuso & J. Adams-Webber (Eds.), *The construing person* (pp. 222-234). Elmsford, NY: Pergamon.

Duck, S. W. (1982b). A topography of relationship disengagement and dissolution. In S. W. Duck (Ed.), *Personal relationships 4: Dissolving personal relationships* (pp. 1-30). London: Academic Press.

Duck, S. W. (1983). Sociality and cognition in personal construct theory. In J. Mancuso & J. Adams-Webber (Eds.), *Applications of personal construct theory* (pp. 37-53). New York: Academic Press

Duck, S. W. (1984). A rose is a rose (is a tadpole is a freeway is a film) is a rose. *Journal of Social and Personal Relationships, 1,* 507-510.

Duck, S. W. (1985). Social and personal relationships. In M. L. Knapp & G. R. Miller (Eds.), *Handbook of interpersonal communication* (pp. 655-686). Beverly Hills, CA: Sage.

Duck, S. W. (1986). *Human relationships.* London: Sage.

Duck, S. W. (1987a). Adding apples and oranges: Investigators' implicit theories about relationships. In R. Burnett, P. McGhee, & D. Clarke (Eds.), *Accounting for relationships* (pp. 215-224). London: Methuen.

Duck, S. W. (1987b). How to lose friends without influencing people. In M. E. Roloff & G. R. Miller (Eds.), *Interpersonal processes: New directions in communication research* (pp. 278-298). Newbury Park, CA: Sage.

Duck, S. W. (1988). *Relating to others.* London: Open University Press, & Monterey, CA: Brooks/Cole/Wadsworth.

Duck, S. W. (1990). Relationships as unfinished business: Out of the frying pan and into the 1990s. *Journal of Social and Personal Relationships, 7,* 5-28.

Duck, S. W. (1991, May). *New lamps for old: A new theory of relationships and a fresh look at some old research.* Paper presented to the Third Conference of the International Network on Personal Relationships, Normal/ Bloomington, IL.

Duck, S. W. (1992a). *Human relationships* (2nd ed.). London: Sage.

Duck, S. W. (1992b, November). *Mental creation of relationships.* Paper presented to the annual convention of the Speech Communication Association, Chicago.

Duck, S. W. (1992c). The role of theory in the examination of relationship loss. In T. L. Orbuch (Ed.), *Close relationship loss: Theoretical approaches* (pp. 3-27). New York: Springer.

Duck, S. W. (1993a). Volume preface. In S. W. Duck (Ed.), *Social contexts and relationships* (Understanding Relationship Processes Series, Vol. 3, pp. ix-xiv). Newbury Park, CA: Sage.

Duck, S. W. (Ed.). (1993b). *Social contexts and relationships* (Understanding Relationship Processes Series, Vol. 3). Newbury Park, CA: Sage.

Duck, S. W. (1993c, March). *Working models of relationships: Discussion points.* Paper presented to Society for Research in Child Development, New Orleans.

Duck, S. W. (1994a). Attaching meaning to attachment. *Psychological Inquiry, 5,* 34-38.

Duck, S. W. (1994b). A multidisciplinary overview of relationships. In A. L. Weber & J. H. Harvey (Eds.), *Introduction to close relationships* (pp. 359-371). Boston: Allyn & Bacon.

Duck, S. W. (1994c). Steady as (s)he goes: Relational maintenance as a shared meaning system. In D. J. Canary & L. Stafford (Eds.), *Communication and relationship maintenance* (pp. 45-60). New York: Academic Press.

Duck, S. W. (1994d). Stratagems, spoils and a serpent's tooth: On the delights and dilemmas of personal relationships. In W. Cupach & B. H. Spitzberg (Eds.), *The dark side of interpersonal communication* (pp. 3-24). Hillsdale, NJ: Lawrence Erlbaum.

Duck, S. W., & Allison, D. (1978). I liked you but I can't live with you: A study of lapsed friendships. *Social Behavior and Personality, 6,* 43-47.

Duck, S. W., & Barnes, M. K. (1992). Disagreeing about agreement: Reconciling differences about similarity. *Communication Monographs, 59,* 199-208.

Duck, S. W., & Condra, M. B. (1989). To be or not to be: Anticipation, persuasion and retrospection in personal relationships. In R. Neimeyer & G. Neimeyer (Eds.), *Advances in personal construct theory* (Vol. 1, pp. 187-202). Greenwich, CT: JAI Press.

Duck, S. W., & Craig, G. (1978). Personality similarity and the development of friendship. *British Journal of Sociology and Clinical Psychology, 17,* 237-242.

Duck, S. W., & Lea, M. (1983). Breakdown of relationships as a threat to personal identity. In G. Breakwell (Ed.), *Threatened identities* (pp. 53-73). Chichester: John Wiley.

Duck, S. W., & Miell, D. E. (1986). Charting the development of personal relationships. In R. Gilmour & S. W. Duck (Eds.), *Emerging field of personal relationships* (pp. 133-144). Hillsdale, NJ: Lawrence Erlbaum.

Duck, S. W., & Montgomery, B. M. (1991). The interdependence among interaction substance, theory, and methods. In B. M. Montgomery & S. W. Duck (Eds.), *Studying interpersonal interaction* (pp. 3-15). New York: Guilford.

Duck, S. W., & Pittman, G. (in press). Social and personal relationships. In M. L. Knapp & G. R. Miller (Eds.), *Handbook of interpersonal communication* (2nd ed.). Thousand Oaks, CA: Sage.

Duck, S. W., & Pond, K. (1989). Friends, Romans, countrymen, lend me your retrospections: Rhetoric and reality in personal relationships. In C. Hendrick (Ed.), *Close relationships* (pp. 17-38). Newbury Park, CA: Sage.

Duck, S. W., Pond, K., & Leatham, G. (1991, May). *Remembering as a context for being in relationships: Different perspectives on the same interaction.* Paper presented to the third conference of the International Network on Personal Relationships, Normal, IL.

Duck, S. W., Pond, K., & Leatham, G. B. (1994). Loneliness and the evaluation of relational events. *Journal of Social and Personal Relationships, 11,* 235-256.

Duck, S. W., Rutt, D. J., Hurst, M., & Strejc, H. (1991). Some evident truths about communication in everyday relationships: All communication is not created equal. *Human Communication Research, 18,* 228-267.

Duck, S. W., & Sants, H. K. A. (1983). On the origin of the specious: Are personal relationships really interpersonal states? *Journal of Social and Clinical Psychology, 1,* 27-41.

Duck, S. W., & Wood, J. T. (in press). *Relationship challenges* (Understanding Relationship Processes Series, Vol. 5). Thousand Oaks, CA: Sage.

Dunn, J. (1992). Siblings and development. *Current Directions in Psychological Science, 1,* 6-9.

Dymond, R. (1954). Interpersonal perception and marital happiness. *Canadian Journal of Psychology, 8,* 164-171.

Edwards, D., & Middleton, D. (1988). Conversational remembering and family relationships: How children learn to remember. *Journal of Social and Personal Relationships, 5,* 3-25.

Feeney, J. A., & Noller, P. (1991). Attachment styles and verbal descriptions of romantic partners. *Journal of Social and Personal Relationships, 8,* 187-215.

Fehr, B. (1993). How do I love thee? . . . Let me consult my prototype. In S. W. Duck (Ed.), *Individuals in relationships* (Understanding Relationship Processes Series, Vol. 1, pp. 87-120). Newbury Park, CA: Sage.

Felmlee, D. (1993, June). *Fatal attractions: Affection and disaffection in intimate relationships.* Paper presented to the Fourth Conference of the International Network on Personal Relationships, Milwaukee, WI.

Festinger, L. (1954). A theory of social comparison processes. *Human Relations, 7,* 117-140.

Fisher, W. R. (1985). The narrative paradigm: An elaboration. *Communication Monographs, 52,* 347-367.

Fitzpatrick, M. A. (1988). *Between husbands and wives: Communication in marriage.* Newbury Park, CA: Sage.

Fitzpatrick, M. A. (1993). Communication and interpersonal relationships: Lust, rust, and dust. In P. Kalbfleisch (Ed.), *Interpersonal communication: Evolving perspectives* (pp. 281-285). Hillsdale, NJ: Lawrence Erlbaum.

Fletcher, G. J. O., & Fitness, J. (1993). Knowledge structures and explanations in intimate relationships. In S. W. Duck (Ed.), *Individuals in relationships* (Understanding Relationship Processes Series, Vol. 1, pp. 121-143). Newbury Park, CA: Sage.

Foa, U. G., & Foa, E. (1974). *Societal structures of the mind.* Springfield, IL: Charles C Thomas.

Fogel, A. (1993). *Developing through relationships: Communication, self, and culture in early infancy.* Hemel Hempstead, UK: Harvester-Wheatsheaf.

Gaines, S. O. (in press). Relationships of cultural minorities. In J. T. Wood & S. W. Duck (Eds.), *Under-studied relationships: Off the beaten track.* (Understanding Relationship Processes Series, Vol. 6). Thousand Oaks, CA: Sage.

Garfinkel, H. (1967). *Studies in ethnomethodology.* Englewood Cliffs, NJ: Prentice Hall.

Genero, N. P., Miller, J. B., Surrey, J., & Baldwin, L. M. (1992). Measuring perceived mutuality in close relationships: Validation of the mutual psychological development questionnaire. *Journal of Family Psychology, 6,* 36-48.

Gergen, K. J. (1990). *The saturated self: Dilemmas of identity in contemporary life.* New York: Basic Books.

Giles, H., & Coupland, N. (1991). *Language in social context.* Milton Keynes, UK: Open University Press.

Ginsburg, G. P. (1988). Rules, scripts and prototypes in personal relationships. In S. W. Duck, D. F. Hay, S. E. Hobfoll, W. Ickes, & B. Montgomery (Eds.), *Handbook of personal relationships: Theory, research and interventions* (pp. 23-40). New York & Chichester: John Wiley.

Glidewell, J. C., Tucker, S., Todt, M., & Cox, S. (1982). Professional support systems—The teaching profession. In A. Nadler, J. D. Fisher, & B. M. De Paulo (Eds.), *Applied research in help-seeking and reactions to aid* (pp. 163-184). New York: Academic Press.

Goffman, E. (1959). *Behavior in public places.* Harmondsworth, UK: Penguin.

Goffman, E. (1971). *Relations in public: Microstudies of the public order.* New York: Harper & Row.

Gottman, J. M. (1979). *Marital interaction: Experimental investigations.* New York: Academic Press.

Gottman, J. M. (1991). Predicting the longitudinal course of marriages. *Journal of Marriage and Family Therapy, 17,* 3-7.

Handel, G. (1993, May). *Contradictions in a children's urban environment in the mid-twentieth century.* Paper presented to the Qualitative Research Conference, University of Waterloo, Canada.

Harré, R. (1977). Friendship as an accomplishment: An ethogenic approach to social relationships. In S. W. Duck (Ed.), *Theory and practice in interpersonal attraction* (pp. 338-254). London: Academic Press.

Harris, L. M., & Sadeghi, A. (1987). Realizing: How facts are created in human interaction. *Journal of Social and Personal Relationships, 4,* 480-495.

Harvey, J. H., Orbuch, T. L., & Weber, A. L. (1992). The convergence of the attribution and accounts concepts in the study of close relationships. In J. H. Harvey, T. L. Orbuch, & A. L. Weber (Eds.), *Attributions, accounts and close relationships* (pp. 1-18). New York: Springer.

Harvey, J. H., Weber, A. L., & Orbuch, T. L. (1990). *Interpersonal accounts: A social psychological perspective.* Oxford: Basil Blackwell.

Hauser, G. (1986). *Introduction to rhetorical theory.* New York: Harper & Row.

Hazan, C., & Shaver, P. R. (1987). Romantic love conceptualized as an attachment process. *Journal of Personality and Social Psychology, 52*, 511-524.

Hecht, M., Marston, P. J., & Larkey, L. K. (1994). Love ways and relationships quality. *Journal of Social and Personal Relationships, 11*, 25-43.

Heider, F. (1958). *The psychology of interpersonal relations.* New York: John Wiley.

Hendrick, C., & Hendrick, S. S. (1986). A theory and a method of love. *Journal of Personality and Social Psychology, 50*, 392-402.

Hendrick, C., & Hendrick, S. S. (1988). Lovers wear rose colored glasses. *Journal of Social and Personal Relationships, 5*, 161-183.

Hendrick, C., Hendrick, S. S., Foote, F., & Slapion-Foote, M. (1984). Do men and women love differently? *Journal of Social and Personal Relationships, 1*, 177-196.

Hendrick, S. S. (1987). Self disclosure and marital satisfaction. *Journal of Personality and Social Psychology, 40*, 1150-1159.

Hendrick, S. S., & Hendrick, C. (1993). Lovers as friends. *Journal of Social and Personal Relationships, 10*, 459-466.

Hewes, D. E., & Planalp, S. (1982). There is nothing as useful as a good theory . . . The influence of social knowledge on interpersonal communication. In M. E. Roloff & C. R. Berger (Eds.), *Social cognition and communication* (pp. 107-150). Beverly Hills, CA: Sage.

Hewstone, M. (1992). Towards a deeper understanding of close relationships. In J. H. Harvey, T. L. Orbuch, & A. L. Weber (Eds.), *Attributions, accounts and close relationships* (pp. 257-268). New York: Springer.

Hill, C. T., Rubin, Z., & Peplau, L. A. (1976). Breakups before marriage: The end of 103 affairs. *Journal of Social Issues, 32*, 147-168.

Hinde, R. A. (1981). The bases of a science of interpersonal relationships. In S. W. Duck & R. Gilmour (Eds.), *Personal relationships 1: Studying personal relationships* (pp. 1-22). New York, San Francisco, London: Academic Press.

Hinkle, D. (1970). The game of personal constructs. In D. Bannister (Ed.), *Perspectives in personal construct theory* (pp. 91-110). London: Academic Press.

Hocker, J., & Wilmot, W. (1989). *Interpersonal conflict* (3rd ed.). Dubuque, IA: William C. Brown.

Hogan, R., & Mankin, D. (1970). Determinants of interpersonal attraction: A clarification. *Psychological Reports, 26*, 235-238.

Holtzworth-Munroe, A. (1992). Attribution and maritally violent men: The role of cognitions in marital violence. In J. H. Harvey, T. L. Orbuch, & A. L. Weber (Eds.), *Attributions, accounts and close relationships* (pp. 165-175). New York: Springer.

Honeycutt, J. M. (1993). Memory structures for the rise and fall of personal relationships. In S. W. Duck (Ed.), *Individuals in relationships* (Understanding Relationship Processes Series, Vol. 1, pp. 60-86). Newbury Park, CA: Sage.

Hopper, R., Knapp, M. L., & Scott, L. (1981). Couples' personal idioms: Exploring intimate talk. *Journal of Communication, 31,* 23-33.

Huesmann, L. R., & Levinger, G. (1976). Incremental exchange theory. In L. Berkowitz & E. H. Walster (Eds.), *Advances in experimental social psychology.* New York: Academic Press.

Ickes, W. (1993, June). *Empathic accuracy in personal relationships.* Invited paper presented to the fourth conference of the International Network on Personal Relationships, Milwaukee, WI.

Ickes, W., & Gonzales, J. (n.d.). *"Social" cognition and SOCIAL cognition: From the subjective to the intersubjective.* Manuscript submitted for publication.

Ickes, W., Robertson, E., Tooke, W., & Teng, G. (1986). Naturalistic social cognition: Methodology, assessment and validation. *Journal of Personality and Social Psychology, 51,* 66-82.

Ickes, W., Tooke, W., Stinson, L., Baker, V. L., & Bissonnette, V. (1988). Naturalistic social cognition: Intersubjectivity in same-sex dyads. *Journal of Nonverbal Behavior, 12,* 58-84.

Ickes, W., & Turner, M. (1983). On the social advantages of having an older, opposite sex sibling: Birth order influences in mixed sex dyads. *Journal of Personality and Social Psychology, 45,* 210-222.

Izard, C. E. (1963). Personality similarity and friendship. *Journal of Abnormal and Social Psychology, 61,* 47-51.

Johnson, M. (1982). Social and cognitive features of dissolving commitment to relationships. In S. W. Duck (Ed.), *Personal relationships 4: Dissolving personal relationships* (pp. 51-74). London: Academic Press.

Jones, W. H., & Burdette, M. P. (1994). Betrayal in close relationships. In A. L. Weber & J. H. Harvey (Eds.), *Perspectives on close relationships* (pp. 243-262). Boston: Allyn & Bacon.

Jones, W. H., Hansson, R. O., & Cutrona, C. E. (1984). Helping the lonely: Issues of intervention with young and older adults. In S. W. Duck (Ed.), *Personal relationships 5: Repairing personal relationships* (pp. 143-162). London: Academic Press.

Jourard, S. M. (1971). *Self-disclosure.* New York: John Wiley.

Katovich, M. A., & Couch, C. J. (1992). The nature of social pasts and their use as foundations for situated action. *Symbolic Interaction, 15,* 25-47.

Keeley, M., & Hart, A. (1994). Nonverbal behavior in interaction. In S. W. Duck (Ed.), *Dynamics of interactions* (Understanding Relationship Processes Series, Vol. 4, pp. 135-162). Thousand Oaks, CA: Sage.

Kelley, H. H. (1967). Attribution theory in social psychology. In D. Levine (Ed.), *Nebraska Symposium on Motivation* (Vol. 15, pp. 192-238). Lincoln: University of Nebraska Press.

Kelley, H. H. (1983). Love and commitment. In H. H. Kelley, E. Berscheid, A. Christensen, J. Harvey, T. L. Huston, G. Levinger, D. McClintock, L. A. Peplau, & D. Peterson (Eds.), *Close relationships* (pp. 265-314). San Francisco: Freeman.

Kelly, G. A. (1955). *The psychology of personal constructs.* New York: Norton.

Kelly, G. A. (1969a). *Clinical psychology and personality* (Posthumous. B. Maher, Ed.). New York: John Wiley.

Kelly, G. A. (1969b). Ontological acceleration. In B. Maher (Ed.), *Clinical psychology and personality: The collected papers of George Kelly* (pp. 7-45). New York: John Wiley.

Kelly, G. A. (1970). Brief introduction to personal construct theory. In D. Bannister (Ed.), *Perspectives in personal construct theory* (pp. 1-26). London: Academic Press.

Kenny, D. A. (1988). The analysis of data from two person relationships. In S. W. Duck, D. F. Hay, S. E. Hobfoll, W. Ickes, & B. Montgomery (Eds.), *Handbook of personal relationships: Theory, research and interventions* (pp. 57-77). New York & Chichester: John Wiley.

Kenny, D. A., & Acitelli, L. K. (1989). The role of the relationship in marital decision-making. In D. Brinberg & J. J. Jaccard (Eds.), *Dyadic decision-making* (pp. 51-62). New York: Springer.

Kerckhoff, A. C. (1974). The social context of interpersonal attraction. In T. L. Huston (Ed.), *Foundations of interpersonal attraction* (pp. 61-77). New York: Academic Press.

Kerckhoff, A. C., & Davis, K. E. (1962). Value consensus and need complementarity in mate selection. *American Sociological Review, 27,* 295-303.

Kidd, V. (1975). Happily ever after and other relationship styles: Advice on interpersonal relations in popular magazines, 1951-1973. *Quarterly Journal of Speech, 61,* 31-39.

Klein, R., & Milardo, R. (1993). Third-party influences on the development and maintenance of personal relationships. In S. W. Duck (Ed.), *Social contexts and relationships* (Understanding Relationship Processes Series, Vol. 3, pp. 55-77). Newbury Park, CA: Sage.

Kovecses, Z. (1986). *Metaphors of anger, pride, and love: A lexical approach to the structure of concepts.* Amsterdam: John Benjamins.

Kovecses, Z. (1991). A linguist's quest for love. *Journal of Social and Personal Relationships, 8,* 77-98.

Krokoff, L., Gottman, J. M., & Roy, A. K. (1988). Blue collar and white collar marital interaction and communication orientation. *Journal of Social and Personal Relationships, 5,* 201-221.

Lacan, J. (1977). *The four fundamental concepts of psychoanalysis.* London: Hogarth.

La Gaipa, J. J. (1977). Interpersonal attraction and social exchange. In S. W. Duck (Ed.), *Theory and practice in interpersonal attraction* (pp. 129-164). London: Academic Press.

Laing, R. D., Phillipson, H., & Lee, C. (1966). *Interpersonal perception.* New York: Harper & Row.

Lakoff, G. (1986). A figure of thought. *Metaphor and Symbolic Activity, 1,* 215-225.

Lakoff, G., & Johnson, M. (1980). *Metaphors we live by.* Chicago: University of Chicago Press.

Lea, M., & Duck, S. W. (1982). A model for the role of similarity of values in friendship development. *British Journal of Social Psychology, 21*, 301-310.

Levinger, G. (1979). A social exchange view of the dissolution of pair relationship. In R. L Burgess & T. L. Huston (Eds.), *Social exchange: Advances in theory and research* (pp. 169-193). New York: Academic Press.

Levinger, G., & Breedlove, J. (1966). Interpersonal attraction and agreement: A study of marriage partners. *Journal of Personality and Social Psychology, 3*, 367-372.

Lewis, C. S. (1960). *The four loves.* New York: Harcourt, Brace, Jovanovich.

Lewis, R. A., & Spanier, G. B. (1973). Theorizing about the quality and stability of marriage. In W. Burr, R. Hill, F. Nye, & I. Reiss (Eds.), *Contemporary theories about the family* (Vol. 1, pp. 268-294). New York: Free Press.

Lyons, R. F. (in press). Remodeling relationships and the handicapped. In S. W. Duck & J. T. Wood (Eds.), *Relationship challenges* (Understanding Relationship Processes Series, Vol. 5). Thousand Oaks, CA: Sage.

Mair, J. M. (1970). Psychologists are human too. In D. Bannister (Ed.), *Perspectives in personal construct theory* (pp. 157-184). London: Academic Press.

Mair, J. M. (1976). Metaphors for living. In A. W. Landfield (Ed.), *Nebraska Symposium on Motivation: Personal construct psychology.* Lincoln: University of Nebraska Press.

Marston, P. J., Hecht, M., & Robers, T. (1987). "True love ways": The subjective experience and communication of romantic love. *Journal of Social and Personal Relationships, 4*, 387-407.

Masheter, C., & Harris, L. (1986). From divorce to friendship: A study of dialectic relationship development. *Journal of Social and Personal Relationships, 3*, 177-190.

McAdams, D. (1993). *Stories we live by: Personal myths and the making of the self.* New York: William Morrow.

McCall, G. J. (1982). Becoming unrelated: The management of bond dissolution. In S. W. Duck (Ed.), *Personal relationships 4: Dissolving personal relationships* (pp. 211-232). London: Academic Press.

McCall, G. J. (1988). The organizational life cycle of relationships. In S. W. Duck, D. F. Hay, S. E. Hobfoll, W. J. Ickes, & B. M. Montgomery (Eds.), *Handbook of personal relationships: Theory, research and interventions* (pp. 467-486). New York & Chichester: John Wiley

McCarthy, B., & Duck, S. W. (1976). Friendship duration and responses to attitudinal agreement-disagreement. *British Journal of Social and Clinical Psychology, 15*, 377-386.

McFarland, C., & Miller, D. T. (1990). Judgements of self-other similarity: Just like other people, only more so. *Personality and Social Psychology Bulletin, 16*, 475-484.

McLaughlin, M. L. (1984). *Conversation: How talk is organized.* Beverly Hills, CA: Sage.

Mead, G. H. (1914). Class lectures in social psychology. In D. L. Miller (Ed.), *The individual and the social self: Unpublished work of G. H. Mead.* Chicago: University of Chicago Press.

Mead, G. H. (1967). *Mind, self, and society: From the standpoint of a social behaviorist* (C. W. Morris, Ed.). Chicago: University of Chicago Press. (Original work published 1934)

Megill, A., & McCloskey, D. N. (1987). The rhetoric of history. In J. S. Nelson, A. Megill, & D. N. McCloskey (Eds.), *The rhetoric of the human sciences: Language and argument in scholarship and public affairs* (pp. 221-238). Madison: University of Wisconsin Press.

Mehrabian, A. (1971). *Silent messages.* Belmont, CA: Wadsworth.

Metts, S., Cupach, W., & Bejlovec, R. A. (1989). "I love you too much to ever start liking you": Redefining romantic relationships. *Journal of Social and Personal Relationships, 6,* 259-274.

Miell, D. E. (1984). *Cognitive and communicative strategies in developing relationships: Converging and diverging social environments.* Unpublished doctoral dissertation, University of Lancaster, UK.

Miell, D. E. (1987). Remembering relationship development: Constructing a context for interactions. In R. Burnett, P. McGhee, & D. Clarke (Eds.), *Accounting for relationships* (pp. 60-73). London: Methuen.

Miell, D. E., & Duck, S. W. (1986). Strategies in developing friendship. In V. J. Derlega & B. A. Winstead (Eds.), *Friendship and social interaction* (pp. 129-143). New York: Springer.

Milardo, R. M. (1992). Comparative methods for delineating social networks. *Journal of Social and Personal Relationships, 9,* 447-461.

Milardo, R. M., Johnson, M. P., & Huston, T. L. (1983). Developing close relationships: Changing patterns of interaction between pair members and social networks. *Journal of Personality and Social Psychology, 44,* 964-976.

Milardo, R. M., & Wellman, B. (1992). The personal IS social. *Journal of Social and Personal Relationships, 9,* 339-342.

Miller, D. L. (1980). (Ed.). *The individual and the social self: Unpublished work of G. H. Mead.* Chicago: University of Chicago Press.

Mills, J., & Clark, M. S. (1982). Communal and exchange relationships. In L. Wheeler (Ed.), *Review of personality and social psychology* (Vol. 3, pp. 121-144). Beverly Hills, CA: Sage.

Monsour, M. (1994). Similarities and dissimilarities in personal relationships: Constructing meaning and building intimacy through communication. In S. W. Duck (Ed.), *Dynamics of interactions* (Understanding Relationship Processes Series, Vol. 4, pp. 112-134). Thousand Oaks, CA: Sage.

Monsour, M., Betty, S., & Kurzweil, N. (1993). Levels of perspectives and the perception of intimacy in cross-sex friendships: A balance theory explanation of shared perceptual reality. *Journal of Social and Personal Relationships, 10,* 529-550.

Montgomery, B. M. (1984). Behavioral characteristics predicting self and peer perception of open communication. *Communication Quarterly, 32,* 233-240.

Montgomery, B. M. (1986, July). *Flirtatious messages*. Paper presented to the Third International Conference on Personal Relationships, Herzlia, Israel.

Montgomery, B. M. (1988). Quality communication in personal relationships. In S. W. Duck, D. F. Hay, S. E. Hobfoll, W. Ickes, & B. Montgomery (Eds.), *Handbook of personal relationships: Theory, research and interventions* (pp. 343-362). New York & Chichester: John Wiley.

Murstein, B. I. (1971). Critique of models of dyadic attraction. In B. I. Murstein (Ed.), *Theories of attraction and love* (pp. 1-30). New York: Springer.

Neimeyer, R. A., & Mitchell, K. A. (1988). Similarity and attraction: A longitudinal study. *Journal of Social and Personal Relationships, 5*, 131-148.

Neimeyer, R. A., & Neimeyer, G. J. (1985). Relational trajectories: A personal construct contribution. *Journal of Social and Personal Relationships, 2*, 325-250.

Newcomb, T. M. (1971). Dyadic balance as a source of clues about interpersonal attraction. In B. I. Murstein (Ed.), *Theories of attraction and love* (pp. 31-45). New York: Springer.

Niven, D. (1974). *Bring on the empty horses*. New York: Fontana.

Noller, P., & Fitzpatrick, M. A. (1990). Marital communication in the eighties. *Journal of Marriage and the Family, 52*, 832-843.

Noller, P., & Guthrie, D. (1992). Studying communication in marriage: An integration and critical evaluation. In W. H. Jones & D. Perlman (Eds.), *Advances in personal relationships* (Vol. 3, pp. 37-74). London: Jessica Kingsley.

Noller, P., & Venardos, C. (1986). Communication awareness in married couples. *Journal of Social and Personal Relationships, 3*, 31-42.

Norton, R. W. (1983). *Communicator style: Theory, applications, and measures*. Beverly Hills, CA: Sage.

O'Keefe, B., & Delia, J. (1982). Impression formation and message production. In M. Roloff & C. R. Berger (Eds.), *Social cognition and communication* (pp. 121-146). Beverly Hills, CA: Sage.

Olson, D. H. (1977). Insiders' and outsiders' views of relationships: Research studies. In G. Levinger & H. Raush (Eds.), *Close relationships: Perspectives on the meaning of intimacy* (pp. 115-135). Amherst: University of Massachusetts Press.

Owen, W. F. (1984). Interpretive themes in relational communication. *Quarterly Journal of Speech, 70*, 274-287.

Owen, W. F. (1985). Thematic metaphors in relational communication: A conceptual framework. *Western Journal of Speech Communication, 49*, 1-13.

Owen, W. F. (1993). Metaphors in accounts of romantic relationship terminations. In P. Kalbfleisch (Ed.), *Interpersonal Communication: Evolving perspectives* (pp. 261-278). Hillsdale, NJ: Lawrence Erlbaum.

Percy, W. (1975). *The message in the bottle*. New York: Farrar, Straus & Giroux.

Philipsen, G. (1987). The prospect for cultural communication. In D. Kincaid (Ed.), *Communication theory: Eastern and Western perspectives* (pp. 245-254). New York: Academic Press.

Planalp, S. (1993). Friends' and acquaintances' conversations II: Coded differences. *Journal of Social and Personal Relationships, 10,* 339-354.

Planalp, S., & Benson, A. (1992). Friends' and acquaintances' conversations I: Perceived differences. *Journal of Social and Personal Relationships, 9,* 483-506.

Planalp, S., & Garvin-Doxas, K. (1994). Using mutual knowledge in conversation: Friends as experts in each other. In S. W. Duck (Ed.), *Dynamics of interactions* (Understanding Relationship Processes Series, Vol. 4, pp. 1-26). Thousand Oaks, CA: Sage.

Planalp, S., & Honeycutt, J. M. (1985). Events that increase uncertainty in personal relationships. *Human Communication Research, 11,* 593-604.

Potter, J., & Wetherell, M. (1987). *Discourse and social psychology.* London: Sage.

Prins, K. S., Buunk, A. P., & vanYperen, N. W. (1993). Equity, normative disapproval and extramarital relationships. *Journal of Social and Personal Relationships, 10,* 39-54.

Prusank, D., Duran, R., & DeLillo, D. A. (1993). Interpersonal relationships in women's magazines: Dating and relating in the 1970s and 1980s. *Journal of Social and Personal Relationships, 10,* 307-320.

Putallaz, M., Costanzo, P. R., & Klein, T. P. (1993). Parental childhood social experiences and their effects on children's relationships. In S. W. Duck (Ed.), *Learning about relationships* (Understanding Relationship Processes Series, Vol. 2, pp. 63-97). Newbury Park, CA: Sage.

Rawlins, W. (1992). *Friendship matters.* Hawthorne, NY: Aldine de Gruyter.

Rawlins, W., & Holl, M. (1988). Adolescents' interaction with parents and friends: Dialectics of temporal perspective and evaluation. *Journal of Social and Personal Relationships, 5,* 27-46.

Reis, H. T., & Shaver, P. R. (1988). Intimacy as an interpersonal process. In S. W. Duck, D. F. Hay, S. E. Hobfoll, W. Ickes, & B. M. Montgomery (Eds.), *Handbook of personal relationships: Theory, research and interventions* (pp. 367-390). New York & Chichester: John Wiley.

Rodin, M. (1982). Nonengagement, failure to engage and disengagement. In S. W. Duck (Ed.), *Personal relationships 4: Dissolving personal relationships* (pp. 31-50). London: Academic Press.

Rosenbaum, M. E. (1986). The repulsion hypothesis: On the non-development of relationships. *Journal of Personality and Social Psychology, 51,* 1156-1166.

Ross, L. (1977). The intuitive psychologist and his shortcomings: Distortions in the attribution process. In L. Berkowitz (Ed.), *Advances in experimental social psychology* (Vol. 10, pp. 173-220). New York: Academic Press.

Rothman, E. (1984). *Hands and hearts: A history of courtship in America.* New York: Basic Books

Rusbult, C. E., & Buunk, A. P. (1993). Commitment processes in close relationships: An interdependence analysis. *Journal of Social and Personal Relationships, 10,* 175-203.

Schonbach, P. (1992). Interaction of process and moderator variables in account episodes. In J. H. Harvey, T. L. Orbuch, & A. L. Weber (Eds.), *Attributions, accounts and close relationships* (pp. 40-51). New York: Springer.

Schultz, A. (1973). *A theory of consciousness.* New York: Philosophical Library.

Shoenewolf, G. (1991). *The art of hating.* New York: Random House.

Shotter, J. (1987). The social construction of an "us": Problems of accountability and narratology. In R. Burnett, P. McGhee, & D. D. Clarke (Eds.), *Accounting for relationships* (pp. 225-247). London: Methuen.

Shotter, J. (1992). What is a "personal" relationship? A rhetorical-responsive account of "unfinished business." In J. H. Harvey, T. L. Orbuch, & A. L. Weber (Eds.), *Attributions, accounts and close relationships* (pp. 19-39). New York: Springer.

Sillars, A. L. (1985). Interpersonal perception in relationships. In W. Ickes (Ed.), *Compatible and incompatible relationships* (pp. 277-305). New York: Springer.

Socha, T. (1991, May). *Children's learning of compliance from their relationships with parents.* Paper presented to the third conference of the International Network on Personal Relationships, Normal, IL.

Spencer, E. E. (1993, February). *New approaches to assessing self-disclosure in conversation.* Paper presented to the Western Speech Communication Association, Albuquerque, NM.

Spencer, E. E. (1994). Transforming relationships through ordinary talk. In S. W. Duck (Ed.), *Dynamics of relationships* (Understanding Relationship Processes Series, Vol. 4, pp. 58-86). Thousand Oaks, CA: Sage.

Spitzberg, B. H., & Cupach, W. (1985). *Interpersonal communication competence.* Beverly Hills, CA: Sage.

Sprecher, S. (1987). The effects of self-disclosure given and received on affection for an intimate partner and stability of the relationship. *Journal of Social and Personal Relationships, 4,* 115-127.

Sprecher, S., & Duck, S. W. (in press). Sweet talk: The role of communication in consolidating relationship. *Personality and Social Psychology Bulletin.*

Stafford, L., & Byers, C. L. (1993). *Interaction between parents and children.* Newbury Park, CA: Sage.

Stein, C. H. (1993). Felt obligation in adult family relationships. In S. W. Duck (Ed.), *Social contexts and relationships* (Understanding Relationship Processes Series, Vol. 3, pp. 78-99). Newbury Park, CA: Sage.

Stephen, T. D. (1985). Fixed-sequence and circular-causal models of relationship development: Divergent views on the role of communication in intimacy. *Journal of Marriage and the Family, 47,* 955-963.

Stinson, L., & Ickes, W. (1992). Empathic accuracy in the interactions of male friends versus male strangers. *Journal of Personality and Social Psychology, 62,* 787-797.

Stromberg, P. (1985). The impression point: Synthesis of symbol and self. *Ethos, 13,* 56-74.

Sunnafrank, M. (1991). Interpersonal attraction and attitude similarity: A communication based assessment. In J. A. Anderson (Ed.), *Communication yearbook 14* (pp. 451-483). Newbury Park, CA: Sage.

Sunnafrank, M. (1992). On debunking the attitude similarity myth. *Communication Monographs, 59,* 164-179.

Surra, C. A. (1984, July). *Attributions about the decision to wed: Variations by style of courtship.* Paper presented to the Second International Conference on Personal Relationships, Madison, WI.

Surra, C. A. (1987). Reasons for changes in commitment: Variations by courtship style. *Journal of Social and Personal Relationships, 4,* 17-33.

Surra, C. A., & Ridley, C. (1991). Multiple perspectives on interaction: Participants, peers and observers. In B. M. Montgomery & S. W. Duck (Eds.), *Studying interpersonal interaction* (pp. 35-55). New York: Guilford.

Surra, C. A., Arizzi, P., & Asmussen, L. (1988). The association between reasons for commitment and the development and outcome of marital relationships. *Journal of Social and Personal Relationships, 5,* 47-63.

Vangelisti, A. L. (1992). Communication problems in committed relationships: An attributional analysis. In J. H. Harvey, T. L. Orbuch, & A. L. Weber (Eds.), *Attributions, accounts and close relationships* (pp. 144-164). New York: Springer.

Vanzetti, N. A., Notarius, C., & NeeSmith, D. (1992). Specific and generalized expectancies in marital interaction. *Journal of Family Psychology, 6,* 171-183.

Waring, E. M., Tillman, M. P., Frelick, L., Russell, L., & Weisz, G. (1980). Concepts of intimacy in the general population. *Journal of Nervous and Mental Disease, 168,* 471-474.

Watzlawick, P., Beavin, J., & Jackson, D. (1967). *Pragmatics of human communication: A study of interactional patterns, pathologies and paradoxes.* New York: Norton.

Weber, A. (1983, May). *The breakdown of relationships.* Paper presented to the Conference on Social Interaction and Relationships, Nags Head, NC.

Wegner, D. M., Raymond, P., & Erber, R. (1990). Transactive memory in personal relationships. *Journal of Personality and Social Psychology, 61,* 923-929.

Werner, C., Altman, I., Brown, B., & Ginat, J. (1993). Celebrations in personal relationships: A transactional/dialectical perspective. In S. W. Duck (Ed.), *Social contexts and relationships* (Understanding Relationship Processes Series, Vol. 3, pp. 109-138). Newbury Park, CA: Sage.

Werner, C., Brown, B., Altman, I., & Staples, J. (1992). Close relationship in their physical and social contexts: A transactional perspective. *Journal of Social and Personal Relationships, 9,* 411-431.

White, J. M. (1985). Perceived similarity and understanding in married couples. *Journal of Social and Personal Relationships, 2,* 45-57.

Wiseman, J. P. (1986). Friendship: Bonds and binds in a voluntary relationship. *Journal of Social and Personal Relationships, 3,* 191-211.

Wiseman, J. P. (1989, May). *Friends and enemies: Are they opposites?* Paper presented to the Iowa Conference on Personal Relationships, Iowa City, IA.

Wiseman, J. P. (in press). Enemies. In S. W. Duck & J. T. Wood (Eds.), *Relationship challenges* (Understanding Relationship Processes Series, Vol. 5). Thousand Oaks, CA: Sage.

Witteman, H. (1988). Interpersonal problem solving: Problem conceptualization and communication use. *Communication Monographs, 55,* 336-359.

Wood, J. T. (1982). Communication and relational culture: Bases for the study of human relationships. *Communication Quarterly, 30,* 75-83.

Wood, J. T. (1993a). Engendered relations: Interaction, caring, power and responsibility in intimacy. In S. W. Duck (Ed.), *Social contexts and relationships* (Understanding Relationship Processes Series, Vol. 3, pp. 26-54). Newbury Park, CA: Sage.

Wood, J. T. (1993b). Enlarging conceptual boundaries: A critique of research in interpersonal communication. In S. P. Bowen & N. J. Wyatt (Eds.), *Transforming visions: Feminist critiques in communication studies* (pp. 27-53). New York: Hampton Press.

Wood, J. T., Dendy, L. L., Dordek, E., Germany, M., & Varallo, S. M. (1994). Dialectic of difference: A thematic analysis of intimates' meanings for difference. In K. Carter & M. Presnell (Eds.), *Interpretive approaches to interpersonal communication* (pp. 115-136). New York: SUNY Press.

Wood, J. T., & Duck, S. W. (in press). *Under-studied relationships: Off the beaten track* (Understanding Relationship Processes Series, Vol. 6). Thousand Oaks, CA: Sage.

Yum, J. O. (1988). The impact of Confucianism on interpersonal relationships and communication patterns in eastern Asia. *Communication Monographs, 55,* 374-388.

Zaidel, S. F., & Mehrabian, A. (1969). The ability to communicate and infer positive and negative attitudes facially and vocally. *Journal of Experimental Research in Personality, 3,* 233-241.

Zajonc, R. B. (1980). Feeling and thinking: Preferences need no inferences. *American Psychologist, 35,* 151-175.

Author Index

Subject Index

About the Author

Steve Duck is the founding editor of the *Journal of Social and Personal Relationship*, the editor of Wiley's *Handbook of Personal Relationships*, and the editor or author of 25 other books on personal relationships. He also founded the International Network on Personal Relationships, the professional organization for the field, and two series of international conferences on relationships. He is presently the Daniel and Amy Starch Research Professor at the University of Iowa, Iowa City.

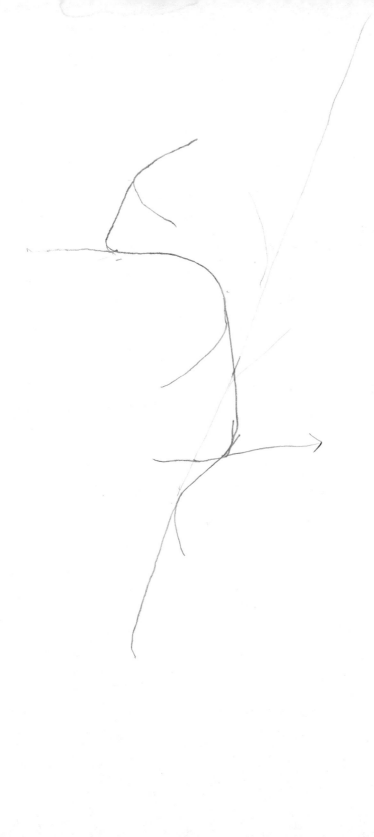

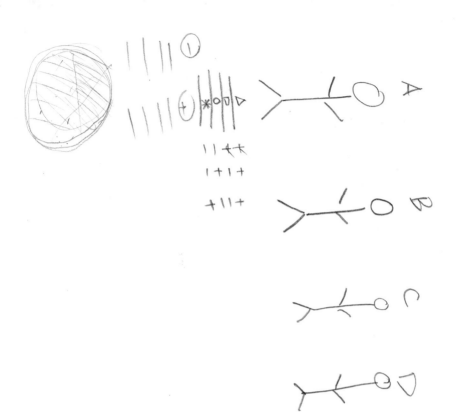